Access
My eLab
leap4

leap4
NEW EDITION
READING AND WRITING
JULIA WILLIAMS
Pearson   CSE

TO REGISTER

❶ Go to **mybookshelf.pearsonerpi.com**

❷ Follow the instructions. When asked for your access code, please type the code provided underneath the blue sticker.

❸ To access **My eLab** at any time, go to http://mybookshelf.pearsonerpi.com. **Bookmark this page for quicker access.**

Access to My eLab is valid for 12 months from the date of registration.

WARNING! This book CANNOT BE RETURNED if the access code has been uncovered.

Note: Once you have registered, you will need to join your online class. Ask your teacher to provide you with the class ID.

TEACHER Access Code

To obtain an access code for My eLab, please contact your Pearson ELT consultant.

 I 800 263-3678, ext. 2
pearsonerpi.com/help

W138566 (A39011)

2691

leap 4
NEW EDITION

READING
AND **WRITING**

JULIA WILLIAMS

Pearson

Product Owner
Stephan Leduc

Managing Editor
Sharnee Chait

Project Editors
Mairi MacKinnon
Emily Harrison

Copy Editor
Mairi MacKinnon

Proofreader
Paula Sarson

Rights and Permissions Coordinator
Aude Maggiori

Text Rights and Permissions
Rachel Irwin

Art Director
Hélène Cousineau

Graphic Design Manager
Estelle Cuillerier

Book and Cover Design
Frédérique Bouvier

Book Layout
Marquis Interscript

Cover Photos
Getty Images © MStudioImages
Shutterstock © TAVEESUK

Dedication

As always, I send more than my thanks to Wayne, Sam, Scott, Carolyn, Ron, Garth, Nicole, Ross, and Mary.

The publisher wishes to thank the following people for their helpful comments and suggestions:

Michelle Duhaney, Seneca College

Eldon Friesen, Brock University

Darlene Murphy, University of Würzburg

Laura Parker, University of Oklahoma

Hélène Prévost, Cégep de L'Outaouais

Bobbi Reimann, Catholic University of Eichstaett-Ingolstadt

Tanya Tervit, Langara College

INTRODUCTION

Welcome to the new edition of *LEAP 4: Reading and Writing*. In this edition, you'll recognize many of the characteristics of the earlier editions:

- engaging chapter topics focused on technology, science, business, and education;
- readings in a variety of genres that reflect interesting and often divergent perspectives;
- Warm-Up Assignments positioned mid-chapter that help you develop the skills you need to succeed in the Final Assignments;
- explicit attention to vocabulary, in particular AWL words, with multiple exercises that allow for lots of practice;
- reading and writing instruction that supports the development of essential academic skills like citing, paraphrasing, and summarizing.

You'll also discover new features that will help you achieve your academic objectives:

- Focus on Critical Thinking sections to encourage you to develop your own opinions about the readings;
- Focus on Accuracy sections to draw your attention to language details.

Several chapter topics are completely new while other topics have been significantly revised based on reviewer feedback.

We hope this new edition will help you reach your academic goals.

ACKNOWLEDGEMENTS

I would like to begin by warmly thanking my former colleagues at Carleton University, who set the stage for the development of the first edition of *Learning English for Academic Purposes*. My colleagues at Renison University College at the University of Waterloo have also supported me with their comments, ideas, and encouragement. My great appreciation goes to my teaching colleagues: Judi Jewinski (in particular for her insightful grammar consultation), Tanya Missere-Mihas, Stefan Rehm, Pat Skinner, Agnieszka Wolczuk, Nancy Ozckowski, Christa Schuller, Maggie Heeney, Maria Pop, Dara Lane, Kent Williams, Xiaoxiao Du, Angie Jeong, Roslyn Zehr, Tony Verbruggen, Elizabeth Matthews, Keely Cook, Stephen Hill, Christine Morgan, Raveet Jacob, Nela Maluckov, Kim Burrell, Margaret Wardell, Dianne Tyers, Audrey Olson, Bruce Russell, Andrea Brandt, and Louann Nhan. Many thanks to Kyle Scholz for finding the Bytheway (2014) reading, Sam Parker for finding the Macur (2017) reading, Wayne Parker for technical consultations on emerging contaminants, Scott Parker for lending his name, and Winona Phachanla for her administrative support and good humour.

A word of thanks is also due to Dr. Ken Beatty, who enthusiastically took on the writing of *LEAP: Listening and Speaking* and who has been instrumental in building the initial books into a full series. Special thanks to Sharnee Chait and the editing team at Pearson ERPI, who have been supportive and patient as we have worked through multiple drafts.

Julia Williams, Renison University College,
University of Waterloo, Canada

HIGHLIGHTS

Gearing Up uses infographics to spark critical thinking, reflection, and discussion about the chapter topic.

Vocabulary Build strengthens comprehension and builds awareness of key vocabulary on the Academic Word List.

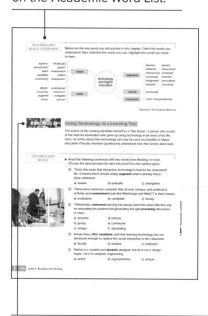

The **overview** outlines the chapter's objectives and features.

Each chapter contains three **readings** from a variety of sources including academic textbooks and journal articles. The readings offer different perspectives on the chapter theme, providing content for writing tasks.

Before, **while**, and **after** reading activities focus on comprehension and critical thinking.

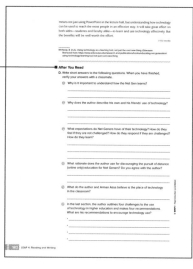

Focus on Reading develops specific strategies you need to fully understand the content and structure of reading texts.

Focus on Writing develops specific skills you need to effectively write about issues using academic English.

My eLab provides practice and additional content.

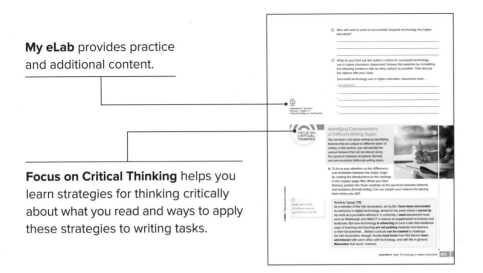

Focus on Critical Thinking helps you learn strategies for thinking critically about what you read and ways to apply these strategies to writing tasks.

The **Warm-Up Assignment** explores a writing task and prepares you for the Final Assignment. Each chapter focuses on a different task.

Focus on Accuracy draws attention to important language details that you can apply when reading and writing academic English.

The **Final Assignment** synthesizes the chapter content and theme into an in-depth writing task. Each chapter focuses on a different type of assignment.

Academic Survival Skill helps you develop essential skills for academic coursework.

Critical Connections allows you to reinvest what you learned by applying critical thinking to a problem related to the chapter theme.

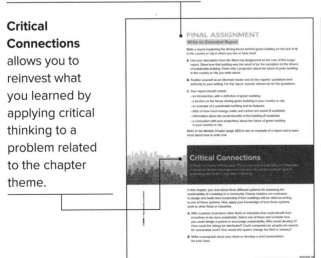

The **Models Chapter** provides instructions and models for the writing tasks in the coursebook.

SCOPE AND SEQUENCE

CHAPTER	READING	CRITICAL THINKING	WRITING
CHAPTER 1 **NATURAL UNEMPLOYMENT** SUBJECT AREAS: business, economics	• Improve comprehension and speed - Learn strategies including skimming and recognizing text type	• Identify economics discourse - Raise your awareness of repeated patterns to recognize this discourse	• Write definitions - Compare different ways to write definitions across disciplines
CHAPTER 2 **ENTREPRENEURSHIP: CREATING YOUR OWN JOB** SUBJECT AREAS: business, economics	• Read journal articles - Learn about the organizational structure and purposes of journal article sections	• Know when and what to cite and reference - Avoid plagiarism and allow readers to find the original source	• Write in-text citations - Learn different ways to introduce citations
CHAPTER 3 **RENEWABLE ENERGY** SUBJECT AREAS: engineering, technology	• Organize information in tables while reading - Learn techniques to summarize complex information	• Inquire further - Consider the relevance of issues to your life and the environment	• Select the optimal organization for your compare and contrast essay - Learn about the standard methods
CHAPTER 4 **SUSTAINABLE BUILDINGS** SUBJECT AREAS: architecture, engineering	• Identify writer perspective in a text - Understand the differences in writers' perspectives	• Apply old knowledge to new information - Develop new ways of thinking	• Use direct quotations and indirect speech - Learn how to integrate these elements in your writing
CHAPTER 5 **SELF-DRIVING CARS** SUBJECT AREAS: engineering, ethics, technology	• Identify paraphrases and summaries - Recognize the differences between these techniques and reasons for using them	• Identify causes and effects - Generate new knowledge and deepen your understanding of issues	• Write conditionally - Review conditional sentence patterns
CHAPTER 6 **HIGH TECHNOLOGY IN HIGHER EDUCATION** SUBJECT AREAS: education, technology	• Maintain authentic voice - Learn why writers include quotes	• Identify characteristics of different writing styles - Understand the differences between informal and academic writing	• Evaluate information for annotated bibliographies - Learn about format and content
CHAPTER 7 **DOPING IN SPORTS** SUBJECT AREAS: ethics, pharmacology	• Compare original and summarized/paraphrased writing - Develop a deeper understanding	• Recognize methods of persuasion - Develop a framework for persuasive arguments	• Synthesize information from multiple sources - Learn how to apply knowledge in a writing task
CHAPTER 8 **EMERGING CONTAMINANTS** SUBJECT AREAS: environmental studies, pharmacology	• Discover the organization of a problem-solution text - Analyze the typical components of this text type	• Express critical thoughts - Learn how to express disagreement or criticism in academic writing	• Analyze critical expression - Identify words/phrases that express criticism

VOCABULARY	ACCURACY	ACADEMIC SURVIVAL SKILL	ASSIGNMENTS
• Explore meaning and context • Find collocations and synonyms • Learn economics terms	• Vary ways to start sentences - Learn how to achieve good flow in your writing	• Identify reliable sources of academic information • Learn how to identify reliable academic sources	• Write a definition of a key economics term • Write a description of a data set

• Explore meaning and context
• Find synonyms and word forms
	• Position the main point for emphasis in a sentence
	  - Learn how to build flow while emphasizing the main point
		• Recognize different styles for in-text citations and references
		  - Learn about different citation systems
			• Write short and extended process essays

• Explore meaning and context
• Find synonyms and word forms
	• Vary grammar and vocabulary to compare and contrast
	  - Review conjunctions and expressions
		• Build your knowledge of discipline-specific vocabulary
		  - Explore techniques to maximize vocabulary acquisition
			• Write short and extended compare and contrast essays

• Explore meaning and context
• Find collocations
• Learn rules about preposition use
	• Integrate quotations in a text
	  - Review punctuation and sentence structure
		• Observe text features to learn about language
		  - Identify grammar points, vocabulary, and text organization
			• Write short and extended reports

• Explore meaning and context
• Find collocations and word forms
	• Express uncertainty
	  - Review modals
		• Use techniques to paraphrase and summarize
		  - Review optimal methods
			• Write a summary
			• Write an extended cause and effect essay

• Explore meaning and context
• Find synonyms and word forms
	• Recognize verb tense patterns in informal and academic writing
	  - Analyze verb tense shifts
		• Exploit your library's resources
		  - Learn tips that apply to most libraries
			• Write short and longer annotated bibliographies

• Explore meaning and context
• Find collocations, synonyms, and word forms
• Learn idioms
	• Use connecting words and phrases common in persuasive writing
	  - Develop a comprehensive list of connectors
		• Persuade by conceding and refuting arguments
		  - Learn a useful technique for essays
			• Write short and longer persuasive essays

• Explore meaning and context
• Find collocations
• Learn technical terms
	• Explore the many uses of *that*
	  - Review sentence structure
		• Combine different organizational patterns to suit your writing purpose
		  - Recognize different organizational patterns
			• Describe and evaluate a solution for a problem-solution text
			• Write a problem-solution essay

TABLE OF CONTENTS

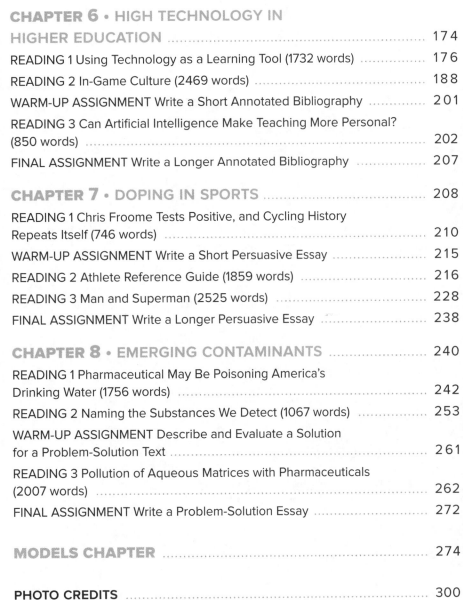

CHAPTER 1
Natural Unemployment

Unemployment is an important issue in every country, and it often affects youth more than other demographic groups. The unemployment rate not only influences a country's quality of life; joblessness may also have significant impacts on individual finances and psychological well-being. In an effort to determine if unemployment can be eliminated, people turn to the field of macroeconomics, which defines unemployment and natural unemployment and explains the root causes. Can unemployment be eliminated to restore young people's confidence in the future?

In this chapter, you will

- learn vocabulary related to economics and unemployment;

- apply strategies to improve comprehension and speed;

- vary ways to start sentences;

- learn about writing definitions;

- identify reliable sources of academic information;

- identify economic discourse;

- write a definition of an economics term and write a description of a data set.

GEARING UP

A. Working in a small group, discuss the following questions. When you have finished, share your answers with the class.

1. How would you define unemployment?

2. How would you define "natural" unemployment?

3. Is unemployment a problem in this country? Why do you think so?

4. Do you believe unemployment is a problem in other countries you have lived in or are familiar with? Why?

5. Can unemployment be eliminated? If so, how? If not, why not?

6. Some people believe that youth unemployment breaks an "unspoken agreement" between society and young people. Do you agree?

Below are the key words you will practise in this chapter. Check the words you understand, then underline the words you use. Highlight the words you need to learn.

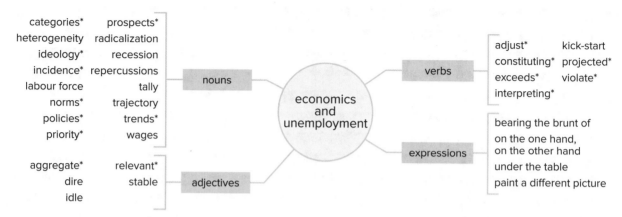

categories*	prospects*
heterogeneity	radicalization
ideology*	recession
incidence*	repercussions
labour force	tally
norms*	trajectory
policies*	trends*
priority*	wages

nouns

economics and unemployment

verbs

adjust*	kick-start
constituting*	projected*
exceeds*	violate*
interpreting*	

expressions

bearing the brunt of
on the one hand, on the other hand
under the table
paint a different picture

aggregate*	relevant*
dire	stable
idle	

adjectives

*Appears on the Academic Word List

FOCUS ON READING

Improving Comprehension and Speed

Reading in a language other than your first can be challenging, but you can apply strategies to improve your comprehension and speed.

A. With your class, discuss what you can do to make reading in English easier and/or faster. Ask one of your classmates (or your instructor) to write the best reading strategies on the board. Copy the list here.

I skim the text before I read in detail.

_____

_____

_____

_____

B. Here are some strategies that students have found helpful; they can be used with almost any type of text.

- Skim the reading to get a sense of the content, length, and text type.
- Consider how the content relates to what you already know or would like to know. This strategy is important because you learn new information better if you connect it to previous knowledge, or if it is about something you are interested in.
- Use your knowledge of the text type to predict how the information is organized. The following table summarizes common text types and their organization.

TEXT TYPE	ORGANIZATION OF INFORMATION
TEXTBOOK	• Logical presentation of information, from simple to complex • Organized by chapters and headings • Main points in topic and concluding sentences of paragraphs
REPORT	• Starts with a summary or highlights section that lists the main points • Body is usually divided into numbered sections with headings • Often presents information through charts, tables, or graphs • May conclude with recommendations for action
ACADEMIC ESSAY	• Follows a formal structure • Thesis (presented at the end of the introduction) previews the content • Paragraphs present content in the order indicated by the thesis • Concluding statement summarizes the content
NEWSPAPER AND MAGAZINE ARTICLES	• Short paragraphs • Main points (*who, what, where, when, why, how*) presented in initial paragraphs • Details and elaboration of points follow • Direct quotations from experts may be included
JOURNAL ARTICLE	• Content previewed in the abstract • Generally organized into sections with headings: abstract, introduction, methods, results, and conclusion
WEBSITE	• Presentation of information varies depending on writer's purpose • Information usually previewed in menus across top and down left-hand side • Related information directly linked to key words in the text for fast access

- Divide a reading into sections and write a heading that reflects the content for each one. If a reading has already been divided into sections, use the writer's headings.

- If you were not given questions to answer, develop a set yourself by turning each heading into a question.

- Read each section carefully to find the answer to your question. If the information is complex, write notes in the margin or on a separate page. Answer the questions as completely as you can.

- Reflect on the content of the reading when you have finished. What did you learn that was new, interesting, or important? What do you not understand or need to ask someone about? What opinion (if any) do you have about the information?

C. Which strategies are new to you and/or your classmates?

_____

_____

_____

_____

D. With your classmates, discuss how these strategies may help when you read in English.

READING ❶   Unemployment and Its Natural Rate

This reading is taken from a popular macroeconomics textbook that you might read for a first-year university course. It provides some useful definitions that will help you understand some of the reasons why unemployment exists.

VOCABULARY BUILD

A. Working with a partner, read the sentences from Reading 1 in the first column. Write the definitions of the key words in bold in the second column. Then work with your class to answer the questions in the third column.

KEY WORDS IN CONTEXT	DEFINITIONS	APPLY WORDS TO YOUR LIFE
❶ In an ideal market, prices **adjust** to bring supply and demand into balance.	*gradually adapt to a new situation*	What do you need to adjust when you start studying at university? *I need to adjust my study habits.*
❷ The problem of unemployment is usefully divided into two **categories**—the long-run problem and the short-run problem.		What categories of subjects do you study?
❸ Sometimes the quantity of labour supplied **exceeds** the quantity demanded.		What exceeds your expectations?
❹ An economy is stronger when people are working than when they are **idle**.		Which companies are never idle?
❺ Statistics on unemployment can be difficult to **interpret**.		What kinds of things can you interpret?
❻ Statistics Canada defines the **labour force** as the sum of the employed and the unemployed.		How many of your friends are in the labour force?
❼ During the recent **recession**, the unemployment rate climbed higher.		Name two things that happen in a recession.
❽ In an ideal labour market, **wages** adjust to balance the quantity of labour supplied and the quantity of labour demanded.		What is a reasonable wage for working in a restaurant?
❾ **On the one hand**, some people who report being unemployed may not, in fact, be trying hard to find a job. **On the other hand**, some people who report being out of the labour force may, in fact, want to work.		Use the two expressions to describe the two sides of an issue. For example, you are trying to save money, but you want to go out with your friends to an expensive restaurant.

KEY WORDS IN CONTEXT	DEFINITIONS	APPLY WORDS TO YOUR LIFE
⑩ Sometimes people report they are unemployed, but they are actually working **under the table** for cash.		Name two kinds of jobs that people work at under the table.
⑪ Alternative measures of unemployment can **paint a different picture** of the unemployment situation.		You may think you are failing a class, but then receive a high score on your exam. Use the expression to describe the new situation.

B. You can further improve your fluency and accuracy in reading and writing (as well as in listening and speaking) by learning to recognize and use collocations: words that are commonly used in combinations.

In the following tables, vocabulary from Reading 1 is divided into two categories: words from the Academic Word List (AWL), and economics-related as well as general vocabulary.

For each word/phrase, read the definition (or quiz yourself on the definition if you think you know it already). Then, locate the word or phrase in Reading 1 using the line number and write the collocations you find in the last column.

Academic Word List Vocabulary

WORDS	DEFINITIONS	COLLOCATIONS
aspects (n.) LINE 45	parts of a situation, plan, idea, that has many parts	*other aspects*
cyclical (adj.) LINE 12	occurring in periods of predictable, repeated increases and decreases	
data (n. pl.) LINES 24, 45, 47, 112	information or facts	
fluctuations (n.) LINES 12, 155	changes in price, amounts, levels	
labour (n.) LINES 45, 53, 69	work or workers (considered collectively)	
policy (n.) LINES 17, 28	officially agreed-upon way of doing something	
structural (adj.) LINE 170	related to how parts of a system connect	
temporary (adj) LINE 55	continuing for a limited time only	

Economics and General Vocabulary

WORDS/PHRASES	DEFINITIONS	COLLOCATIONS
alleviate (v.) LINE 37	make something less painful	*alleviate the hardships*
determinants (n.) LINES 1, 139, 140	strong influences or causes	
equilibrium (n.) LINES 173, 174	relatively stable balance between competing groups	
frictional (adj.) LINE 164	describes the unemployment that results from the time it can take people to find the job they are most suited for	
goods (n.) LINE 3	things that are produced in order to be sold	
impervious (adj.) LINE 17	not influenced by something	
spell (n.) LINES 41, 165, 171	period of time of a particular type of activity	

Before You Read

A. To help you think about the content of the reading, consider the following descriptions of people with different employment situations. Work with a classmate and for each short description, indicate whether you believe this person is employed, unemployed (i.e., looking for work), or not in the labour force (i.e., not looking for work).

DESCRIPTION	EMPLOYED	UNEMPLOYED	NOT IN THE LABOUR FORCE
❶ An adult who has a full-time job	✓		
❷ A fourteen-year-old high school student who delivers papers after school one day a week			
❸ A full-time student, nineteen years old, looking for a part-time job			
❹ A recent college or university graduate looking for a full-time job			
❺ A woman who lost her job and is looking for another one			
❻ A man who lost his job and is taking a few months to travel before searching for another job			
❼ An adult who is working under the table for cash and who is not looking for other work			

While You Read

Use the strategies in Focus on Reading (page 4) to help you read quickly and with good comprehension.

B. Skim Reading 1 to find the answers to questions 1 to 5.

1 a) What is the topic of the reading? _____

    b) How long is it? _____

    c) What type of text is it? How do you know?

    _____

    _____

2 What do you already know about the topic? Your discussion from Gearing Up may help you answer this question.

    _____

3 Based on the text type, how will the content most likely be organized?

    _____

4 This reading is already divided into sections. List the four section headings.

    Unemployment and Its Natural Rate

    _____

    _____

    _____

5 Turn each of the section headings into questions. The first one is done for you. Then copy the questions on a separate page.

    What is unemployment and what is its natural rate?

    _____

    _____

    _____

C. Now read the text more carefully and highlight the answers to the questions you wrote.

Unemployment and Its Natural Rate

An obvious determinant of a country's standard of living is the amount of unemployment it typically experiences. People who would like to work but cannot find jobs are not contributing to the economy's production of goods and services. Although some degree of unemployment is inevitable in a complex economy with thousands of firms
5 and millions of workers, the amount of unemployment varies substantially over time and across countries. When a country keeps its workers as fully employed as possible, it achieves a higher level of **Gross Domestic Product (GDP)** than it would if it left many of its workers **idle**.

Gross Domestic Product (GDP): market value of all final goods and services produced within a country in a given period of time

natural rate of unemployment: rate of unemployment to which the economy tends to return in the long run

cyclical unemployment: deviation of unemployment from its natural rate

… The problem of unemployment is usefully divided into two **categories**—the long-
10 run problem and the short-run problem. The economy's **natural rate of unemployment** refers to the amount of unemployment that the economy normally experiences. **Cyclical unemployment** refers to the year-to-year fluctuations in unemployment around its natural rate and is closely associated with the short-run ups and downs of economic activity … In this chapter, we will discuss the determinants of an economy's
15 natural rate of unemployment. As we will see, the term *natural* does not imply that this rate of unemployment is desirable. Nor does it imply that it is constant over time or impervious to economic policy. It merely means that this unemployment does not go away on its own even in the long run.

We begin the chapter by looking at some of
20 the relevant facts that describe unemployment. In particular, we examine three questions: How does the government measure the economy's rate of unemployment? What problems arise in **interpreting** the unemployment data? How long
25 are the unemployed typically without work?

We then turn to the reasons why economies always experience some unemployment and the ways in which policy-makers can help the unemployed. We discuss [three] explanations for the economy's
30 natural rate of unemployment: job search, minimum-wage laws, and unions. As we will see, long-run unemployment does not arise from a single problem that has a single solution. Instead, it reflects a variety of related problems. As a result,
35 there is no easy way for policy-makers to reduce the economy's natural rate of unemployment and, at the same time, to alleviate the hardships experienced by the unemployed.

We begin this chapter by examining more precisely what the term *unemployment*
40 means. We consider how the government measures unemployment, what problems arise in interpreting the unemployment data, how long the typical spell of unemployment lasts, and why there will always be some people unemployed.

Measuring Unemployment

In Canada, measuring unemployment is the job of Statistics Canada. Every month,
45 Statistics Canada produces data on unemployment and on other aspects of the labour market, such as types of employment, length of the average workweek, and the duration of unemployment. These data come from a regular survey of about 54,000 households, called the ***Labour Force*** *Survey*.

Based on answers to survey questions, Statistics Canada places each adult (aged fifteen
50 and older) in each surveyed household into one of three categories:

- employed
- unemployed
- not in the labour force

A person is considered employed if he or she spent some of the previous week
55 working at a paid job. A person is unemployed if he or she is on temporary layoff or
is looking for a job. A person who fits neither of the first two categories, such as a
full-time student, homemaker, or retiree, is not in the labour force. Figure 1.1 shows
this breakdown for 2014.

Figure 1.1: The Breakdown of the Population in 2014

Statistics Canada divides the adult population into three categories: employed, unemployed, and not in the labour force.

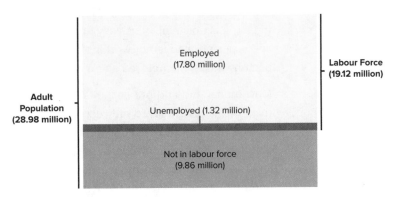

Source: Statistics Canada, CANSIM database.

Once Statistics Canada has placed all the individuals covered by the survey in a category,
60 it computes various statistics to summarize the state of the labour market. Statistics
Canada defines the labour force as the sum of the employed and the unemployed:

$$\text{Labour force} = \text{number of employed} + \text{number of unemployed}$$

unemployment rate:
percentage of the labour
force that is unemployed

Statistics Canada defines the **unemployment rate** as the percentage of the labour
force that is unemployed:

65

$$\text{Unemployment rate} = \frac{\text{Number of unemployed}}{\text{Labour force}} \times 100$$

Statistics Canada computes unemployment rates for the entire adult population and
for more narrowly defined groups—young, old, men, women and so on.

Statistics Canada uses the same survey to produce data on labour-force participation.
The **labour-force participation rate** measures the percentage of the total adult
70 population of Canada that is in the labour force:

**labour-force participation
rate:** percentage of the
adult population that is
in the labour force

$$\text{Labour-force participation rate} = \frac{\text{Labour force}}{\text{Adult population}} \times 100$$

This statistic tells us the fraction of the population that has chosen to participate in
the labour market. Like the unemployment rate, the labour-force participation rate
is computed both for the entire adult population and for more specific groups.

75 To see how these data are computed, consider the figures for 2014. In that year,
17.80 million people were employed, and 1.32 million people were unemployed. The
labour force was

$$\text{Labour force} = 17.80 + 1.32 \text{ million} = 19.12 \text{ million}.$$

The unemployment rate was

80

$$\text{Unemployment rate} = (1.32/19.12) \times 100 = 6.90 \text{ percent}.$$

Because the adult population was 28.98 million, the labour-force participation rate was

$$\text{Labour-force participation rate} = (19.12/28.98) \times 100 = 65.98 \text{ percent.}$$

Hence, in 2014, two-thirds of Canada's adult population was participating in the labour market, and 6.9 percent of those labour-market participants were without work.

...

85 Challenges of Measuring Unemployment

Measuring the amount of unemployment in the economy might seem straightforward. In fact, it is not. While it is easy to distinguish between a person with a full-time job and a person who is not working at all, it is much harder to distinguish between a person who is unemployed and a person who is not in the labour force.

90 Movements into and out of the labour force are, in fact, common. More than one-third of the unemployed are recent entrants into the labour force. These entrants include young workers looking for their first jobs, such as recent university and college graduates. They also include, in greater numbers, older workers who had previously left the labour force but have now returned to look for work. Moreover, not all 95 unemployment ends with the job seeker finding a job. Almost half of all spells of unemployment end when the unemployed person leaves the labour force.

Because people move into and out of the labour force so often and for such a variety of reasons, statistics on unemployment can be difficult to interpret. **On the one hand**, some of those who report being unemployed may not, in fact, be trying hard to find 100 a job; for example, they might be on temporary layoff and are waiting to be recalled to work. Or perhaps they are calling themselves unemployed because they want to qualify for Employment Insurance or because they are actually working and being paid "**under the table**." It may be more realistic to view these individuals as out of the labour force or, in some cases, employed.

105 **On the other hand**, some of those who report being out of the labour force may, in fact, want to work. These individuals may have tried to find a job but have given up after an unsuccessful search. Such individuals, labelled **discouraged searchers** by Statistics Canada, do not show up in unemployment statistics, even though they are truly workers without jobs. Similarly, some workers may be working part-time when 110 in fact they want to work full-time. Although such workers are working less than they want to and so are underemployed, they do not show up in unemployment statistics.

discouraged searchers: individuals who would like to work but have given up looking for a job

The bottom part of Table 1.1, which provides 2014 data, shows the official unemployment rate for Canada as well as several alternative measures of labour underutilization calculated by Statistics Canada. The table shows that these alternative 115 measures can **paint quite a different picture** of the unemployment situation. In the end, it is best to view the official unemployment rate as a useful but imperfect measure of joblessness.

TABLE 1.1: ALTERNATIVE MEASURES OF LABOUR UNDERUTILIZATION	
MEASURE AND DESCRIPTION	**PERCENTAGE OF THE LABOUR FORCE**
Unemployed 1 to 4 weeks	2.3 %
Unemployed 5 to 13 weeks	2.3 %
Unemployed 14 to 25 weeks	1.9 %

TABLE 1.1: ALTERNATIVE MEASURES OF LABOUR UNDERUTILIZATION	
MEASURE AND DESCRIPTION	PERCENTAGE OF THE LABOUR FORCE
Unemployed 26 to 52 weeks	1.0 %
Unemployed more than 52 weeks	0.8 %
Official Unemployment Rate	**6.9 %**
Discouraged searchers	0.1 %
Those awaiting recall	0.5 %
Involuntary part-time workers	1.8 %
Official rate + discouraged searchers + those awaiting recall + involuntary part-time workers	9.3 %

Sources: Statistics Canada, CANSIM database and authors' calculations.

...

Causes of Natural Unemployment

We have discussed how the government measures the amount of unemployment,
120 the problems that arise in interpreting unemployment statistics, and the findings of labour economists on the duration of unemployment. You should now have a good idea about what unemployment is.

This discussion, however, has not explained why economies experience unemployment. In most markets in the economy,
125 prices **adjust** to bring quantity supplied and quantity demanded into balance. In an ideal labour market, **wages** would adjust to balance the quantity of labour supplied and the quantity of labour demanded. This adjustment of wages would ensure that all workers are always fully employed.

130 Of course, reality does not resemble this ideal. There are always some workers without jobs, even when the overall economy is doing well. Figure 1.2 shows Canada's observed unemployment rate and an estimate of Canada's natural unemployment rate. The natural rate of unemployment is what economists judge to be the rate of unemployment to which the economy tends to return in the long run.
135 The exact value of the natural unemployment rate is unknown, but most economists estimate the rate in Canada to be currently 6 to 7 percent. Economists form estimates of the natural unemployment rate based on those variables they believe are the underlying determinants of the natural rate of unemployment. We will discuss these
140 underlying determinants in the remainder of this chapter.

The values of the natural unemployment rate shown in Figure 1.2 represent the authors' opinions. Because the natural unemployment rate is only an estimate, there may be some disputes about the level of the rate at any particular time. However, the movements shown in the figure represent a fairly widespread view among economists about what
145 has happened to Canada's natural unemployment rate since 1966. During the 1970s and 1980s, the natural unemployment rate roughly doubled, from about 4 percent to over 8 percent, and began falling in the mid-1990s. Most economists would agree that by 2014, the natural rate had fallen to between 6 percent and 7 percent.

Figure 1.2: Observed and Natural Unemployment Rates, 1966–2014

*Most economists agree that the natural unemployment rate increased during the 1970s, stabilized at about 8 percent in the 1980s, and has followed a slow downward path since the mid-1990s. The difference between the observed unemployment rate and the natural unemployment rate is the cyclical unemployment rate. The **recessions** in the early 1980s, the early 1990s, and most recently in 2008–2009 are identified in this figure by the jump in the observed unemployment rate well above the natural unemployment rate.*

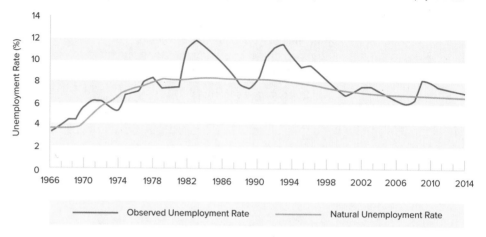

Sources: Statistics Canada, CANSIM database and authors' assumptions.

Figure 1.2 also shows that the observed
150 unemployment rate fluctuates around the natural rate. The observed unemployment rate differs from the natural rate due to the existence of cyclical unemployment. Cyclical unemployment arises due to
155 short-run economic fluctuations …

To preview our conclusions, we will find that there are [three] ways to explain unemployment in the long run. The first explanation is that it takes time for
160 workers to search for the jobs that are best suited for them. The unemployment that results from the process of matching workers and jobs is sometimes called **frictional unemployment**, and it is often
165 thought to explain relatively short spells of unemployment.

frictional unemployment: unemployment that results due to time it takes workers to find the jobs that best suit their tastes and skills

structural unemployment: unemployment that results when the quantity of jobs available in the labour market is less than the quantity of jobs needed to meet the demand

The next [two] explanations for unemployment suggest that the number of jobs available in some labour markets may be insufficient to give a job to everyone who wants one. This occurs when the quantity of labour supplied **exceeds** the quantity
170 demanded. Unemployment of this sort is sometimes called **structural unemployment**, and it is often thought to explain longer spells of unemployment. As we will see, this kind of unemployment results when wages are, for some reason, set above the level that brings supply and demand into equilibrium. Later in this section, we will examine [two] possible reasons for an above-equilibrium wage: minimum-wage laws and unions.

(1949 words)

Mankiw, N. G., Kneebone, R. D., & McKenzie, K. J. (2017). *Principles of macroeconomics* (7th Canadian ed., pp. 179–188). Toronto, ON: Nelson Education.

After You Read

D. Compare the answers you highlighted in the text with your classmate's. Are they the same? If not, work together to verify the answers to your questions. Next, working on your own, write the answers on a separate page where you listed your questions in While You Read.

E. To demonstrate your understanding of the reading, write short answers to the questions below.

1. If a country has a high GDP, what can we assume?

   _____

2. What is the difference between the unemployment rate and the natural rate of unemployment?

   _____

   _____

   _____

   _____

3. According to Statistics Canada, from what age can people potentially be considered as part of the labour force? Do you agree that this is the appropriate age to be considered eligible to work?

   _____

   _____

4. a) According to the Labour Force Survey, what are the three employment categories used to classify people?

   _____

   b) Based on the information in Reading 1, return to task A in Before You Read (page 8), and verify that your answers are correct.

5. Using the following numbers, calculate the following rates for country Z:
   People employed: 27.22 million
   People unemployed: 1.67 million
   Adult population: 35.11 million

   a) Total labour force: _____

   b) Unemployment rate: _____

   c) Labour-force participation rate: _____

   d) Do you think country Z has a high GDP? _____

   _____

6. Why is the unemployment rate an "imperfect measure" of joblessness?

   _____

   _____

   _____

⑦ Why can economists only estimate the natural rate of unemployment?

_____

_____

_____

⑧ What explains short and long spells of unemployment?

_____

_____

_____

⑨ How many data sets (groups of information) can you find in this reading represented in figures or tables? In the Final Assignment, you will work with a data set you find yourself.

_____

MyBookshelf > My eLab > Exercises > Chapter 1 > Unemployment and Its Natural Rate

F. When you have finished, reflect on the reading. What did you learn that was new, interesting, or important? What would you like to learn more about? Compare your thoughts with those of your classmates.

FOCUS ON ACCURACY

Varying Ways to Start Sentences

Writers are often encouraged to vary their sentence structure so their text has good flow (or cohesion). What is good sentence flow? And how can you achieve good flow in your own writing?

Flow makes writing easier to understand. One way to create good flow is by starting your sentence with a grammar structure that links it to the preceding sentence. There are a variety of structures that achieve this goal.

A. In this paragraph from Reading 1, sentences *A, B, C,* and *D* start with grammar structures (underlined) that help build good flow. Match the letter of each grammar structure to the correct description below.

> The labour-force participation rate measures the percentage of the total adult population of Canada that is in the labour force:
>
> Labour-force participation rate = labour force/adult population × 100
>
> A) This statistic tells us the fraction of the population that has chosen to participate in the labour market. B) Like the unemployment rate, the labour-force participation rate is computed both for the entire adult population and for more specific groups.
>
> C) To see how these data are computed, consider the figures for 2014. D) In that year, 17.80 million people were employed, and 1.32 million people were unemployed.

❶ Prepositional phrase (there are two) _____ and _____

❷ This/these + noun (to refer to something just mentioned) _____

❸ Infinitive phrase of purpose _____

To be explicit:

- *This statistic* in sentence A refers to *the labour-force participation rate* in the preceding sentence.
- *Like the unemployment rate* in sentence B refers to *the unemployment rate* that was discussed in the preceding paragraph.
- *To see how these data are computed* in sentence C refers to the *unemployment rate* and the *labour-force participation rate* in the preceding paragraph and sentence.
- *In that year* in sentence D refers to 2014 in the preceding sentence.

The writers very skillfully use a variety of grammar structures to create flow. Refer to the Reading 1 line numbers indicated in the first column of the table to find examples of sentences with good flow. Write them in the second column. Underline the grammar structures that illustrate this technique.

LINE NUMBERS	PREPOSITIONAL PHRASES
75–76	*In that year, 17.80 million people were employed, and …*
98–99	
100	
124–125	
145–146	

LINE NUMBERS	ADVERB CLAUSES
6–8	
15–16	*As we will see, the term natural does not imply that this rate of unemployment is desirable.*
97–98	
110–111	

LINE NUMBERS	DETERMINERS + NOUNS
44–45	*Every month, Statistics Canada produces data on unemployment and…*
107–108	

LINE NUMBERS	ONE-WORD ADVERBS
109	*Similarly*, some workers may be working part-time when …*
143–144	

LINE NUMBERS	INFINITIVE PHRASES OF PURPOSE
75	*To see how these data are computed*, consider the figures for 2014.*
156–157	

Keep these grammatical structures in mind when you write and revise, and use them to improve flow in your writing.

B. To increase your understanding of this writing technique, read these three paragraphs adapted from Reading 2 and underline the grammatical structures the authors use at the beginning of their sentences. When you have finished, discuss the structures you have underlined with your class.

> In 2016, youth accounted for over 35 percent of unemployed people globally, despite representing just over 15 percent of the world's labour force. In regions such as Southern Asia, Northern Africa, and the Arab States, youth comprise more than 40 percent of the total unemployed population despite constituting only 17 percent or less of the labour force within their respective regions. As a point of comparison, in Europe youth represent around 20 percent of the total unemployed and around 10 percent of the total labour force.
>
> These data show how much more likely it is for young, economically active people to find themselves in unemployment in comparison to the rest of the population. The ratio of the youth to adult unemployment rate globally is estimated at 2.9 in 2016. This remains comparable to the 2007 ratio, with significant differences across regions. For instance, as of 2016, youth unemployment rates are five times higher than those of adults in South-Eastern Asia and the Pacific. Meanwhile, in the Arab states, Southern Asia, and Northern Africa, the ratio is between 3.5 and 4.3. The youth to adult unemployment ratio is comparatively lower in Sub-Saharan Africa and Central and Western Asia as well as in Europe and Northern America.
>
> In addition to the high youth unemployment rates, the growing duration of unemployment spells among young workers is of equal concern, especially in many of the developed countries. For instance, across the Organization for Economic Cooperation and Development (OECD) countries, more than two out of every ten unemployed youth have been without work for a year or more in 2015. While the incidence of long-term unemployment among youth is lower than among the prime age unemployed, extended periods of unemployment for young workers can lead to skills decline, and result in growing discouragement. This unfortunate situation can have long-lasting negative consequences on young people's future employability and earning capacity as well as on aggregate productivity and economic growth.

MyBookshelf > My eLab >
Exercises > Chapter 1 >
Accuracy Review

Writing Definitions

In Reading 1, some key economics terms are defined in the margin. While definitions are not always so conveniently highlighted in academic texts, key terms are often defined. It is important to note definitions as they are often tested in exams. Furthermore, including definitions in your writing gives it one of the characteristics of academic discourse.

A. The following table includes economics definitions from Reading 1, as well as some definitions from other academic fields. Compare how they are written across disciplines. Look closely at the definitions in the table and find the following:

1. the term defined by an equation: *unemployment rate* _____

2. the term with the most descriptive definition: _____

3. the term whose definition starts with a reference to a word root: _____

4. the term whose definition describes its evolution: _____

5. the term with a definition describing what it is and what it is not: _____

6. the term defined by the description of a process: _____

7. the term defined by a noun phrase positioned between commas and directly following it: _____

8. terms with definitions introduced by the verb *be* (*is*): _____
_____

DISCIPLINE	TERM	DEFINITION
BUSINESS	ProSnack Natural Foods (the name of a business)	Despite some success, Vancouver-based ProSnack Natural Foods, a provider of energy bars with natural ingredients, is having difficulty placing its snacks with big stores that could increase sales. (adapted from Griffin, Ebert, Starke, & Lang, 2014)
COMPUTER SCIENCE	Hypertext transfer protocol (HTTP)	The conventions that govern this dialogue [between web servers and individual computers] constitute the hypertext transfer protocol (HTTP). A protocol is a list of rules that defines an agreed way of exchanging information. In HTTP, the browser first opens a connection, specifying the address of the desired server. Then, it makes its request. After delivering the response, the server closes down the connection. Once the transaction is complete, that is the end of the matter (Witten, Gori, & Numerico, 2007).
ECONOMICS	Unemployment rate	This rate represents the percentage of the labour force that is unemployed: $$\text{Unemployment rate} = \frac{\text{Number of unemployed}}{\text{Labour force}} \times 100$$
	Natural rate of unemployment	The economy's natural rate of unemployment refers to the amount of unemployment that the economy naturally experiences (Mankiw, Kneebone, & McKenzie, 2017).

DISCIPLINE	TERM	DEFINITION
ECOLOGY	Boreal forest	The boreal forest or taiga is a world of wood and water that covers over 11 percent of the Earth's land area. On the surface, the boreal forest is the essence of monotony. However, if you pay attention, you are rewarded with plenty of variety. In places, the trees stand so close together you can barely walk through them. Elsewhere, so many trees have been toppled by wind that you can walk on their piled trunks, one to two metres above the ground, for many kilometres. In still other places, the forest is open and you can wander wherever you like on its soft floor of needles and duff. A trek through a boreal forest eventually leads to the shore of a lake or river, where shade and cover give way to light and space (Molles, 2008).
ENGINEERING	Engineer	The term engineer comes to English from the Latin word ingenium, meaning "talent," "genius" or "native ability." Its first use was to describe those who had an ability to invent and operate weapons of war. Later, the word came to be associated with design and construction as in ships, roads, canals and bridges, and the people skilled in these fields were non-military, or civil, engineers (Andrews, Aplevich, Fraser, & MacGregor, 2009).
HUMAN RESOURCE MANAGEMENT	Employment equity program	An employment equity program is a detailed plan designed to identify and correct existing discrimination, redress past discrimination and achieve a balanced representation of designated group members in the organization (Dressler & Cole, 2011).
PHYSICS	Mass	In the International System of Units (SI), mass is measured in kilograms. Unlike the metre, the kilogram is not based on any natural physical quantity. By convention, the kilogram has been defined as "the mass of a particular platinum-iridium alloy cylinder" by the International Bureau of Weights and Standards in Sèvres, France. Weight and mass are quite different quantities, even though they are often confused in everyday language. Mass is an intrinsic, unchanging property of an object. Weight, in contrast, is a measure of the gravitational force acting on an object, which can vary depending on the object's location. For example, if you are fortunate enough to travel to Mars someday, you will find that your weight is less than on Earth, though your mass is unchanged (Walker, 2010).

It would be oversimplifying to say that all definitions are written the same way, or even that definitions within a single discipline all follow the same pattern. For example, some definitions in engineering and physics are presented as equations. And in some disciplines, it is appropriate to use the second person *you* in definitions (e.g., the ecology and physics definitions above).

References

Andrews, G., Aplevich, J. D., Fraser, R., & MacGregor, C. (2009). *Introduction to professional engineering in Canada* (3rd ed., p. 1). Toronto, ON: Pearson Prentice Hall.

Dressler, G., & Cole, N. (2011). *Human resources management in Canada* (11th Canadian ed., p. 41). Toronto, ON: Pearson Canada.

Griffin, R. W., Ebert, R. J., Starke, F. A., & Lang, M. D. (2014). *Business* (8th Canadian ed., pp. 110–119). Toronto, ON: Pearson Education Canada.

Mankiw, N. G., Kneebone, R. D., & McKenzie, K. J. (2017). *Principles of macroeconomics* (7th Canadian ed., pp. 179–188). Toronto, ON: Nelson Education.

Molles, M. C. (2008). *Ecology: Concepts and applications* (4th ed., p. 36). New York, NY: McGraw Hill Higher Education.

Walker, J. (2010). *Physics* (4th ed., p. 3). San Francisco, CA: Pearson Addison-Wesley.

Witten, K., Gori, M., & Numerico, T. (2007). *Web dragons* (p. 64). San Francisco, CA: Elsevier.

MyBookshelf > My eLab >
Exercises > Chapter 1 >
Focus on Writing

WARM-UP ASSIGNMENT

Write a Definition for a Key Economics Term

Working with a partner, write a one-paragraph definition for one of the key terms at the end of Reading 1 (lines 167–174): *minimum wage* or *unions*.

A. Review the models of definition writing below or in Focus on Writing (page 19) to determine which will work best for your term. You may want to use more than one model to extend your definition to a full paragraph.

- Equation
- Process description
- Reference to the word root
- Description of the evolution of the term (over time)
- Description of what the term is and what it is not
- Detailed description

> When you receive feedback from your instructor or your classmates on this Warm-Up Assignment, you will have information that you can use to improve your writing on the Final Assignment.

B. Include the name of your key term in your definition and write in the third-person objective perspective. Consult reliable sources for help with your definition. However, for this assignment, do not use quotations from outside sources. State the definition in your own words so you do not accidentally plagiarize. (Refer to the Academic Survival Skill on paraphrasing techniques in Chapter 5, page 152.)

Refer to the Models Chapter (page 274) to see an example of a definition and to learn more about how to write one.

Academic Survival Skill

Identifying Reliable Sources of Information

When you communicate in an academic environment, you must base your factual statements on reliable information. How do you know what sources are reliable? In almost all cases, reliable sources contain information that has been reviewed by experts in the field. Therefore, when you are searching for information, it is useful to know how the findings were generated. Here are some notes on several common sources of academic information to give you an idea of their reliability.

DICTIONARIES: Published dictionaries have been written and reviewed by experts. Online dictionaries may not have been reviewed. To combine the convenience of an online dictionary with the reliability of a published dictionary, look for a reliable dictionary that you can access on your computer or electronic device.

TEXTBOOKS: Published textbooks have been written and reviewed by experts. They are reliable sources of information.

PEER-REVIEWED JOURNAL ARTICLES: Articles in peer-reviewed journals have been written and reviewed by experts (academic peers or colleagues). They are also reliable sources of information.

NEWSPAPERS AND MAGAZINES: Newspaper and magazine articles are as reliable as the organizations that produce them. Generally, larger or well-known organizations produce reliable information. If you use a newspaper or magazine article as a source, it is advisable to verify that information in an alternate source. If you are not sure whether a newspaper or magazine article is reliable, don't use it.

WEBSITES: Like newspapers and magazines, websites are as reliable as the bodies that produce them. Some come from large organizations, like Statistics Canada, and must meet high standards of review before information is posted. Others are created by individuals or organizations with specific perspectives or opinions; these websites may provide biased information. In these cases, the information is not reliable.

Students often ask about the reliability of information on *Wikipedia*. Currently, information on *Wikipedia* is reviewed but not necessarily by experts. *Wikipedia* is a good place to begin your search, but it is best to confirm information you find using an alternate or original source.

In considering the reliability of sources on which to base your academic work, ask yourself these questions:

• Who are the authors or creators of the information?
• Do they have a specific purpose or opinion that might influence the reliability of the information?
• Was the information reviewed by experts?

For this exercise, your instructor will present you with a set of texts. You may be able to add other textbooks or articles that you have with you.

A. With a partner, review the texts and determine which ones are reliable sources and which are not.

B. Discuss your reasons with the class.

  **READING ②**

World Employment Social Outlook: Trends for Youth

The International Labour Office, located in Geneva, Switzerland, produces annual global labour force statistics. This text contains information about global youth unemployment rates.

A. Replace the bold word(s) in each sentence with the appropriate academic or economics-related word from the box. This practice will prepare you for Reading 2.

> ~~aggregate~~   constituting   heterogeneity   incidence   projected
> tally   trajectory   trend   relevant   repercussions   stable

1. Unemployment can have negative effects on young people's future employment and financial security as well as on **total combined**
   _____*aggregate*_____ productivity and economic growth.

2. Youth unemployment is expected to climb further to 17.1 percent
   in 2017, implying an increase in the regional **count** _____
   of unemployed young people of about 0.8 million in comparison
   to 2015 figures.

3. Unemployment can have long-lasting negative **effects** _____
   on young people's future employability and earning capacity.

4. The ratio of the youth to adult unemployment rate globally is estimated
   at 2.9 although there is considerable **difference** _____
   across regions.

5. Youth unemployment in Eastern Europe and Central and Western Asia is
   predicted _____ to reach 16.6 percent in 2016, half a percentage
   point lower than 2015 estimates, with a further decrease to 16.2 percent
   expected in 2017.

6. In regions such as Southern Asia, Northern Africa, and the Arab States,
   youth comprise more than 40 percent of the total unemployed population
   despite **making up** _____ only 17 percent or less of the labour
   force within their respective regions.

7. In most regions, youth unemployment rates have remained relatively
   unchanged _____, with some evidence of a decline in rates
   in Europe and Northern America.

8. The youth unemployment rate in Eastern Asia is expected to edge up
   slightly to 10.7 percent in 2016, from 10.6 percent in 2015, continuing
   the upward **movement** _____ that has been evident since 2011.

9. Extended periods of unemployment for young workers can lead to skills
   decline, and prevent efforts to gain **suitable** _____ labour
   market experience.

10. The youth unemployment rate in Sub-Saharan Africa is expected
    to continue on its downward **path** _____.

11. The **amount** _____ of unemployment among youth will remain
    a pressing issue in Northern, Southern, and Western Europe.

B. For further practice, fill in the blanks in the paragraph below with the best word from the word box in task A above. When you have finished, check your answers with a classmate.

Youth unemployment can be damaging for both a country's youth and

its economy. In Canada, Statistics Canada measures the _____ unemployment rate for people in a variety of categories: youth, older people, men, and women. Statistics Canada also reports the unemployment rate for

each province, and there is considerable _____ across regions.

In the past, in some regions, such as the Maritime provinces, the _____ of unemployment has been consistently high; in other provinces, such

as the mid-western provinces, the _____ has been toward low unemployment. At times like this, people from the Maritimes have travelled

to the western provinces to find _____ work. However, what can

seem like a _____ market can change rapidly. More recently,

a downward _____ in oil prices has had negative _____ for the economy in the western provinces. Although oil prices are

_____ to rise again, the _____ of unemployed youth in Alberta and Saskatchewan rose during this period. The natural resource

_____ the greatest income for the western provinces in Canada is oil; however, a diverse economy is the best protection from the fluctuations that can cause economic instability.

Before You Read

A. Discuss with your classmates whether youth unemployment is a problem in the countries in which you live, study, or work. Answer these questions.

1. Do you know (approximately) the youth unemployment rate for the country you are in now?

2. Can you find this information in a reliable source? Where could you look for it?

B. Once you have identified a reliable source (or two), find the youth unemployment rate for your own country or another country you might like to live in.

While You Read

Use the strategies you learned in Focus on Reading (page 4).

C. Skim Reading 2 to answer the questions.

1. a) What is the topic of the reading? _____

   b) How long is it? _____

   c) What type of text is it? How do you know? _____

   _____

2. What do you already know about the topic?

   _____

   _____

3 Based on the text type, how will the content most likely be organized?

_____

D. While you read, complete the chart by adding arrows that indicate upward (↑), downward (↓), or no (=) change in global youth unemployment rates.

REGION	UPWARD CHANGE (↑) DOWNWARD CHANGE (↓) NO CHANGE (=)
Northern Africa	= *(remain high)*
Sub-Saharan Africa	
Latin America and the Caribbean	
North America	
Arab States	
Eastern Asia	
Southern Asia	
South-Eastern Asia and the Pacific	
Eastern Europe	
Central and Western Asia	
Northern, Southern, and Western Europe	

World Employment Social Outlook: Trends for Youth

Regional Trends in Youth Unemployment

Global youth unemployment is again on the rise, largely due to a significant economic slowdown in some major emerging countries

The global youth unemployment rate is expected to reach 13.1 percent in 2016, an
5 increase of 0.2 percentage points in comparison to 2015 values (and the number of unemployed youth is **projected** to rise by half a million to 71 million). The upturn in the youth unemployment rate represents a return to a level close to the twenty-year peak of 13.2 percent, which was observed in 2013 (Table 2). However, a closer look at the global picture reveals considerable **heterogeneity** in youth unemployment
10 **trends** across regions, in terms of both rates and levels. In particular, much of the increase in the 2016 global figures appears to be due to growing youth unemployment in Latin America and the Caribbean, Central and Western Asia and South-Eastern Asia and the Pacific. In most other regions, youth unemployment rates have remained relatively **stable**, with some evidence of a decline in rates in Europe and Northern
15 America. Individual regions are considered separately below.

Africa

• **Northern Africa:** The **incidence** of unemployment among youth in the region is expected to remain elevated at 29.3 percent in 2016, representing the second highest rate across all regions. The slight improvement in the regional figures during

2016 stems from improvements in Egypt and Tunisia, two countries that experienced recent declines but where youth unemployment rates still remain high. A further decline in the regional youth unemployment rate is expected in 2017 when it should reach 29.2 percent.

- **Sub-Saharan Africa:** The youth unemployment rate in sub-Saharan Africa is expected to continue on its downward **trajectory**, which began in 2012, reaching 10.9 percent in 2016 and decreasing slightly to 10.8 percent in the following year. However, the unemployment outlook for youth in major countries of the region remains quite mixed. In South Africa, more than half of all active youth are expected to remain unemployed in 2016, representing the highest youth unemployment rate in the region.

Americas

- **Latin America and the Caribbean:** The region is expected to show the largest increase in the youth unemployment rate, which is estimated to reach 16.8 percent in 2016, up from 15.7 percent in 2015—this compares with a low of 13.8 percent achieved in 2008. It is expected to climb further to 17.1 percent in 2017, implying an increase in the regional **tally** of unemployed young people of about 0.8 million in comparison to 2015 figures. The impact of the uncertain economic situation in Brazil is a major factor in the overall regional estimates for 2016, together with growing youth unemployment rates in Argentina (which are only partially offset by declining rates in Chile and Mexico).

- **North America:** The youth unemployment rate in the region is likely to decrease slightly to 11.5 percent in 2016 from 11.8 percent in 2015. This reduction is driven by declining youth unemployment in the United States. Conversely, in 2017, a slight rise in the regional unemployment rate to 11.7 percent is anticipated.

Arab States

- The youth unemployment rate in the Arab States will remain the highest globally, at 30.6 percent in 2016 (although a slight improvement to 29.7 percent by 2017 is anticipated). Oil exporting countries—notably Oman, Qatar and Saudi Arabia— are projected to see an increase in the youth unemployment rate in 2016, mainly as a result of a slowdown in growth and tighter fiscal policy (ILO, 2016). Geopolitical tensions will continue to weigh on youth unemployment prospects in other countries of the region.

Asia

- **Eastern Asia:** The youth unemployment rate is expected to edge up slightly to 10.7 percent in 2016, from 10.6 percent in 2015, continuing the upward trend that has been evident since 2011. However, the number of unemployed youth in the region is expected to decrease to 11 million in 2017, down from 11.9 million in 2015 (due to a decline in the number of youth participating in the labour market and remaining in education instead).

- **Southern Asia:** The share of unemployed youth in the region should remain stable at 10.9 percent in 2016 and 2017. Consequently, the total number of unemployed youth—representing nearly 20 percent of unemployed youth worldwide—will remain just below 14 million. The youth unemployment rate in the region's largest economy, India, is expected to remain slightly below the regional average in 2016. Youth unemployment rates in Pakistan and Bangladesh are expected to decline, though remaining slightly above the average rate.

Table 2: Youth unemployment trends and projections to 2017, by region

REGION	UNEMPLOYMENT RATE, 2007–17 (PERCENTAGES)				UNEMPLOYMENT YOUTH, 2015–17 (MILLIONS)		
	2007–14	2015	2016	2017	2015	2016	2017
World		12.9	13.1	13.1	70.5	71.0	71.0
AFRICA							
Northern Africa		29.4	29.3	29.2	3.7	3.7	3.7
Sub-Saharan Africa		10.9	10.9	10.8	11.1	11.3	11.6
AMERICAS							
Latin America and the Caribbean		15.7	16.8	17.1	8.5	9.2	9.3
North America		11.8	11.5	11.7	3.0	2.9	2.9
ARAB STATES		30.6	30.6	29.7	2.6	2.7	2.6
ASIA							
Eastern Asia		10.6	10.7	10.9	11.9	11.4	11.0
South-Eastern Asia and the Pacific		12.4	13.0	13.6	7.4	7.7	8.0
Southern Asia		10.9	10.9	10.9	13.7	13.8	13.9
EUROPE AND CENTRAL ASIA							
Central and Western Asia		16.6	17.1	17.5	2.1	2.1	2.2
Eastern Europe		17.1	16.6	16.2	2.0	1.8	1.7
Northern, Southern and Western Europe		20.6	19.7	18.9	4.5	4.3	4.1

Source: ILO calculations based on ILO Research Department's Trends Econometric Models, April 2016.

- **South-Eastern Asia and the Pacific:** The region is expected to show a steady increase in the youth unemployment rate over the coming years: rising from 12.4 percent in 2015 to 13.0 percent in 2016 and reaching 13.6 percent in 2017. This means that, by 2017, more than half a million youth will have joined the pool of unemployed in the region. This increase is largely driven by adverse developments in Indonesia, where youth unemployment is currently above 20 percent and expected to rise considerably over the next two years.

Europe and Central Asia

- **Eastern Europe and Central and Western Asia:** Youth unemployment is expected to decline in Eastern Europe despite the recent adverse economic developments in the Russian Federation. Youth unemployment in the region is projected to reach 16.6 percent in 2016, half a percentage point lower than 2015 estimates, with a further decrease to 16.2 percent expected in 2017. In Central and Western Asia, however, youth unemployment is expected to rise to 17.1 percent in 2016, from 16.6 percent in 2015.

- **Northern, Southern and Western Europe:** The incidence of unemployment among youth will remain a pressing issue in Northern, Southern and Western Europe, despite some signs of normalization beginning to emerge. Indeed, the youth

85 unemployment rate is projected to decline from 19.7 percent in 2016 to 18.9 percent in 2017. A large proportion of this reduction is due to developments in certain high unemployment countries, such as Italy, Portugal, and Spain, which are expected to see sizable reductions in the youth unemployment rates during 2017. Overall, the youth unemployment rate in the EU-28 is expected to reach 19.2 percent in
90 2016 and 18.4 percent in 2017, down from 20.3 percent in 2015. This means that the number of unemployed youth in the region is expected to decline by half a million, from 4.7 million in 2015 to 4.2 million in 2017.

Young people are over-represented among the unemployed, a trend which has strengthened in several regions

95 As of 2016 youth accounted for over 35 percent of unemployed people globally, despite representing just over 15 percent of the world's labour force and 21 percent of the global working-age population. In regions such as Southern Asia, Northern Africa and the Arab States, youth comprise more than 40 percent of the total unemployed population despite **constituting** only 17 percent or less of the labour force within their
100 respective regions. To a lesser degree, in Europe youth represent around 20 percent of the total unemployed and around 10 percent of the total labour force.

As such, these data show how much more likely it is for young, economically active people to find themselves in unemployment in comparison to the rest of the population. The ratio of the youth to adult unemployment rate globally is estimated at 2.9 in 2016.
105 This remains comparable to the 2007 ratio, with considerable heterogeneity across regions. For instance, as of 2016, youth unemployment rates are five times higher than those of adults in South-Eastern Asia and the Pacific (Figure 2). Meanwhile, in the Arab states, Southern Asia and Northern Africa, the ratio is between 3.5 and 4.3. The youth to adult unemployment ratio is comparatively lower in Sub-Saharan Africa
110 and Central and Western Asia as well as in Europe and Northern America.

In addition to the high youth unemployment rates, the growing duration of unemployment spells among young workers is of equal concern, especially in many of the developed countries. For instance, across the Organization for Economic Cooperation and Development (OECD) countries, more than two out of every ten
115 unemployed youth have been without work for a year or more in 2015 (in the EU-28,

Figure 2: Youth to adult unemployment rate ratios by region, 2007–2016

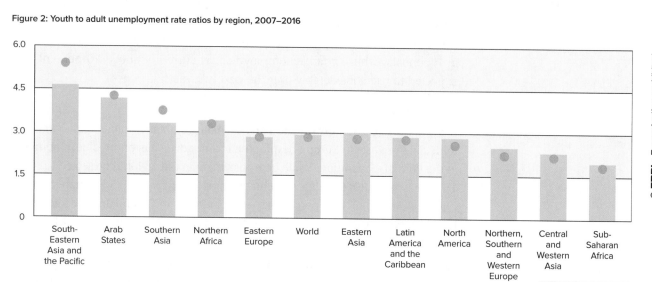

Source: ILO calculations based on ILO Research Department's Trends Econometric Models, April 2016.

2007   2016

this share reached almost one-third of unemployed youth in 2015). While the incidence of long-term unemployment among youth is lower than among the prime age unemployed, i.e., aged 25 to 54 (37.3 percent in the OECD countries in 2015), extended periods of unemployment for young workers can lead to skills deterioration,

120 hinder efforts to gain **relevant** labour market experience and result in growing discouragement, especially among those young workers seeking their first job. This can have long-lasting negative **repercussions** on young people's future employability and earning capacity as well as on **aggregate** productivity and economic growth.

(1459 words)

Reference

International Labour Office (ILO). (2016). *World employment social outlook: Trends 2016*. Geneva.

International Labour Organization. (2016). *World employment social outlook: Trends for youth* (pp. 5–7). Geneva: International Labour Office.

UNIVERSITY

After You Read

E. Answer the following questions to demonstrate your understanding of the reading.

1. How does the average global youth unemployment rate in 2016 compare to the 2015 numbers? How does this compare to the rate over the past twenty years?

_____

_____

2. Is the average global youth unemployment rate a good representation of what is happening with youth employment in each region? Why?

_____

_____

_____

3. Based on the information in this reading, if you were a youth looking for work in 2016, where would be the best place for you to live?

_____

_____

4. How does the youth unemployment rate that you found for your own country in Before You Read compare with the information in this 2016 reading?

_____

_____

5. How do youth unemployment rates compare with unemployment rates for adults?

_____

_____

6 What is the only advantage that youth seem to have in the global unemployment context?

_____

_____

7 What are the negative consequences of long-term unemployment for both youth and older workers and for society in general?

_____

_____

_____

8 Why do you think it is important to record and track global trends in youth unemployment?

_____

_____

_____

MyBookshelf > My eLab > Exercises > Chapter 1 > World Employment Social Outlook

FOCUS ON CRITICAL THINKING

Identifying Economics Discourse

Discourse refers to the language that is used in a specific discipline. Being able to identify discourse typical of a specific discipline can help you write and speak like an expert. As you read textbooks and listen to lectures, be aware of repeated patterns in language that will help you recognize the discourse.

In this chapter, we can identify discourse commonly used in the field of economics. Economists measure variables that influence economic health and report on how those variables have *increased* or *decreased*. Because they frequently need to express these concepts, they use synonyms extensively to add variety and interest.

A. Reread lines 1 to 93 of Reading 2 (page 25); this time, underline the words and expressions that mean "increasing," "decreasing," or "staying the same." Then, categorize the words and expressions in the following table (page 31) or on a separate page. Include the adjectives, adverbs, or prepositions that precede or follow the expressions; these words are as important to accurate written expression as the terms themselves. When you have finished, check with the class to ensure your lists are complete.

B. As a class, review your lists and circle the discourse that uses passive voice to emphasize the information rather than the people who are expecting or anticipating the information.

C. Highlight the two expressions (one in each of the first two columns) that show the increase or reduction is driven by something else. These are useful expressions to show cause and effect.

WORDS OR EXPRESSIONS MEANING "INCREASING"	WORDS OR EXPRESSIONS MEANING "DECREASING"	WORDS OR EXPRESSIONS MEANING "STAYING THE SAME"
• *on the rise* • *is expected to reach*	• *economic slowdown* • *some evidence of decline in*	• *a return to the level of* • *remained relatively stable*

D. Using this data set, select words or expressions from the table above to show the relationships between the variables. Working with a partner, on a separate page, write six sentences using two expressions from each column. Write your best sentences on the board to share with the class.

Hypothetical Unemployment Rate for Men and Women

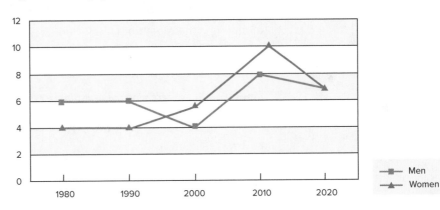

Example: *In 2000, the unemployment rate for women was on the rise.*

 **READING ❸**   **The "Jobless Recovery"**

This reading is an excerpt from a popular book that is sold in bookstores around the world. In it, the authors refer to a global youth protest movement that was partly driven by high youth unemployment. Read the excerpt to learn how high youth unemployment breaks the unspoken promise that society has with young people.

A. Label the graph with the following expressions: *baby boom, baby boom echo,* and *demographic bulge*. With a partner, discuss the possible causes of the baby boom and the baby boom echo.

B. Choose the best answer to replace the bold word(s) in each sentence, then give another synonym for the best choice.

1 Young people are **bearing the brunt of** the failures of previous generations.

　a) suffering the most from

　b) working with

　c) managing to work with

　Other synonym: *receiving the worst impact from*

2 Youth unemployment is similarly **dire** in other parts of the world.

　a) low

　b) high

　c) serious

　Other synonym: _____

3 The '60s baby boomer radicalization was based on youthful hope and social **ideology**.

　a) thoughts that constitute the political system of Marxism

　b) ideas that support the economic system of capitalism

　c) set of beliefs that influence how people behave

　Other synonym: _____

4 We need to reinvent our institutions—everything from the financial industry to our models of education and science—to **kick-start** a new global economy.

　a) initiate slowly

　b) start off quickly

　c) begin gradually

　Other synonym: _____

5 Fifty years ago, baby boomers had access to information through the new marvel of television, and as they became university-age and delayed having families, many had time to challenge government **policies** and social **norms**.

For policies:

a) official ways of doing something

b) officially written in law

c) official plans for the future

Other synonym: _____

For norms:

a) government rules

b) accepted standards

c) written agreements

Other synonym: _____

6 We need to make the creation of new jobs a top **priority**.

a) one of the first to start

b) something of high action

c) one of the most important things to do

Other synonym: _____

7 Without job **prospects**, young people may decide to immigrate to countries where they can find relevant work.

a) policies

b) opportunities

c) priorities

Other synonym: _____

8 Youth **radicalization** swept the world, ending in explosive protests, violence, and government restrictions across Europe, Asia, and North America.

a) process of adopting extreme political, social, or religious ideas

b) desire to learn about different ideas

c) wish to respect other people's ideas

Other synonym: _____

9 Such high rates of unemployment **violate** the unspoken agreement society has with young people.

a) decline

b) support

c) destroy

Other synonym: _____

MyBookshelf > My eLab > Exercises > Chapter 1 > Vocabulary Review

Before You Read

A. Skim Reading 3 and share your answers with your class.

1 a) What is the topic of the reading? _____

_____

b) How long is it? _____

c) What type of text is it? _____

2 What do you already know about the topic?

_____

_____

3 Based on the text type, how will the content most likely be organized?

_____

_____

While You Read

B. While you read, demonstrate your understanding of the text by indicating whether the following statements are true or false. For questions 10 and 11, explain your choice.

STATEMENTS	TRUE	FALSE
1 High youth unemployment was a catalyst for the revolutions in Tunisia and Egypt.	✓	
2 Society's unspoken agreement with young people is that if they study and work hard, they will find a job and become productive citizens.		
3 Once youth unemployment is solved, the rest of our problems will be solved.		
4 The unhappiness that unemployed youth are experiencing today has a precedent in the radicalization that occurred fifty years ago.		
5 As there are so few young people today, they do not have much power.		
6 Poor voter turnout among young people suggests that they are not involved in the political processes in their countries.		
7 Youth do not have the ability to work together or become informed.		
8 The author suggests that young people should pay higher tuition fees.		
9 If youth remain unemployed and uninvolved in society, they will rebel against the older generation.		
10 The authors of this text are young people. (How can you tell if this is true or false?) _____ _____		
11 This reading tries to make readers take action to change things. (How can you tell if this is true or false?) _____ _____		

The "Jobless Recovery"

A common thread to the revolutions in Tunisia and Egypt and protests elsewhere in the Middle East and North Africa is the soul-crushing high rate of youth unemployment. Twenty-four percent of young people in the region cannot find jobs. To be sure, protesters were also agitating for democracy, wanting the full rights of citizenship and not to be treated as subjects. But non-existent employment opportunities were a powerful catalyst.

Youth unemployment is similarly **dire** in other parts of the world. In Spain, more than 40 percent of young people are unemployed. In France, the rate is more than 20 percent, and in the United States, it's 21 percent. In country after country, many young people have given up looking for work. A recent survey in the UK revealed that more than half of the eighteen- to twenty-five-year-olds questioned said they were thinking of immigrating because of the lack of job **prospects** ("The outsiders," 2011).

Such high rates of unemployment **violate** the unspoken agreement society has with young people: if they are industrious, law-abiding and diligent students, their lives will be prosperous. That's why it's hardly surprising that unemployed young people are fuelling a growing protest movement around the world. To make matters worse, widespread youth unemployment is just one sign of a deeper failure. The society we are passing to today's young people is seriously damaged. And as we explain in *Macrowikinomics*, many institutions that have served us well for decades, even centuries, seem frozen and unable to move forward. The global economy, our financial services industry, governments, health care, the media and our global problem-solving institutions like the UN are all struggling.

Young people are **bearing the brunt** of our failures. Full of enthusiasm and relatively free of responsibilities, youth are traditionally the generation most inclined to question the status quo and authority. Fifty years ago, baby boomers had access to information through the new marvel of television, and as they became university-age and delayed having families, many had time to challenge government **policies** and social **norms**.

Youth **radicalization** swept the world, culminating in explosive protests, violence and government crackdowns across Europe, Asia and North America.

In Paris in May 1968, protests that began as student sit-ins challenging the Charles de Gaulle government and the capitalist system culminated in a two-week general strike involving more than eleven million workers. Youth played a key role in the so-called Prague Spring in Czechoslovakia that same year. In West Germany, the student movement gained momentum in the late '60s. In the United States, youth radicalization began with the civil rights movement and extended into movements for women's rights and other issues and culminated in the Vietnam War protests.

Young people today have a demographic influence similar to that of their once-rebellious parents. In North America, the baby boom echo is larger than the boom itself. In South America, the demographic bulge is huge and even bigger in Africa, the Middle
50 East, and Asia. Approximately 52 percent of the world population is under the age of thirty and a whopping 27 percent under the age of fifteen (US Census Bureau, 2011).

The '60s baby boomer radicalization was based on youthful hope and social **ideology**. Protesters championed the opposition
55 to war, a celebration of youth culture and the possibilities for a new kind of social order. Today's simmering youth radicalization is much different. It is rooted not only in unemployment but personal broken hopes, mistreatment and injustice. Young people are alienated; witness the dropping young voter turnout
60 for elections. They are turning their backs on the system. And we shouldn't forget that today's youth have at their fingertips the most powerful tools ever for finding out what's going on, informing others and organizing collective responses.

We need to make the creation of new jobs a top **priority**. We need to reinvent our
65 institutions—everything from the financial industry to our models of education and science—to **kick-start** a new global economy. We need to engage today's young people, not jack up tuition fees and cut back on retraining. We need to encourage their drive, passion, and expertise. We need to help them take advantage of new web-based tools and become involved in making the work more prosperous, just,
70 and sustainable. If we don't take such measures, we run the risk of a generational conflict that could make the radicalization of youth in Europe and North America in the 1960s seem insignificant in comparison.

(748 words)

References

The outsiders: Where the financial crisis has hit hardest. (2011, July 5). *Economist*. Retrieved from http://www.economist.com/blogs/dailychart/2011/07/youth-unemployment

US Census Bureau, 2011.

Tapscott, D., & Williams, A. D. (2012). *Macrowikinomics: New solutions for a connected planet* (pp. xiv–xvi). Toronto, ON: Portfolio Penguin.

After You Read

C. Working with a partner, answer the following questions. When you are finished, discuss your answers with two other classmates.

1 In the first two paragraphs, what information do the authors cite to show the seriousness of the global economic situation for youth?

_____

_____

_____

2 What is society's "unspoken agreement" with its young people?
Do you believe in this agreement?

_____

_____

_____

3 What institutions do the authors believe are struggling and not progressing?

_____

_____

4 According to the authors, what characterized the youth radicalization
movement fifty years ago?

_____

_____

_____

5 In which countries did youth radicalization appear in the 1960s?

_____

6 Why do the authors believe that young people today have the power
to influence governments and change society?

_____

_____

_____

7 Do the authors believe that the current protests are the result of the same
problems that existed fifty years ago?

_____

_____

8 What do the authors believe needs to be done to solve the problem
of youth unemployment?

_____

_____

_____

9 With your class, discuss what you learned that was new, interesting,
or important. What would you like to learn more about? Do you disagree
with any issues that were raised in this reading? Do you have other
thoughts about what could be done to reduce youth unemployment?

_____

_____

D. Reading 3 was published in 2012 (with data from 2011) and Reading 2, in 2016. In the five intervening years, youth unemployment rates changed. Scan Readings 2 and 3 to complete the table and generate a data set. Add two more countries that particularly interest you. Use what you know about reliable sources to locate information to complete the table.

This is the data set you will work with for your Final Assignment.

COUNTRIES	2011 YOUTH UNEMPLOYMENT RATE (READING 3 DATA)	2016 YOUTH UNEMPLOYMENT RATE (READING 2 DATA)	CURRENT YOUTH UNEMPLOYMENT RATE (FIND RELIABLE SOURCES)
Tunisia and Egypt	*24 percent*		
Spain (Western Europe)			
France (Western Europe)			
United States (North America)			
Other country of interest to you			
Other country of interest to you			

MyBookshelf > My eLab > Exercises > Chapter 1 > The "Jobless Recovery"

FINAL ASSIGNMENT
Write a Description of a Data Set

Using the above data set (customized to include your interests), write a description of the increases and decreases you can observe.

A. Begin with a definition of youth unemployment.

B. Continue with a description of the data that matches your definition.

C. Use your knowledge of economic discourse to describe the increases and decreases in the data.

D. Use a variety of grammatical structures at the start of your sentences to build flow.

E. Finish with a recommendation for steps that should be taken to reduce youth unemployment in the future.

Refer to the Models Chapter (page 274) to learn more about how to describe a data set and to see an example.

Critical Connections

Find two other texts on economics-related topics. These could be from a textbook or from a reliable newspaper or journal.

A. Read the texts, looking for definitions and examples of economic discourse such as expressions indicating upward or downward changes, or stability.

List the definitions here:

_____

_____

_____

List the examples of economics discourse here:

_____

_____

_____

B. When you have finished, compare the definitions and discourse from these two texts with the discourse from Reading 2. Finally, compare your definitions and examples with those of your classmates.

Continue to build your awareness of the conventions of writing definitions and discipline-related discourse as you work through the following chapters.

CHAPTER 2

Entrepreneurship: Creating Your Own Job

Finding employment can be difficult, but you can increase your chances of finding a job by becoming better educated, building a network of friends, professors, and supervisors, and developing job search documents like cover letters and résumés. You might also think about creating your own job. With an innovative idea and some entrepreneurial skills, you may even end up creating jobs for others. Do you have what it takes to be a successful entrepreneur?

BEGIN.

In this chapter, you will

- learn vocabulary related to entrepreneurship and job creation;

- position main points for emphasis in sentences;

- recognize different styles for in-text citations and references;

- learn how and what to cite and reference;

- learn how to read journal articles;

- discover common organizational patterns in academic articles;

- learn ways to introduce in-text citations in your writing;

- write short and extended process essays.

GEARING UP

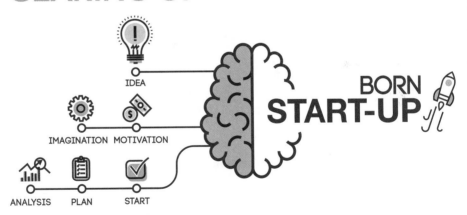

IDEA

IMAGINATION MOTIVATION

ANALYSIS PLAN START

BORN START-UP

A. This infographic shows some of the resources and skills needed to start a successful business. Using it as a starting point, work with a small group of classmates and think of all the resources you might need if you were planning to start your own business.

_____

_____

_____

_____

B. Are you familiar with any entrepreneurs? Discuss with your class any ones you know or have heard of. What companies did they start and how successful are they?

Below are the key words you will practise in this chapter. Check the words you understand, then underline the words you use. Highlight the words you need to learn.

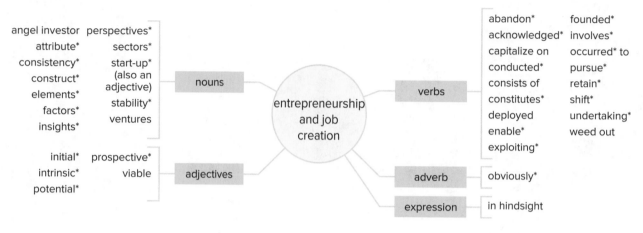

angel investor	perspectives*
attribute*	sectors*
consistency*	start-up* (also an adjective)
construct*	
elements*	stability*
factors*	ventures
insights*	

initial*	prospective*
intrinsic*	viable
potential*	

nouns

entrepreneurship and job creation

adjectives

verbs

abandon*	founded*
acknowledged*	involves*
capitalize on	occurred* to
conducted*	pursue*
consists of	retain*
constitutes*	shift*
deployed	undertaking*
enable*	weed out
exploiting*	

adverb   obviously*

expression   in hindsight

*Appears on the Academic Word List

READING ❶   Jason Njoku and iROKO: A Success Story

In this reading, you will meet a young entrepreneur called Jason Njoku, who has started multiple companies. Here, he talks mostly about iROKO, a Netflix-like company that provides Nollywood (Hollywood-type movies made in Nigeria) content to Africans. Written in interview format, the article reveals the challenges and rewards of entrepreneurial life.

A. Complete each sentence in a way that demonstrates you understand the meaning of the word in bold. When you have finished, compare your sentences with two other classmates. Do you agree on the definitions of the words?

❶ Even if their companies are not doing well, entrepreneurs don't want to **abandon** their companies because *they want to stick with their companies until they become successful.*

❷ An **angel investor** can help an entrepreneur by _____ _____

❸ An entrepreneur will **deploy** her resources quickly as she _____ _____

❹ Experienced entrepreneurs often hope to **enable** the next generation of entrepreneurs by _____

❺ Elon Musk **founded** TESLA motors to _____

❻ Entrepreneurs may learn valuable business lessons **in hindsight** after _____

❼ **Obviously**, not all entrepreneurs _____

Mark Zuckerberg

⑧ It never **occurred to** Mark Zuckerberg to quit because _____

_____

⑨ The **perspective** of an experienced business person can be useful

to an entrepreneur because _____

_____

⑩ There are many **potential** ideas that entrepreneurs might be interested in,

but _____

⑪ A **start-up** company is different from an established company because

_____

B. While you may be familiar with the meaning of the words in the table below, it might be helpful to practise their spelling as the words change from noun to verb to adjective forms. You will see most of these forms in Reading 1.

Fill in the table with the missing word forms next to the bullets; if necessary, consult a dictionary or ask a classmate for help.

NOUN	VERB	ADJECTIVE
•	• access	• *accessible*
• *blogger* •	• blog	
•	• create	•
• entrepreneur • entrepreneurship		•
• •	• invest	
•	• participate	•
• •	• subscribe	

Before You Read

A. Based on information from Gearing Up, consider what personality traits successful entrepreneurs must have, and which traits would be nice to have (but are not essential). Working in a small group, list your top five for each category. Then, compare answers with another group.

PERSONALITY TRAITS ENTREPRENEURS ...	
MUST HAVE (ESSENTIAL)	**MIGHT HAVE (NOT ESSENTIAL)**
hard-working	

While You Read

B. As you read, answer the following questions.

1 What the personality traits make Jason Njoku a successful entrepreneur?

_____

_____

_____

2 What start-up companies has he developed?

_____

_____

3 How did he raise money (resources) to start the companies?

_____

_____

When you have finished, compare your answers with those of a classmate.

Jason Njoku and iROKO: A Success Story

If you watch a lot of Nigerian movies, or follow the Nigerian Internet **start-up** scene, chances are either iROKO or Jason Njoku need no introduction.

In 2010, Jason Njoku **founded** iROKO—an online platform that offers its worldwide audience
5 subscription-based access to stream Nollywood movies (primarily)—with the help of his friend and business partner, Bastian Gotter.

Jason Njoku

Seven years on, iROKO has grown to become possibly the biggest online repertoire of African movies. The
10 company has gone through a lot of drastic changes in the past year—shutting down its London head-quarters (HQ), shifting focus to a premium-only business model, expanding to East Africa, **cutting** bundled Internet deals with local telcos, and just
15 recently, enabling offline viewing—all in a **bid** to reposition itself as the market leader.

cutting (v.): making (arranging)

bid (n.): effort

Techpoint spent an afternoon chatting with Jason Njoku at the iROKO headquarters in Lagos.

Muyiwa Matuluko of Techpoint: For those who may not know who you are, could
20 you give us a little background on yourself?

Jason Njoku of iROKO: They exist? [Laughs]. I was born and bred in London, UK. I studied chemistry at the University of Manchester. In 2004, I started trying to build start-ups—mostly offline traditional kind of start-ups. In 2009–2010, I founded iROKO, which was just to connect Africans with content that they love.

25 **MM:** It appears that you never for a single day had a regular job. Have you always been an entrepreneur right from day one?

JN: I had jobs, but I was always fired from them. I've never really had a job for more than three to four months maximum.

MM: Interesting. Some claim people are born to be entrepreneurs. Would you agree
30 with them?

JN: I'm probably just incredibly difficult in employment. I think that's just my very nature. I think most people can be entrepreneurs; I just think that some personality traits **enable** some people to deal better with aspects of entrepreneurial life.

I am a workaholic so I have no problem working a hundred hours a week. I also have
35 a huge tolerance for pain and risk—which is what entrepreneurship is all about—and I'm just a terrible employee. So all those things together make me think I was always going to be an entrepreneur. Whether I was going to be a successful one or not would have been the difference.

MM: You founded many failed start-ups before iROKO. What was your biggest failure
40 and what did you learn from it?

JN: My biggest failure definitely was *Brash*, a magazine that I founded straight out of university in 2005. I ran it for three years—it literally took over my life for three years.

All of my experiences with all the other start-ups combined were compressed into that three-year period. From raising or not being able to raise money, to the challenge
45 of building a team, losing a team, running out of money, missing payroll, all of these things combined have basically taught me the hard lessons of start-up life.

…

MM: iROKO has grown a lot over five years. The company has gone through a lot of changes in the past year, and you recently hit over a billion views on the YouTube Multi-Channel Network alone. What's the big picture for iROKO in the coming years?

50 **JN**: Our goal is really simple—to get to a million paid subscribers. We're trying to connect a million people to content that they love. That's basically it.

MM: You probably are the most **vocal** CEO in the Nigerian Internet start-up scene. Some are of the opinion that a person in your position shouldn't be blogging so much about your company. Why do you blog?

55 **JN**: I started in 2004. By 2010, I had gone through six years of doing entrepreneurial things. I read a book a week; I read all of the tech blogs, all of the different stories of people who are trying to do things. They inspire me; they help me understand things. They've helped me become a better person and a better business person if you will.

But they are always **perspectives** of non-black people. I'm black; these are my
60 experiences. Where were the people I was supposed to look to, to help me understand how to run a start-up in an environment where essentially all the participants are black? There was no perspective on that.

I think building a business is hard enough with no information. So I think if there's any information out there, it's great. I enjoy reading and writing but at the same time,
65 I think every single Internet company in Nigeria is going through the exact same big internal changes as iROKO is. I'm just public with mine, and I'm comfortable with that.

I think any consistency cannot be built unless more and more people share information. People talk about Silicon Valley; Silicon Valley exists because people share information …

vocal (adj.): not afraid to speak

70 I think that's why when possible, I will help people out. I am very accessible. If someone wants to meet me, and I think I can help them, somehow I will definitely try to help them out. That's how ecosystems are built. I often talk about the mentors that I have in the West who have built huge video companies and sold them for over a hundred million dollars. They gave me the benefit of the doubt; they gave me time.

75 I respect that, and I think if people have helped me, I [want to] pass that on to other people. That's how you build an ecosystem. I would hope that my blogging is more a net positive to the ecosystem than not.

MM: Speaking about building the ecosystem, you and Bastian made a foray into angel investing with Spark. Could you tell us a little more about that? How and why was

80 Spark started and how many start-ups have you invested in so far?

JN: Obviously, Bastian and I believe in wealth creation from the Internet because that is where a lot of our wealth has come from. How it started was really simple. One of our **angel investors**

85 invested $80,000 in iROKO in January 2011. By January 2013, one of our other investors wanted to buy them out for a couple of million dollars, so we thought that's quite an interesting business to be in. If we can enable the next wave

90 of Internet companies being built, or at least create a **fertile** environment for people to get funding and to move on, then we can participate in wealth creation.

The fact that we're sitting here in Nigeria means

95 we can have more impact. We were fortunate to know some wealthy people who gave us two and a half million dollars. We **deployed** all of that money very quickly. I believe we invested in nine or ten companies in the beginning. We made

100 every single mistake that every incubator or angel investor would make in Nigeria. But we are fortunate to have three or four companies, which we see as big **potential** companies, in terms of growing into iROKO-sized opportunities.

105 Hotels.ng for example will be a big business. So will ToLet.com.ng and Drinks.ng. Foto.com.ng is another company I'm really excited about. The other ones, for whatever reason, they haven't worked out quite as well as we would have [liked]. We have to be quite narrow in our ability to keep on supporting companies that don't really work any more.

110 **MM: In hindsight**, considering your vast experience in the Internet start-up scene, what would you say most young entrepreneurs aren't doing well enough?

JN: I think there needs to be more patience. Patience is probably one of the most underrated virtues. iROKO was not a success straightaway. I spent eighteen months and about $150,000 of Bastian's money before I figured it out. Then it took another

115 six months to determine, "Now it's ripe."

fertile (adj.): successful and productive

Obviously, we've [moved] on from there, but I think sometimes you literally can spend two years doing something that doesn't appear like it makes sense. It's just about you getting an understanding of what direction to go … You should ask people and spend some time trying to figure stuff out. But that could take two years.

propensity (n.): tendency

120 I have always had a propensity to not kill companies fast enough. Most smart people told me to kill iROKO a long time ago. If I had listened to them, I wouldn't be here today. Most people **abandon** ideas too early. I think that's a very dangerous thing. It's all about patience. These things take time. The worst entrepreneurs I hear of are people who say, "I'm going to try this thing for six months; if doesn't work, I'll do
125 something else."

I've been doing this since 2004, and it never **occurred to** me to quit. [Although] when I literally couldn't afford to eat, I told myself, "Let me go get a job for three months and then I'll leave after." Otherwise, that's the only way it's always worked for me.

MM: One last thing. What's your biggest fear for iROKO?

130 **JN**: My biggest fear is that Nollywood becomes less popular. I know that's not happening at all, which is great. I think competition is competition; it will always be there. You just have to have a very strong perspective or vision. We have a very long-term perspective, which gives our investors confidence, which gives us confidence.

(1563 words)

Matuluko, M. (2015, March 23). My biggest fear is that Nollywood becomes less popular–Jason Njoku. *Techpoint. africa*. Retrieved from: https://techpoint.africa/2015/03/23/jason-njoku-iroko-fears-nollywood-less-popular/

After You Read

C. To demonstrate your comprehension, write short answers to the following questions.

1 Why does Njoku believe he is well suited for entrepreneurship?

_____

_____

2 Why does Njoku not believe that people are born to be entrepreneurs?

_____

_____

3 What challenges of entrepreneurship did Njoku learn from his *Brash* magazine start-up?

_____

_____

4 Why does Njoku believe that it is good to blog about his experiences with start-ups?

_____

_____

⑤ At the end of the interview, what characteristic does Njoku suggest new entrepreneurs need to have, and why?

_____

_____

_____

⑥ In this interview, Njoku reveals many of the experiences that have made him a successful entrepreneur. What were some of the stages on his journey to success?

_____

_____

_____

_____

_____

MyBookshelf > My eLab >
Exercises > Chapter 2 >
Jason Njoku

 **READING ②**   **Entrepreneurship**

The authors of this reading believe that founding a start-up is a process, like a journey. They identify three important elements in the entrepreneurial process: the entrepreneur, the opportunity, and the resources (financing).

VOCABULARY BUILD

A. Working with a classmate, read the sentences in the first column. Each sentence is missing a key word. Try to guess the missing word by looking at its synonym in the second column. If neither of you can guess, use the line number indicated to find the sentence in the reading. Write the key word in the blank.

WORDS/PHRASES IN CONTEXT	SYNONYMS
❶ Many successful managers in large organizations in both the public and private ___*sectors*___ also exhibit similar entrepreneurial characteristics.	parts of an industry LINE: 16
❷ Estimating market demand requires an _____ understanding of who the customers are.	first LINE: 104
❸ Lacking a competitive advantage or developing one that is not sustainable _____ two fatal flaws of many new businesses.	makes up LINE: 99
❹ The Heritage Foundation assesses the extent to which entrepreneurs have freedom to _____ new business opportunities.	follow LINE: 4
❺ Approximately half of all new business ideas come from _____ gained or skills learned at a previous job.	understandings LINE: 53

WORDS/PHRASES IN CONTEXT	SYNONYMS
6 The faster you can _____ the "dead-end" venture ideas, the more time and effort you can devote to the ones that remain.	eliminate LINE: 70
7 As they have been employees, _____ entrepreneurs are familiar with the product or service and with the customers, suppliers, and competitors.	future LINE: 48
8 Typically, generating ideas _____ abandoning traditional assumptions about how things work and how they ought to be.	includes LINE: 42
9 Most new _____ do not emerge from a deliberate search for _____ business ideas but from events relating to work or everyday life.	businesses LINE: 51 financially workable LINE: 52
10 The entrepreneur must identify a business opportunity and access the resources needed to _____ it.	make money from LINE: 2
11 We will focus our attention on understanding the three key process _____ —the entrepreneur, the opportunity, and the resources.	features LINE: 26

Before You Read

Use reading strategies to help you read quickly and with good comprehension.

A. Skim Reading 2 to find the answers to the following questions.

    1   a) What is the topic of the reading? _____

           b) How long is it? _____

           c) What type of text is it? How do you know?

               _____

    2   What do you already know about the topic?

               _____

               _____

    3   Use your knowledge of the text type to predict the organization.

               _____

In this reading, the authors use a different system of citing sources than the one most often used in this book. Both systems are correct. (See Academic Survival Skill, page 57.)

B. The authors use headings to divide the content into sections. On a separate page, write your own set of questions by turning the section headings into questions. Check your questions with a classmate to make sure they are accurate before you read the text.

While You Read

C. Read the text and answer the questions you developed in task B. When you have finished, confirm your answers with your class.

1. Entrepreneurship is the process of identifying an opportunity in the marketplace and accessing the resources needed to **capitalize on** that opportunity. "An entrepreneur is someone who perceives an opportunity and creates an organization to **pursue** it."[1] For example, Mark Zuckerberg created Facebook, and in 2011 it had
5 over 750 million active users. He is one of the richest people in the world under the age of thirty. Zuckerberg works long hours and he is constantly tailoring the website to suit its expanding audience.[2]

...

2. Each year, the Heritage Foundation publishes an index of economic freedom, which assesses the extent to which entrepreneurs have freedom to pursue new business
10 opportunities. In 2011, the top three countries were Hong Kong, Singapore, and Australia ... Canada ranked sixth ... and North Korea ranked last.[3]

3. Creativity is an important personal attribute that has come to be associated with entrepreneurs, and small businesses provide a great environment to use creativity.[4] However, do not assume that only small business owners exhibit entrepreneurial
15 characteristics. Many successful managers in large organizations in both the public and private **sectors** also exhibit similar characteristics.[5] Entrepreneurship is evident in a wide range of contexts: in small or new firms, in old firms, in large firms, in firms that grow slowly, in firms that grow rapidly, in non-profit organizations, and in the public sector.[6]

...

20 The Entrepreneurial Process

4. The entrepreneurial process is like a journey. To get to the destination (the start-up of a new venture), the entrepreneur must identify a business opportunity and access the resources needed to capitalize on it. Along the way, social, economic, political, and technological factors in the
25 broader environment will have an influence, but we will focus our attention on understanding the three key process **elements**—the entrepreneur, the opportunity, and the resources—and how they interact.

...

The Entrepreneur

5. Since the entrepreneur is at the heart of the entrepreneurial process, researchers
30 have paid considerable attention to identifying the personal characteristics of entrepreneurs ... Some are behavioural (for example, high energy level), others are personality traits (for example, independence), and still others are skills (for example, problem-solving).[7]

6. While the idea that people are "born" entrepreneurs is still quite popular, nothing
35 could be further from the truth.[8] In fact, entrepreneurial characteristics are widely distributed in the population.[9] We also know that personal characteristics often have less impact on a person's actions than the situation a person is in.[10] In other words, the important thing is not who the person *is*, but what the person *does*.[1] The two main things that entrepreneurs need to do are identify an opportunity
40 and access resources.

Identifying Opportunities

7. Identifying opportunities **involves** generating ideas for new (or improved) products, processes, or services, then screening those ideas so that the one that presents the best opportunity can be developed, and then developing the opportunity.

Idea generation

45

8. Typically, generating ideas involves abandoning traditional assumptions about how things work and how they ought to be, and involves seeing what others do not. If the **prospective** new (or improved) product, process, or service can be profitably produced and is attractive relative to other potential venture ideas, it

50 might present an opportunity.

9. Where do ideas come from? Most new **ventures** do not emerge from a deliberate search for **viable** business ideas but from events relating to work or everyday life.[11] Approximately half of all new business ideas come from **insights** gained or skills learned at a previous job. As employees, prospective entrepreneurs are

55 familiar with the product or service and with the customers, suppliers, and competitors. They can relate those needs to their own personal capabilities and can determine whether they are capable of producing products or services that can fill the void.

10. For example, Jay Hagan and Scott Gaidano learned how to recover data from

60 damaged hard drives while working for a company that manufactured them. When that company went bankrupt, they started their own business and called it DriveSavers.

...

11. The next most frequent sources of venture ideas are a personal interest / hobby (16 percent) and a chance happening (11 percent).[12] A chance happening refers

65 to a situation where a venture idea comes about unexpectedly. For example, while on vacation in another country, you might try a new snack food that you feel would be in demand if introduced to [your home] market.

Screening

12. Entrepreneurs often generate many ideas, and screening them is a key part of the

70 entrepreneurial process. The faster you can **weed out** the "dead-end" venture ideas, the more time and effort you can devote to the ones that remain. The more of the following characteristics that an idea has, the greater the opportunity it presents.

13. *The Idea Creates or Adds Value for the Customer*. A value-added product or service is one that solves a significant problem or meets a significant need in new or

75 different ways. Consider Polar Mobile, a Toronto-based developer of mobile applications that has made great strides since launching a few years ago. Polar provides a software platform called SMART TM that makes it easy for media companies to launch apps for all types of smartphones and tablet devices. The company must be doing something right because major companies are finding

80 value in this relatively new company. In 2011, just four years since its inception, Polar had over three hundred customers in ten countries and powered over one thousand mobile apps with its platform. Among its clients, Nokia signed a deal for Polar to build three hundred mobile apps .... Polar also signed a deal with Dubai-based Emitac Mobile, a large distributor of smartphones with more than

85 seventy mobile operators in fifty countries, so Polar could distribute its apps more

efficiently in the Middle East, North Africa, and Central Asia. It would seem that Polar has clearly shown the capacity to add value based on this impressive list of partners.[13]

14. *The Idea Provides a Competitive Advantage That Can Be Sustained.* A competitive advantage exists when potential customers see the product or service as being better than that of competitors. Toronto-based Sentinelle Medical is counting on a very important sustainable advantage. Cameron Piron spent ten years developing a better cancer detection technology and another two years convincing General Electric to use it in its MRI machines. He recently received the Ontario government Innovation Award.[14] Sustaining a competitive advantage involves maintaining it in the face of competitors' actions or changes in the industry. All other things being equal, the longer markets are in a state of flux, the greater the likelihood of being able to sustain a competitive advantage. Lacking a competitive advantage or developing a competitive advantage that is not sustainable **constitutes** two fatal flaws of many new ventures.[15]

15. *The Idea Is Marketable and Financially Viable.* While it is important to determine whether there are enough customers who are willing to buy the product or service, it is also important to determine whether sales will lead to profits.[16] Estimating market demand requires an **initial** understanding of who the customers are, what their needs are, and how the product or service will satisfy their needs better than competitors' products. Customers define the competition in terms of who can satisfy their needs best. However, success also requires a thorough understanding of the key competitors who can provide similar products, services, or benefits to the target customer. For example, despite some home-grown success, Vancouver-based ProSnack Natural Foods, a provider of energy bars with organic ingredients, is having difficulty accessing large retailers like MEC that would take them to the next level of sales. The problem is that the market is oversaturated, with more than fifty brands of energy bars lining the shelves of MEC; unfortunately, ProSnack is not one of them.[17]

. . .

16. *The Idea Has Low Exit Costs.* The final consideration is the venture's exit costs. Exit costs are low if a venture can be shut down without a significant loss of time, money, or reputation.[18] If a venture is not expected to make a profit for a number of years, its exit costs are high since the project cannot be reasonably abandoned in the short term. However, if the venture is expected to make a profit quickly, its exit costs will be lower, making the idea more attractive. For example, zero-emission car manufacturer Zenn Motors has very long-term projections: an investor in this company must understand that it will not be profitable for many years. Therefore, they must be patient and invest based on its long-term potential.

. . .

Financial Resources

17. There are two main types of financing—*debt* and *equity*. Briefly, *debt financing* refers to money that is borrowed. The borrower is obliged to repay the full amount of the loan in addition to interest charges on the debt. The most common sources of debt financing are banks (which provide personal loans), trust companies, cooperatives, finance companies, equipment companies, credit unions, government

130 agencies, and suppliers (who provide goods such as inventory to the entrepreneur with an agreement to bill the entrepreneur later).

18. *Equity financing* refers to money that the entrepreneur (or others) invests in a business in return for an ownership interest. Equity investors, as owners, are keenly interested in how any profit will be distributed. The most common sources 135 of equity financing are personal savings (new venture founders draw heavily on their own finances to start their businesses), love money (investments from friends, relatives, and business associates), venture capitalists (who loan money to promising new ventures in return for a share of ownership in the business), and private investors (also known as *angels*), who are financially well-off entrepreneurs 140 who wish to recycle their wealth by investing in new businesses.

19. Choosing between debt and equity financing involves trade-offs with regard to potential profitability, financial risk, and control. On the one hand, borrowing money increases the potential for higher rates of return to the entrepreneur when the business is performing well. On the other hand, equity makes it possible to 145 reduce risk by giving up some control. Since a business is at its riskiest point during the start-up phase, equity is usually more appropriate and accessible than debt. However, most new venture founders prefer debt because they are reluctant to give up any control to outsiders.

(1691 words)

Notes

1. Bygrave WD, Hofer CW. Theorizing about entrepreneurship. *Entrep Theory Practice*. 1991;16(2):14.

2. Vogelstein F. How Mark Zuckerberg turned Facebook into the web's hottest platform. *Wired*. www.wired.com / techbuz / startups / news / 2007 / 09 / ff_facebook?currentPage=3. Published September 6, 2007.

3. Heritage Foundation Index of Economic Freedom. www.heritage.org/index/topten. Accessed September 26, 2011.

4. Dale A. Self-Employment and Entrepreneurship: Notes on Two Problematic Concepts. In: Burrows R, ed. *Deciphering the Enterprise Culture*. London: Routledge; 1991:45–48.

5. Sexton D, Bowman-Upton, N. *Entrepreneurship: Creativity and Growth*. New York, NY: MacMillan Publishing Company; 1991:11.

6. Gibb AA. The enterprise culture and education: Understanding enterprise education and its links with small business, entrepreneurship and wider educational goals. *Int Small Bus J*. 1993;11(3):13–34.

7. Kuratko DF, Hodgetts RM. *Entrepreneurship: Theory, Process and Practice*. 7th ed. Mason, OH: Thomson South-Western; 2007:118–125.

8. Timmons JA, Spinelli S. *New Venture Creation: Entrepreneurship for the 21st Century*. 7th ed. Boston, MA: McGraw-Hill/Irwin; 2007:19.

9. Kyle JD, Blais R, Blatt R, Szonyi AJ. The culture of the entrepreneur: Fact or fiction. *J Small Bus Entrep*.1991:3–14.

10. Brockhaus RH, Horwitz PS. The Psychology of the Entrepreneur. In: Sexton DL, Smilor RW, eds. *The Art and Science of Entrepreneurship*. Cambridge, MA: Ballinger Pub. Co; 1986.

11. Good W. *Building a Dream*. Toronto, ON: McGraw-Hill Ryerson; 1998:40.

12. Long WA, McMullan WE. *Developing New Ventures*. San Diego, CA: Harcourt Brace Jovanovich; 1990:374–375.

13. Jeong M. Fast-growing apps developer Polar Mobile looks east. *Globe and Mail*. August 24, 2011:B4.

14. Mourtada R. Tested to the limit. *Globe and Mail*. April 14, 2009:B4.

15. Porter ME. Know your place: How to assess the attractiveness of your industry and your company's position in it. *Inc*. 1991; 13(9):90–93.

16. Stevenson HH, Grousbeck HI, Roberts MJ, Bhide A. *New Business Ventures and the Entrepreneur*. Boston, MA: McGraw-Hill/Irwin; 1999:19.

17. Braga M. The fight for shelf space. *Globe and Mail*. May 4, 2011: B10.

18. Ibid. 21.

Griffin, R. W., Ebert, R. J., Starke, F. A., & Lang, M. D. (2014). *Business* (8th Canadian ed., pp. 110–119). Toronto: Pearson Education Canada.

After You Read

D. To increase your awareness of some of the features of this reading, complete the following tasks.

① Look at paragraphs 1 and 13 and highlight the descriptive definitions you find. What terms are defined?

_____

_____

② In paragraphs 13 and 15, highlight the definitions that are provided by noun phrases positioned between commas. What terms are defined? Why did the authors choose to define them in this way?

_____

_____

E. Answer these questions to demonstrate what you have learned in Reading 2 that has not been stated explicitly.

① In the opening paragraph, the authors refer to Mark Zuckerberg (creator of Facebook) as an example of a successful young entrepreneur. What do you know about Zuckerberg that might make him a less appealing example?

_____

_____

_____

② This reading focuses on three aspects of the entrepreneurial journey: the characteristics of the entrepreneur, identification of the opportunity, and access to financial resources. Are there other factors that could influence the entrepreneur's success?

_____

_____

_____

MyBookshelf > My eLab >
Exercises > Chapter 2 >
Entrepreneurship

FOCUS ON
ACCURACY

Positioning Main Points for Emphasis in a Sentence

A technique to build flow or cohesion in your text is to start sentences with short phrases or clauses (see Chapter 1, page 16). When using this technique, note that the main point of your sentence should be placed in the main clause, before or after the short phrase or clause.

Look at the following sentence from Reading 2; the main point is underlined.

> To get to the destination (the start-up of a new venture), <u>the entrepreneur must identify a business opportunity and access the resources needed to capitalize on it.</u>

▶

The authors start the sentence with an infinitive phrase of purpose (followed by a comma) and position the main point in the independent clause to emphasize its importance.

Here is another example from Reading 2 with the main point underlined.

> While the idea that people are "born" entrepreneurs is still quite popular, <u>nothing could be further from the truth</u>.

The authors start with a subordinate (adverb) clause (followed by a comma) and again put the main point in the independent clause. This places a strong emphasis on the main point, particularly as it contradicts the idea in the subordinate clause.

Look at the next sentence and notice the main idea.

> <u>Entrepreneurship is evident in a wide range of contexts</u>: in small or new firms, in old firms, in large firms, in firms that grow slowly, in firms that grow rapidly, in non-profit organizations, and in the public sector.

You can see that the main idea is contained in the independent clause. Additional information (a list of possible contexts) is added after the independent clause (and after a colon).

Here is another example.

> For example, <u>Jay Hagan and Scott Gaidano learned how to recover data from damaged hard drives</u> while working for a company that manufactured them.

Again, the main idea is located in the independent clause while additional information is added in the subordinate clause (starting with *while*). Notice that no comma is required when the subordinate clause follows the independent clause.

A. Use the additional information given below (based on content from Readings 1 and 2) to write sentences; remember that the independent clauses should emphasize the main points. Share your best sentences on the board with your class.

1 Additional information: ToLet.com.ng, Drinks.ng, Foto.com.ng

Possible answer: *Jason Njoku and his partner Bastian Gotter founded several start-up companies: ToLet.com.ng, Drinks.ng, and Foto.com.ng.*

2 Additional information: While running his first start-up, called *Brash* ...

Possible answer: _____

_____

3 Additional information: ... since no one else writes about the experiences of black entrepreneurs

Possible answer: _____

_____

④ Additional information: Although entrepreneurs may have many ideas ...

Possible answer: _____

_____

⑤ Additional information: ... to understand the journey of a successful entrepreneur.

Possible answer: _____

_____

MyBookshelf > My eLab > Exercises > Chapter 2 > Accuracy Review

WARM-UP ASSIGNMENT
Write a Short Process Essay

Using information from Reading 1, write a short process essay explaining Jason Njoku's entrepreneurial journey.

A. Focus on the three key elements in the entrepreneurial process: the entrepreneur (characteristics), the opportunity (how the idea developed and grew), and the resources (how it was financed).

B. To emphasize your main ideas, place them in independent clauses; build flow (cohesion) by starting your sentences with short phrases and clauses, and add additional information at the end of your sentences when appropriate.

A process essay explains how something is done—the steps or stages of a process. Like all essays, it has three sections: an introduction, a body, and a conclusion. The introduction ends with a thesis statement that clearly identifies the topic of the essay. The body of the essay outlines the steps of the process; generally, one step corresponds to one paragraph. The conclusion summarizes the main points in a single paragraph and reminds the reader of the importance of the process.

Refer to the Models Chapter (page 276) to see an example and to learn more about how to write a process essay.

When you receive feedback from your instructor or your classmates on this Warm-Up Assignment, you will have information that you can use to improve your writing on the Final Assignment.

Recognizing Different Styles for In-Text Citations and References

In-text citations and references provide information about sources cited in a text. Both can be written in various styles (or formats). This textbook uses the American Psychological Association (APA) format, although in Reading 2 in this chapter, you can see an example of the American Medical Association (AMA) style (used in business as well as scientific fields).

In-Text Citations

In-text citations provide brief information about the source of the original material and are indicated in the body of the text by either a *number* or an *author-date combination*. You can see examples of these two citation types in Readings 2 and 3.

- Reading 2 (page 50) uses a numbered system. Each number in the text corresponds to an entry in a Notes section at the end of the text.
- Reading 3 (page 65) uses an author-date system. Each in-text citation corresponds to an entry in a References section.

References, Works Cited, and Bibliography

References provide complete information to help the reader locate the original source; they appear at the end of the text. A References or Works Cited list includes all the sources that are cited while a Bibliography lists all the cited sources as well as all others the writer consulted for background information.

Accurate references include the author's name, date of publication, title of the work, page number(s), publisher, location of publisher (for books), issue and volume number (for journals, magazines, or newspaper articles) or URL (if found on a website). Entries are listed in alphabetical order according to the author's last name.

Citation Styles

For both numbered and author-date citation systems, several different styles can be used, each following slightly different formatting rules. For example, if you look closely at the references in Readings 2 and 3, you will see that information is arranged in a different order for similar sources and that the punctuation and use of italics varies.

Follow the specific rules for information order and punctuation established by the citation style you are using. The choice of style will depend on your field of study or the preferences of your instructors. If you are not sure which style to use, ask your instructor or a librarian.

Visit My eLab Documents for more information about different citation formats and to see some useful citation guides.

DISCIPLINE	CITATION STYLE	CITATION SYSTEM
BUSINESS, MEDICINE, HEALTH, BIOLOGICAL SCIENCES	American Medical Association (AMA)	Numbered (as in Reading 2)
PSYCHOLOGY, EDUCATION, SOCIAL SCIENCES, ENGINEERING	American Psychological Association (APA)	Author-date (as in Reading 3)
HISTORY (AND OFTEN USED IN NEWSPAPERS, MAGAZINES, TEXTBOOKS)	Chicago Manual of Style (CMS)	Numbered or author-date
SCIENCES AND MATHEMATICS	Council of Science Editors (CSE)	Author-date-page number

DISCIPLINE	CITATION STYLE	CITATION SYSTEM
ELECTRICAL ENGINEERING	Institute of Electrical and Electronics Engineers (IEEE)	Numbered
LITERATURE, ARTS, HUMANITIES	Modern Languages Association (MLA)	Author-page number
ALL DISCIPLINES	Turabian	Numbered or author-date-page number

A. Look through a textbook or journal article, either one of yours or a classmate's. Which citation style is used? Survey your class to determine which styles seem to be most commonly used.

Citation Formatting Made (Relatively) Easy

Writing accurate citations according to the style required by your discipline used to be quite complex and laborious. While attention to detail is still important, it is now relatively easy to generate accurate references. You can use one of the following methods.

- Citation Machine is available for free online. Click the citation style you want to use, type in the identifying information, and the software will format the information for you.

- RefWorks and EndNote are two examples of citation management software packages that are available for free.

- Mendeley and Zotero are examples of reference management systems that are available free online.

- Library databases may provide a link to citation software when you search and find library items. Click on Cite and select your preferred citation style.

- Current versions of Microsoft Word help format citations. Find the Document Elements tab and click on References.

- The associations that have developed citation systems publish style manuals and guides that give examples of citations. Many of these are online, or the library will link to them through its website. Paper copies are also available through the library.

FOCUS ON CRITICAL THINKING

Knowing When and What to Cite and Reference

Citing sources allows readers to find the original source in case they want further information on the subject. Knowing what type of information is necessary to cite will help you avoid plagiarizing or copying another writer's words or ideas without giving that author credit.

In most cases, you do *not* need to cite general information or information that is commonly known in your discipline if you present it in your own words. For example, the following sentence does not need a citation.

> Entrepreneurs bring creativity and energy to the marketplace in hopes of making money.

This is a general statement about entrepreneurs that is well understood by a wide range of people.

However, there are still many cases where you do need to provide an in-text citation and a reference, for example, if you quote directly from a source. The following sentence requires an in-text citation (including page number) because it is copied directly from Reading 2 (lines 46–48). In general, it is a good idea not to quote too often, or too much.

> Typically, generating ideas involves abandoning traditional assumptions about how things work and how they ought to be and involves seeing what others do not (Griffin, Ebert, Starke, & Lang, 2014, p. 115).
>
> _____
> Griffin, R. W., Ebert, R. J., Starke, F. A., & Lang, M. D. (2014). *Business* (8th Canadian ed., p. 110–119). Toronto: Pearson Education Canada.

In addition, in-text citations and references are essential when you refer to specific information from another text, even if you are paraphrasing. Here is an example of a paraphrase of a sentence from Reading 2.

> According to the Heritage Foundation Index of Economic Freedom (2011), entrepreneurs have the most freedom to pursue their businesses in Hong Kong, Singapore, and Australia, and the least freedom to do so in North Korea.[1]
>
> _____
> [1]Griffin, R. W., Ebert, R.J., Starke, F. A., & Lang, M. D. (2014). *Business* (8th Canadian ed., p. 110). Toronto: Pearson Education Canada.

It is sometimes difficult to be sure what is considered general or common knowledge, but the more you study and write in your discipline, the more confident you will become about recognizing information you need to cite. When in doubt, it's always best to provide a reference.

The following sources must be cited and referenced:

- exact quotations;
- specific ideas;
- specific facts learned from another source of information;
- specific research results;
- specific statistics;
- specific examples from another source of information.

To write an in-text citation for a source with up to five authors, the first time, include all the authors' last names. The second time, use the first author's last name followed by the abbreviation "et al.," which means "and others." In the reference, include the names and initials of all the authors.

A. The content below is based on the first reading in this chapter. Read the text and use your critical thinking skills to determine whether you need to provide in-text citations and references. Explain your reasoning in the right-hand column.

TEXT	EXPLANATION
Increasingly, young people around the world are turning to entrepreneurship as a way to pursue their career goals _(Global Entrepreneurship Monitor, 2018)_. A formal definition of entrepreneurship states that, "An entrepreneur is someone who perceives an opportunity and creates an organization to pursue it" ___(Griffin, Ebert, Starke, & Lang, 2014, p. 110)___ ; however, this definition fails to convey the liveliness and get-up-and-go spirit of young entrepreneurs. A better description might be as follows: entrepreneurs bring creativity and energy to the marketplace in hopes of making money (_____). Jason Njoku is an example of a young entrepreneur who, along with his partner Bastian Gotter, has brought his creativity and energy to the Nigerian marketplace. His media-streaming platform, called iROKO, provides Nigerian content to subscribers around the world (_____). Born in London, England, and a former chemistry student at the University of Manchester, Njoku suggests that he is an entrepreneur because he didn't have the characteristics to be a good employee, saying, "I'm probably just incredibly difficult in employment" (_____). Njoku is an example of a successful entrepreneur as defined by any standards (_____). Not only does he manage iROKO, he also runs several other start-ups, including Hotels.ng, ToLet.ng, Drinks.ng, and Foto.com.ng (_____). His success may be an example to many other young entrepreneurs around the globe (_____).	_Paraphrased, requires in-text citation and reference_ _Quote, requires in-text citation, page number, and reference_ _General knowledge, no in-text citation or reference required_

References

Global Entrepreneurship Research Association. (2018). *Global Report 2017/18*. Retrieved from http://www.gemconsortium.org/report

Griffin, R. W., Ebert, R. J., Starke, F. A., & Lang, M. D. (2014). *Business* (8th Canadian ed., pp. 110–119). Toronto: Pearson Education Canada.

Matuluko, M. (2015, March 23). My biggest fear is that Nollywood becomes less popular– Jason Njoku. *Techpoint.africa*. Retrieved from https://techpoint.africa/2015/03/23/jason-njoku-iroko-fears-nollywood-less-popular/

Secondary Purposes of Citations

Although citations provide essential identifying information about the sources of the information, writers also use them to

• demonstrate their knowledge about a subject;

• show that they can write like other authors in the discipline;

• show respect for other writers;

• support colleagues in the discipline.

B. Discuss with your class the importance of providing citations for these purposes.

Reading Journal Articles

As you progress in your academic career, you will be required to read journal articles to get the most reliable and current information about a topic. Journal articles usually report the results of specific research and, even across disciplines, typically follow the same organizational structure: they are divided into predictable sections, each with a specific purpose.

A. Working with a partner, skim Reading 3 (pages 65) and complete the first column, matching the major sections of the journal article with their purposes. When you have finished, confirm your answers with the class.

B. Skim Reading 3 again, this time looking for features common to the different sections, as shown in the third column. In the SECTION PURPOSE column, write the line numbers where each feature is found. This will help you understand the structure of a journal article.

ARTICLE SECTION	SECTION PURPOSE	COMMON FEATURES
ABSTRACT	• Summarizes the article to provide readers with enough information to decide if it will be useful to them. LINES _____	• Often not labelled with a heading but inset from the rest of the text or in italics.
_____	• Explains why this research is important. LINES _____ • Identifies a knowledge gap in the current research literature—something that is unknown. LINES _____ • Summarizes the research literature that is relevant to the problem the authors are trying to solve. LINES _____ • States the research question that will guide the researchers in their work. LINES _____	• Often introduced with a subordinate conjunction (although/while/despite). • Contains in-text citations that refer to other research.
_____	• Describes the process the authors used to discover the information they are searching for. LINES _____	• May be written in the passive voice.
_____	• Summarizes the results of the research and compares them to previous research. LINES _____	• Often written in the present tense. • Often contains in-text citations that refer to other research.
_____	• Explains the important contributions this research has made. LINES _____ • States the limitations of the research project and possible opportunities for further research. LINES _____	• Often written in the present tense.

Towards an Explanation of the Growth in Young Entrepreneur Activities

The authors explore the differences between South African and American undergraduate business college students in their attitudes toward work and entrepreneurship. As you read, you may be surprised by both the similarities and differences in their opinions.

VOCABULARY BUILD

A. Fill in the blanks in the following sentences with the appropriate words from the table. Use your knowledge of word form to determine if you are looking for a noun, a verb, or an adjective, then select the word from the appropriate column. When you have finished, check your answers with a classmate, and write a definition of the word under each sentence.

NOUNS	VERBS	ADJECTIVES
~~attributes~~ construct consistency factors stability	acknowledged conducted consists of exploiting retain shift undertaking	consistent with intrinsic

① Among South African students, interesting and motivating opportunities for promotion and economic prospects are the most desirable job

_____*attributes*_____.

Definition: *characteristics* _____

② Entrepreneurship researchers have attempted to identify the situational and

environmental _____ that predict entrepreneurial activity.

Definition: _____

③ Survey data is collected through a self-administered questionnaire, an approach found appropriate given the limited use of alternative

methods of data collection, and the need for _____.

Definition: _____

④ Job challenge and interest are variables that address _____ rewards linked to job satisfaction.

Definition: _____

⑤ American students are attracted to the possibility of _____ personal creativity within the work environment.

Definition: _____

⑥ There are many variables within the _____ of a social workplace environment.

Definition: _____

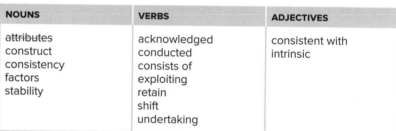

7　Around the globe, there is a growing interest in _____ actions to show entrepreneurship as an attractive alternative to organizational employment.

Definition: _____

8　There is a need for attitudinal change if organizations are going to attract

and _____ top talent.

Definition: _____

9　The important role of entrepreneurship to any economy is widely

_____.

Definition: _____

10　The findings of this study are _____ the results of other research studies that come to similar conclusions.

Definition: _____

11　This attitudinal change will indicate an important _____ on the part of employers who should know how essential it is to keep well-trained workers.

Definition: _____

12　For South African students, job _____ is the least important factor to consider in their employment decisions.

Definition: _____

13　The sample _____ undergraduate student subjects facing important career decisions.

Definition: _____

14　Although significant research has been _____ in the field of entrepreneurship, writers continue to emphasize that studies on entrepreneurial motivation are still limited.

MyBookshelf > My eLab >
Exercises > Chapter 2 >
Vocabulary Review

Definition: _____

Before You Read

A. Using the line numbers as a guide, scan Reading 3 to quickly identify the following pieces of important information. When you have finished, compare your answers with those of a classmate.

1　Line 6: This article compares attitudes of students from which two countries?

_____

_____

2　Lines 19–21: What is the aim of this research?

_____

_____

3 Lines 34–35: What are the two additional research questions the authors address?

_____

_____

4 Lines 38–40: Which seven employment attitude factors do the authors research in this study?

_____

_____

5 Line 67: How did the authors collect data for this study?

_____

_____

6 Lines 146–148 (and table): Do you think the results in the final table show more similarities or more differences?

_____

_____

While You Read

B. Before reading the article, look at the following sentences from Reading 3, two from each of the four main sections of the article: introduction, methodology, results, and discussion. Use your knowledge of the features of article sections (Focus on Reading, page 61), and match the sentence numbers with the appropriate sections in the table below. Once complete, this table will reflect the organization of the whole article. Then read the article and confirm that you have paired the sentences with the correct sections.

1 Interest in entrepreneurship among young people is reported to be growing (Scarborough et al., 2009), prompting increased research interest in the area (Harris and Gibson, 2008).

2 Another limitation is that because of the survey nature of the research, it has not been possible to make follow-up questions to uncover the reasoning behind the attitudes.

3 A basic survey analysis tool is used to generate the career preference patterns.

4 The responses [in lines 13–16] show the respondents disagreeing with statements suggesting avoiding responsibility as a factor in career choice, an average of 2.59 for US students and 2.57 for South African students.

5 This research makes three important contributions.

6 Although significant research has been conducted in the field of entrepreneurship, writers continue to emphasize that studies on entrepreneurial motivation are still limited (van Gelderen et al., 2008).

7 Table 2, lines 1–2, show the importance attached to job security.

8 The sample population is built from graduating students from two partner universities, one in South Africa and one in the US.

SENTENCE NUMBERS	MAIN JOURNAL ARTICLE SECTIONS
1,	Introduction
	Methodology
	Results
	Discussion

Towards an Explanation of the Growth in Young Entrepreneur Activities: A Cross-Country Survey of Work Values of College Students

This short exploratory paper aims to study job attitudes of business college students with a view to contributing to the explanation of the reported global growth in young entrepreneur activities. Seven career attitude **factors** *adapted from the theory of planned behaviour are used to conduct a comparative study of work attitudes of university business students in the United States and South Africa to establish if there are significant differences across nations. The results show similarity in what the students expect from their future careers but do not necessarily provide an explanation for the observed increase of young entrepreneurs.*

Introduction

Entrepreneurship is an important career option. In the past few years, successive Results Reports from the Global Entrepreneurship Monitor have indicated that throughout the world, entrepreneurs are pursuing new ventures out of both necessity and opportunity. Around the globe, public policy **rhetoric** in the area of job creation in different countries has pronounced a growing interest in **undertaking** actions to portray entrepreneurship as an attractive alternative to organizational employment among students (Schwarz et al., 2009). Interest in entrepreneurship among young people is reported to be growing (Scarborough et al., 2009), prompting increased research interest in the area (Harris and Gibson, 2008). This paper aims to study job attitudes of business graduates with a view to contributing to the explanation of the reported global growth in young entrepreneur activities. Starting up a new venture is **acknowledged** to be an individual decision (Littunen, 2000). This makes the individual entrepreneur central in the investigation of entrepreneurial activities. Research has encouraged a continuous study and refinement of the entrepreneurial profile. In examining the global landscape, it is clear that some cultures produce many more entrepreneurs than others, and finding possible explanations continues to be of increasing importance in the global economy.

Although significant research has been **conducted** in the field of entrepreneurship, writers continue to emphasize that studies on entrepreneurial motivation are still limited (van Gelderen et al., 2008). Research on work values of young college graduates has shown that they desire work which provides a feeling of accomplishment, job security, and the opportunity for advancement. Much of this research has been done

rhetoric (n.): language used to persuade or influence people

in developed … economies. Also, with the reported increase in entrepreneurial activity among young people, research questions that arise are whether the work values reported earlier still hold and whether there are differences across countries.

40 The objective of this exploratory comparative study is to contribute to entrepreneurship research through establishing the work attitudes of today's undergraduate college business students across countries. Seven employment attitude factors of job security, workload, social environment, responsibility, opportunity, job challenge, and self-direction, adapted from the theory of planned behaviour, are used to conduct a
45 comparative study of work attitudes of university business students in the United States of America (US) and South Africa (SA) to establish if there are significant differences across nations.

While entrepreneurship is important to all economies, businesses need employees. Some young people opting for entrepreneurship may actually have great potential
50 as employees. A skilled, knowledgeable, and committed workforce is an essential resource of successful businesses. Business leaders need to know today's young employee expectations and motivations. The results of this exploratory research make an important contribution in this regard.

…

Entrepreneurship research has attempted to identify the situational and environmental
55 factors that predict entrepreneurial activity. Using contingency theory, Gilad and Levine (1986) proposed the "push" and "pull" theories as possible explanations of entrepreneurial motivation. The "push" theory suggests that a person can opt for entrepreneurship as a result of unfavourable environmental conditions like job dissatisfaction, while the "pull" theory argues that people can find entrepreneurship
60 attractive. Despite research indications that individuals become entrepreneurs mainly because of "pull" factors, college graduates and students are reported to be increasingly **disenchanted** with career prospects as organizational employees (Orham, 2001), seemingly suggesting a "push" factor **scenario**.

…

Methodology

65 The sample population is built from graduating students from two partner universities, one in South Africa and one in the US. Country selection is based on the need to have a developing and developed nation representation, and the two universities are chosen for ease of access. An existing partnership between the two universities made them a preferred choice. The sample **consists of** undergraduate student subjects facing
70 imminent career decisions.

Survey data is collected through a self-administered questionnaire, an approach found appropriate given the limited use of alternative methods of data collection, like online surveys in developing nations like South Africa, and the need for **consistency**.

… Our basic proposition is that a partial explanation for the increase in entrepreneurial
75 activity among young people is that compared to organizational employment, entrepreneurship better meets the career aspirations of the young people of today and that this **phenomenon** cuts across nations …

A basic survey analysis tool is used to generate the career preference patterns. The questions allow assessment of job attitudes along seven identifiable categories.
80 The aggregate tables generated by the two data sets representing responses from the

disenchanted (adj.): disappointed; unhappy

scenario (n.): situation that could happen

phenomenon (n.): something that is studied because it is difficult to understand

two universities studied are used to discuss the results along seven employment attitude factors of job security, workload, social environment, responsibility, opportunity, job challenge, and self-
85 direction. In the analysis, we use the overall rating average. For the overall rating average, given that in our scale 1 = agree and 3 = disagree, the smaller the overall rating average, the higher the extent of agreement with the statement and vice versa.

90 Results

... Participants were US students n = 71, South African students n = 33, and rating scale 1 = agree, 2 = neutral and 3 = disagree.

[Table 2, lines 1–2,] show the importance attached
95 to job security. Overall attitude to job security is the average response to the two questions related to job security as shown [in line 3]. Job security is an important factor in career choice to both the US students (1.48), and South African students
100 (1.44), with the South African students seemingly attaching more importance to job security than the US students.

[Lines 4–8] show scores for workload factors. The average score for workload factors [shown in line 9] is 1.99 for US students and 1.75 for South African students. For the
105 US students surveyed, job simplicity has the lowest rating at 2.38. The results show a higher preference for fixed working hours for the South African students (1.48), compared to 1.93 for the US students. The respondents agree on their level of concern for leisure (1.73). The responses also show that for the South African students, job-related stress, at 1.76, may be a concern in career choice.

110 [Lines 10 and 11] show the scores for work social environment. The social environment **construct** takes care of people as social beings. The overall ratings, ... [line 12,] for the groups are close at 1.8 and 1.9 and lean more toward being neutral than having a clear positive concern. Although the overall averages are close on the individual items, the South African students show a higher concern to be part of the social
115 environment (1.5) than the US students, with only 1.77 agreeing with the statement.

The responses [in lines 13–16] show the respondents disagreeing with statements suggesting avoiding responsibility as a factor in career choice, an average of 2.59 for US students and 2.57 for South African students.

[Lines 17–21] show results of responses to organizational human resources management
120 practices of rewarding employees. From [line 18] it can be seen that opportunity as represented by promotional possibilities is 1.37 for US students and 1.33 for South African students surveyed. The South African students show a high concern for compensation based on merit, 1.24, against 1.66 for US students.

Job challenge and interest are variables that address **intrinsic** rewards linked to job
125 satisfaction. The results [in line 24] show an average overall rating closer to agreeing than neutral, 1.43 for US students and 1.23 for South African students.

The final set of variables addresses entrepreneurial orientation construct. They are about self-direction as represented by the freedoms associated with the entrepreneurship career. The results are summarized in [lines 25–29]. The overall rating for US students is 1.63, and for South African students is 1.52. The specific entrepreneurial area where the US students score highest is the desire to create something new (1.57). Results in the other three areas of evidence of being one's own boss, independence, choosing one's own tasks and **exploiting** personal creativity are close, averaging 1.65. For the South African students, the lowest score is in the area of choosing one's own tasks (1.76), with the other three areas very close at 1.45.

Table 2: Scores for all factors considered in choosing a career among US and SA students

	UNITED STATES				SOUTH AFRICA			
	AGREE (%)	NEUTRAL (%)	DISAGREE (%)	AV.	AGREE (%)	NEUTRAL (%)	DISAGREE (%)	AV.
① JOB SECURITY	71.8	12.7	15.5	1.44	72.7	9.1	18.2	1.45
② JOB STABILITY	63.4	21.1	15.5	1.52	72.7	12.1	15.2	1.42
③ **OVERALL JOB SECURITY**	67.6	16.9	15.5	1.48	72.7	10.6	16.7	1.44
④ NOT HAVING LONG HOURS	30.0	45.7	24.3	1.94	42.4	24.2	33.3	1.91
⑤ TO HAVE LEISURE	43.7	38.4	16.9	1.73	45.5	36.4	18.2	1.73
⑥ TO HAVE FIXED WORKING HOURS	35.2	36.6	28.2	1.93	60.6	30.3	9.1	1.48
⑦ NOT TO HAVE A STRESSFUL JOB	31.0	42.3	26.8	1.96	48.5	27.3	24.2	1.76
⑧ TO HAVE A SIMPLE JOB	11.3	39.4	49.3	2.38	36.4	36.4	27.3	1.91
⑨ **OVERALL WORKLOAD INFLUENCES**	30.2	40.7	29.1	1.99	46.7	30.9	22.4	1.75
⑩ PARTICIPATE IN SOCIAL ENVIRONMENT	39.4	43.7	16.9	1.77	60.0	30.0	10.0	1.50
⑪ BE MEMBER OF SOCIAL MILIEU	25.7	55.7	18.6	1.93	35.5	22.6	41.9	2.06
⑫ **OVERALL SOCIAL ENVIRONMENT**	32.6	49.7	17.8	1.85	47.8	26.3	26	1.78
⑬ AVOID RESPONSIBILITY	11.3	18.3	70.4	2.59	12.1	3.0	84.8	2.73
⑭ NOT TAKING ON TOO MUCH RESPONSIBILITY	8.5	23.9	67.6	2.59	9.4	25.0	65.6	2.56
⑮ AVOID COMMITMENT	11.3	19.7	69.0	2.58	18.8	21.9	59.4	2.41
⑯ **OVERALL RESPONSIBILITY**	10.4	20.6	69.0	2.59	13.4	16.6	69.9	2.57
⑰ OPPORTUNITY FOR CAREER PROGRESS	81.4	2.9	15.7	1.34	78.8	9.1	12.1	1.33
⑱ PROMOTION	78.9	5.6	15.5	1.37	78.8	9.1	12.1	1.33
⑲ ECONOMIC OPPORTUNITY	69.0	16.9	14.1	1.45	87.9	6.1	6.1	1.18
⑳ COMPENSATION BASED ON MERIT	49.3	35.2	15.5	1.66	81.8	12.1	6.1	1.24
㉑ **OVERALL ECONOMIC OPPORTUNITY**	65.7	19.2	15.03	1.49	82.8	9.1	8.1	1.25
㉒ CHALLENGE AND EXCITEMENT	67.1	21.4	11.4	1.44	84.8	3.0	12.1	1.27
㉓ INTERESTING AND MOTIVATING JOB	71.8	14.1	14.1	1.42	87.9	6.1	6.1	1.18
㉔ **OVERALL JOB CHALLENGE**	69.5	17.8	12.8	1.43	86.4	4.6	9.1	1.23
㉕ FREEDOM, INDEPENDENCE, OWN BOSS	49.3	38	12.7	1.63	69.7	12.1	18.2	1.48

		UNITED STATES				SOUTH AFRICA			
		AGREE (%)	NEUTRAL (%)	DISAGREE (%)	AV.	AGREE (%)	NEUTRAL (%)	DISAGREE (%)	AV.
26	ABILITY TO CHOOSE OWN WORK TASKS	47.9	36.6	15.5	1.68	54.5	15.2	30.3	1.76
27	CREATE SOMETHING NEW	54.3	34.3	11.4	1.57	69.7	18.2	12.1	1.42
28	TAKE ADVANTAGE OF CREATIVE NEEDS	47.9	40.8	11.3	1.63	68.8	21.9	9.4	1.41
29	**OVERALL NEED FOR SELF-DIRECTION**	49.9	37.4	12.7	1.63	65.7	16.9	17.5	1.52

SCALE: AGREE = 1   NEUTRAL = 2   DISAGREE = 3

. . .

In this final section, we use results from responses to [all the] questions … to show the top-rated preferred career **attributes**. Top for the South African students is an interesting and motivating job (1.18), with promotional opportunities (1.18). These fall into two categories: the nature of the job and potential rewards from the job. In
140 second place is economic opportunity (1.24). A close third position at 1.27 is the challenge and excitement associated with the job. This attribute, as with interest and motivation, is about the nature of the job. Fourth is opportunity for career progress (1.33), and the last in the top five is job security and **stability**, both at 1.45.

As can be seen in Table 2, the responses from US students show a strong preference
145 for opportunities in the career. In first place is opportunity for career progress (1.34), and second is promotion opportunity (1.37). In third place are two factors in different categories. The students are interested in a job that is interesting and motivational (1.42), a job characteristic factor, and job security (1.42). In fourth position, at 1.44, is challenge and excitement. Last in the top five preferences for the US students is
150 the importance of economic opportunity (1.45). The following table is a summary of the top-ranked preferred career attributes as found by this study of college students in the United States and in South Africa.

Top-ranked preferred career attributes among US and SA students

RANK	UNITED STATES	SOUTH AFRICA
1	Opportunity for career progress	Promotion/Interesting and motivating job
2	Promotion	Economic opportunity
3	Interesting and motivating job/Job security	Challenge and excitement
4	Challenge and excitement	Opportunity for career progress
5	Economic opportunity	Job stability/Job security

Discussion

Analysis of the results of this exploratory study reveals two interesting patterns. First is the universality of the broad career expectations of today's young people, and
155 second is the important differences in attitude in the South African and US students. This is **consistent with** Harris and Gibson's (2008) finding that collectively the students **exhibit** similar attitudes but that differences do exist.

exhibit (v.): clearly show

. . .

This research makes three important contributions. First, it highlights what young business students expect from their careers. Second, it provides a comparative
160 perspective of the career preferences of young people. The important role of entrepreneurship to any economy is widely acknowledged. Economic and community development hinges on growing business formation and growth. To encourage economic development in the form of new businesses, it is necessary to have information on factors that exert a positive influence on attitudes toward self-
165 employment. Information that helps enhance entrepreneurship should be of interest to a range of stakeholders including researchers, educators, and policy-makers. Understanding differences in work attitudes across nations will make a contribution toward explaining differences in rates of firm start-ups across nations, which is an important consideration in this age of globalization.

paradigm shift (n.): significant change in the way things are done or the way people think

170 Third, the research has a message for business leaders. There is a need for a paradigm shift if organizations are going to attract and **retain** top talent. Today's young people believe they can take a heavy workload provided it is exciting. They also have the propensity to look for alternative opportunities if the organization fails to meet their expectations. A possible contribution of this study is that in addition to the
175 traditional rewards, organizations should consider making the work environment an interesting place.

One limitation of this exploratory study is its cross-sectional nature. It does not provide a direct link between job attitude and active business founding. As such, conclusions linking job attitudes to levels of entrepreneurship are theoretically based. Another
180 limitation is that because of the survey nature of the research, it has not been possible to make follow-up questions to uncover the reasoning behind the attitudes. The results suggest potentially interesting explanatory research to provide detailed information of the career intentions of today's business students and country differences as shown by this study, and attempt to answer the questions raised in the discussion section
185 above. It is also important to provide longitudinal studies in this area to follow the career paths of the respondents.

(2655 words)

References

Gilad, B., & Levine, P. (1986). A behaviour model of entrepreneurial supply. *Journal of Small Business Management, 24*, 45–51.

Harris, M. L., & Gibson, S. G. (2008). Examining the entrepreneurial attitudes of US business students. *Education + Training, 50*(7), 568–581.

Littunen, H. (2000). Entrepreneurship and the characteristics of the entrepreneurial personality. *International Journal of Entrepreneurial Behaviour and Research, 6*(6), 295–301.

Orham, Scott D. (2001). Why women enter into entrepreneurship: An explanatory model. *Women in Management Review, 16*(5), 232–243.

Scarborough, N. M., Wilson, D. L., & Zimmerer, T. W. (2009). *An effective small business management: An entrepreneurial approach* (9th ed.). Toronto: Pearson, Prentice Hall.

Schwarz, E. J., Wdowiak, M. A., Almer-Jarz, D. A., & Breitenecker, R. J. (2009). The effects of attitudes and perceived environment conditions on students' entrepreneurial intent: An Austrian perspective. *Education + Training, 51*(4), 272–291.

van Gelderen, M., Brand, M., van Praag, M., Bodewes, W., Poutsma, E., & van Gils, A. (2008). Explaining entrepreneurial intentions by means of the theory of planned behavior. *Career Development International, 13*(6), 538–559.

Mboko, S. (2011). Towards an explanation of the growth in young entrepreneur activities: A cross-country survey of work values of college students. *Journal of Marketing Development and Competitiveness, 5*(4), 108–118.

After You Read

C. Demonstrate your understanding of the article by indicating whether the following statements are true or false. Confirm your answers with your classmates and as a class. On a separate page, rewrite any false statements to make them true.

STATEMENTS	TRUE	FALSE
❶ In the abstract, the author, Mboko, states that the research provides an explanation for the growth in young entrepreneurship.		
❷ There have not been many research studies about entrepreneurship.		
❸ There have not been many research studies about what motivates young people to become entrepreneurs.		
❹ There have not been many research studies that compare student attitudes to entrepreneurship in developed and developing countries.		
❺ Gilad and Levine suggest that young people become entrepreneurs because they can't get employment elsewhere. This is the "pull" theory of entrepreneurial motivation.		
❻ Mboko believes that entrepreneurship meets the career aspirations of young people more than jobs with established organizations.		
❼ Mboko uses an online survey to collect data.		
❽ The results show that business students in the US and SA generally have similar motivation to become entrepreneurs.		
❾ The differences in student attitudes toward entrepreneurship may be a result of culture, but this was not a major focus of this study.		
❿ The study connected student attitudes toward young entrepreneurship to the founding of businesses.		

MyBookshelf > My eLab > Exercises > Chapter 2 > Towards an Explanation of the Growth in Young Entrepreneur Activities

Writing In-Text Citations

There are several ways to introduce in-text citations; each places a different degree of emphasis on the original author(s).

A. Read these sentences from Readings 2 and 3, paying particular attention to the *presence* (and *position*) or *absence* of the author's name. Then, answer the questions that follow.

  a) Creativity is an important personal attribute that has come to be associated with entrepreneurs, and small businesses provide a great environment to use creativity.

b) While the idea that people are "born" entrepreneurs is still quite popular, nothing could be further from the truth.

c) Interest in entrepreneurship among young people is reported to be growing (Scarborough et al., 2009), prompting increased research interest in the area (Harris and Gibson, 2008).

d) This is consistent with Harris and Gibson's (2008) finding that collectively the students exhibit similar attitudes but that differences do exist.

e) Using contingency theory, Gilad and Levine (1986) proposed the "push" and "pull" theories as possible explanations of entrepreneurial motivation.

1 Which examples emphasize the author(s) the most? _____

2 Which examples minimize the author(s) the most? _____

3 Which verb tense is used in each example?

_____

_____

B. Refer to Reading 1 (page 44) and, on a separate page, provide concise answers to these questions in which you cite the sources of the information. Vary your citation formats to emphasize or de-emphasize the author's name. Pay careful attention to your verb tenses.

1 According to the *Techpoint* interview, when did Jason Njoku found iROKO?

Matuluko (2015) states that Njoku founded iROKO in 2010.

2 What were some of the drastic changes that iROKO experienced in the year before the interview took place?

3 What does the *Techpoint* interview reveal about Njoku's previous jobs working for other people?

4 What goal do Njoku and his partner, Bastian Gotter, have for iROKO?

MyBookshelf > My eLab >
Exercises > Chapter 2 >
Focus on Writing

FINAL ASSIGNMENT
Write an Extended Process Essay

Find an example of a young entrepreneur. Search "profiles of young entrepreneurs" on the Internet or ask your instructor for a suggestion. Write a longer process essay about this person, describing his or her entrepreneurial development. Include citations and references.

A. Learn as much as you can about the entrepreneur's background, education, and experience. Remember to use reliable sources and to keep track of citation and referencing information.

B. In the introduction, define *entrepreneur* or *entrepreneurship*. In the body of your essay, discuss the entrepreneur's characteristics, business opportunity (how the idea was generated), and resources (how the business was financed).

C. Use the citation style that is preferred in your discipline. Follow the correct format for either numbered or author-date citations and finish your essay with a corresponding reference section. On the front of your paper, clearly indicate the citation style you are following.

Refer to the Models Chapter (page 276) to see an example of a process essay and to learn more about how to write one.

Critical Connections

Work with a partner (or two), and complete the table, indicating the key knowledge writers must consider to determine how and when to cite their sources. When you have finished, confirm your answers with your class.

QUESTIONS ABOUT CITATIONS	KEY KNOWLEDGE FOR CITATIONS
❶ How can you discover which citation style to use?	
❷ What citation style should you use in your field of study?	
❸ What are the characteristics of reliable sources of information?	
❹ Where can you find reliable sources?	
❺ Do you need to provide a citation for a) a direct quote? b) a paraphrase? c) a summary? d) general knowledge?	

CHAPTER 3

Renewable Energy

How the world produces energy to feed its increasing hunger for power is one of the defining issues of our time. The vast majority of the power we consume is generated by burning fossil fuels: oil, coal, or natural gas. However, the appeal of these energy sources is decreasing as scientists point to how they pollute our environment. This, and the threat of their eventual depletion, is the inspiration for innovation with renewable energy sources. When scientists and engineers talk about diversifying "the energy mix," they speak of how a combination of renewable energy sources can supplement the use of fossil fuels. Which sources of renewable energy will best replace the burning of fossil fuels to meet our energy needs?

In this chapter, you will

- learn vocabulary related to renewable energy sources;
- organize information in tables while you read;
- vary grammar and vocabulary to compare and contrast;
- select the optimal organization for your compare and contrast essays;
- learn how to build your knowledge of discipline-specific vocabulary;
- inquire further about how issues will impact you;
- write short and extended compare and contrast essays.

GEARING UP

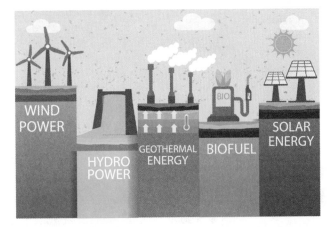

A. Working in a group of three students, look at the infographic and identify the five sources of renewable energy. Then brainstorm answers to the following questions.

1 What do you think makes an energy source renewable?

_____

2 Do you know of other sources of renewable energy?

_____

3 What are some sources of non-renewable energy?

_____

4 What are the benefits and challenges of renewable and non-renewable energy? List them in the table. When you have finished, discuss your answers with the rest of the class.

TYPE OF ENERGY	RENEWABLE ENERGY	NON-RENEWABLE ENERGY
Benefits	*Less pollution*	
Challenges		

Below are the key words you will practise in this chapter. Check the words you understand, then underline the words you use. Highlight the words you need to learn.

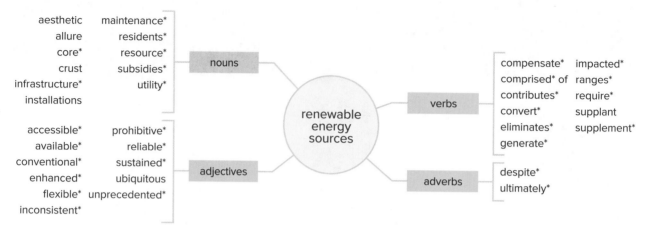

nouns

aesthetic
allure
core*
crust
infrastructure*
installations

maintenance*
residents*
resource*
subsidies*
utility*

adjectives

accessible*
available*
conventional*
enhanced*
flexible*
inconsistent*

prohibitive*
reliable*
sustained*
ubiquitous
unprecedented*

renewable energy sources

verbs

compensate*
comprised* of
contributes*
convert*
eliminates*
generate*

impacted*
ranges*
require*
supplant
supplement*

adverbs

despite*
ultimately*

*Appears on the Academic Word List

READING ❶ So Fresh and So Clean

Wind and solar power have great appeal. Gradually, these forms of renewable energy are being used alongside traditional non-renewable sources. However, wind and solar energy have some challenges: this first reading introduces both their advantages and disadvantages.

VOCABULARY BUILD

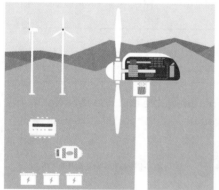

A. Below are some key words and phrases used to describe wind and solar power generation. Underline any that are unfamiliar and look them up in a dictionary.

copper wire coil	photovoltaic cells	transmission lines
electrical grid	shaft	turbine blades
electromagnets	solar array	wafers of silicon
magnetic field	solar panel	wind turbine

B. Working with a partner and referring to the pictures (page 76) as a guide, use the key words and phrases to briefly explain how wind and solar power are generated and transmitted to homes.

> Examples: *When the wind blows, the **turbine blades** spin, …*
> *When the sun shines, light hits the **solar array** …*

C. The author uses a variety of words to present the advantages and disadvantages of renewable energy. You will use these words in your own writing too. With your partner, write the following synonyms in the appropriate column of the table.

~~upside~~ pitfall benefit drawback gain weakness pro downside strength challenge plus con minus

SYNONYMS FOR *ADVANTAGE*	SYNONYMS FOR *DISADVANTAGE*
upside	

D. The box below contains key words from Reading 1. Match each word to its definition in one of the three tables that follow. Then label each table with the part of speech (adjective, noun, or verb) corresponding to the words in the table. When you have finished, compare your answers with your class.

compensate contributes conventional convert generate infrastructure require subsidies supplant supplement sustained ubiquitous

_____ **Table**

KEY WORDS	DEFINITIONS
compensate	replace or balance something bad with something good
	take the place of a person or thing so they are no longer needed
	add something to something else to increase or improve it
	gives ideas, money, or help to something other people are also involved in
	need something
	produce or cause something
	change something to a different form

_____ Table

KEY WORDS	DEFINITIONS
	continuing for a long time
	used for a long time and considered usual
	seeming to be everywhere

_____ Table

KEY WORDS	DEFINITIONS
	money paid by governments to reduce prices or production costs
	the basic structures and systems a country or organization needs to work well

Before You Read

Use reading strategies (see Chapter 1, page 4) to help you understand this text.

A. Skim Reading 1 to find the answers to the questions.

1 What is the topic of the reading? _____

2 How long is it? _____

3 What type of text is it? _____

4 What do you already know about the topic?

_____

_____

While You Read

B. Reading 1 has been divided into sections, with suggested headings given below. Read the text and choose the heading that best represents each section. Write the heading in the space provided in the reading.

> The Disadvantages of Wind and Solar Power
>
> The Place of Wind and Solar Power in the "Energy Mix"
>
> Challenges for Wind and Solar Power
>
> ~~World Use of Renewable Energy and How Wind and Solar Power Work~~
>
> The Advantages of Wind and Solar Power

So Fresh and So Clean

Section 1: _World Use of Renewable Energy and How Wind and Solar Power Work_ _____

The first step to adopting more … renewable power is to understand how the various technologies work and what challenges they face. Historically, most renewable electricity has come from hydroelectric dams, which now provide about 16 percent
5 of the world's electricity. Today, the sources growing the fastest and receiving the most investor attention are wind and solar power.

Wind power, which **generates** about 1.4 percent of the world's electricity, is produced as pinwheel-style turbines spin atop towers that rise hundreds of feet
10 above the ground. Solar power provides an even smaller share of global electricity: just 0.1 percent. Techniques for generating it vary; the most popular uses panels containing wafers of silicon thinner than a fingernail to **convert** sunlight into electrical
15 current. A few of these photovoltaic panels, as they are known, can be mounted directly on a building's roof, letting the occupants produce at least some of their own power. Or hundreds of panels can be grouped together on the ground in vast arrays that
20 funnel power into the electrical grid—sprawling, centralized power plants of a new sort.

Section 2: _____

Although wind power is more widespread today, solar power is theoretically more attractive. The sun emits a nearly limitless supply of energy, and it does so during
25 the daytime, when people use the most electricity. (Wind tends to blow most strongly at night.) Solar power also is easily distributed—panels can be placed on a streetlight or a soldier's backpack—whereas wind power is mostly a centralized energy source, requiring clumps of turbines to generate sizable amounts of power. But both wind and solar energy offer big advantages over fossil fuels. Wind and sunshine are clean,
30 emitting neither the pollutants that cause smog nor the carbon dioxide that **contributes** to climate change. They are **ubiquitous**, providing a domestic energy source even in places with no indigenous fossil fuels. And they are essentially never-ending.

Section 3: _____

caveats (n.): warnings that something may not be completely effective

There are huge caveats to this rosy assessment, and they come down mostly to money.
35 In most places, producing electricity from new wind and solar projects is more expensive than making it in new **conventional** power plants. Wind and solar power are younger technologies, with much work left to be done to wring out cost. The downsides of fossil fuels, notably their geopolitical and environmental risks, are not fully reflected in their market prices. And everything about the modern electrical
40 system is predicated on the use of fossil fuels: the coal mines and gas fields that produce them; the railroads, pipelines, and ships that transport them and the power plants that burn them. That system has been built up and its costs largely paid down over decades.

Wind and solar power enjoy no such entrenched **infrastructure**. The challenge of
45 making and installing the wind turbines and solar panels is just the start. Massive new transmission lines must be built to move large amounts of renewable electricity from the out-of-the-way places where it is generated to the metropolitan areas where it is consumed. This new equipment costs money and it often stokes opposition from people who are not used to living near industrial-scale energy infrastructure of any
50 sort. Along with other opponents, a group of landowners in Cape Cod, Massachusetts, for instance, has managed to delay the construction of an offshore wind farm that was proposed back in 2001. Even environmental activists often fight large renewable-energy projects, out of concern for local landscapes or animals.

Section 4: _____

55 Taking wind and solar power mainstream will also **require** better ways to get it to consumers when they need it, since the times when wind turbines and solar panels generate the most electricity are not necessarily the times when people use electricity most. Power

60 plants fired by natural gas can be dialed up or down to meet changing electricity demand, but the sun shines and the wind blows only at certain times. One potential solution is to stockpile renewable power— either in large-scale storage equipment, such as

65 massive batteries, or in smaller-scale devices, such as people's plug-in hybrid cars. Other approaches include better technologies to predict gusts and rays and "smart" electrical-transmission grids that could tie together far-flung renewable-power projects. Both

70 could help **compensate** in one place for … grey skies somewhere else. Scientists are working to bring down the cost of all these ideas. For now, in some places with dense concentrations of wind turbines, some of the power they could produce is wasted; the turbines

75 are shut off when the wind is blowing so hard that the turbines would produce more power than the grid could handle.

Section 5: _____

Wind and solar power will not replace fossil fuels anytime soon—not by a long shot.

80 The International Energy Agency (IEA) projects that by 2035, wind and solar could be producing 10 percent of global electricity, up from 1.5 percent now, and that renewables of all sorts could be generating 31 percent of the world's electricity, up from about 19 percent now. But even that expansion would require an increase in **subsidies**—"support that in some cases," the IEA notes, "cannot be taken for granted

85 in this age of fiscal austerity." Some countries with particularly generous subsidies and high electricity prices have made wind and solar power big enough to matter. Denmark gets 18 percent of its electricity from wind, and Spain gets 2 percent from the sun—the world's leaders by share, according to the IEA's latest figures. But even that renewable electricity is backed up by fossil-fuel power plants. Last year, fully

90 one-third of the new electricity-generating capacity brought on line in the United States came from wind and solar projects. Even so, given the vastness of the conventional energy system, wind and solar power remained relatively tiny, accounting for just 3 percent of the electricity the country actually produced. For the foreseeable future, renewable power is likely to **supplement**, not **supplant**, conventional energy …

95 Considering what renewable power is up against, the drive for it might seem a folly. But giving up now would be a mistake. As a result of recent technological improvements, the prospect of renewable power as an economically competitive part of the energy mix is no longer a **pipe dream**. Wind turbines and solar panels have gotten more efficient and less expensive … Solar power remains more expensive than conventional

pipe dream (exp.): hope or plan that will probably never happen

100 power (except in a few sunny places with high power prices, such as Hawaii), but its costs, too, are falling rapidly. Now more than ever, **sustained** but strategic support could produce blockbuster innovations with the potential to meaningfully change the energy mix.

(1129 words)

Ball, J. (2012, May/June). Tough love for renewable energy. *Foreign Affairs, 91*(3), 122–133.

After You Read

C. Work with a partner to answer the following questions. Then compare answers with another pair of students.

1 List the percentage of the world's electricity each of these renewable energy sources generates: hydroelectricity, wind power, and solar power.

_____

2 Put a check mark in the appropriate column of the table to identify the differences and similarities between wind and solar power mentioned in Section 2 of the reading.

POINTS OF COMPARISON	WIND	SOLAR
❶ Most widespread source	✓	
❷ Most popular source		
❸ Provides electricity when people need it most		
❹ Easily distributed		
❺ Mostly centralized		
❻ Clean energy		
❼ Can be installed where there are no fossil fuels for energy		
❽ Renewable source		

3 Why do conventional methods of generating energy (i.e., burning fossil fuels) seem cheap compared to the costs of renewable forms of energy?

_____

_____

_____

_____

_____

_____

_____

④ Why do some people, sometimes even environmentalists, fight against the development of renewable energy infrastructure?

_____

_____

_____

_____

⑤ What is one significant disadvantage of wind and solar energy? How could this be overcome?

_____

_____

_____

_____

_____

_____

_____

⑥ By 2035, what percentage of the world's electricity might wind and solar power contribute? Does this mean that we can eliminate the use of non-renewable energy sources?

_____

_____

_____

_____

⑦ Does the article end on a positive or negative note? Why?

_____

_____

_____

_____

⑧ What is your opinion about the future of wind and solar power?

_____

_____

_____

_____

Organizing Information in Tables

Recording information as you read is an efficient way to remember a large amount of material, which you can then refer to when you write. You have already practised this skill in this chapter in task C, question 2, on page 81.

Summarizing information in tables is especially useful if it is technical or complicated or if it is extensive.

The tables you create might look different depending on your purpose. If you want to take notes on step-by-step information to explain a process or classification or to write a definition essay, a useful table might look like this.

SOURCES	INFORMATION
Write citation information here. Keeping accurate references will save you time when you write.	*Write what you want to remember here. A linear or step-by-step presentation of information clarifies its order.*

If you want to write about similarities and differences in characteristics, your table might look like the one below. This type of table can help you organize and remember information for a compare and contrast essay (for example, for writing assignments in this chapter).

CHARACTERISTICS FOR COMPARISON OR CONTRAST	ITEM TO COMPARE OR CONTRAST (E.G., SOLAR POWER)	ITEM TO COMPARE OR CONTRAST (E.G., WIND POWER)	SOURCES
CHARACTERISTIC 1: (E.G., AMOUNT OF ENERGY AVAILABLE)	*Write information about solar power here.*	*Write information about wind power here.*	*Write citation information here.*
CHARACTERISTIC 2: (E.G., EXPENSE OF EQUIPMENT)			

A. Can you think of information on other subjects that might be useful to summarize in a compare and contrast table? Discuss this with your class.

MyBookshelf > My eLab > Exercises > Chapter 3 > So Fresh and So Clean

Reading 2 is about solar and wind power that can be generated on rooftops (as opposed to large wind or solar farms). While the idea of displaying a visible sign of one's commitment to the environment is appealing, there are some factors to consider before installing a home wind turbine or solar panel.

VOCABULARY BUILD

A. Work with a partner and read the sentences with key words from Reading 2 in bold in the first column. Write the definitions of the key words in the second column. Then work with your class to answer the questions in the third column.

WORDS IN CONTEXT	DEFINITIONS	APPLY WORDS TO YOUR LIFE
❶ Some wind turbines have a more pleasing **aesthetic** than other models.	*appearance connected with beauty*	What items do you purchase where aesthetics is a factor?
❷ The **allure** of renewable energy is great.		Some foreign countries have a greater allure than others when we think about travel. What countries do you find most alluring?
❸ In optimum circumstances, a 6 kW turbine **comprised of** a rotating blade and generator will produce 15,000 kWh per year.		What objects are comprised of two or more parts?
❹ The Honeywell Wind Turbine has a design that **eliminates** mechanical resistance and drag.		How can we eliminate energy waste in our homes?
❺ Technology has also been improving rapidly, decreasing the cost and making the solar cells smaller and more **flexible**.		What are two things that are flexible?
❻ Home wind turbines that have a vertical axis are **impacted** less by winds that change directions.		What factors impacted your decision to study English?
❼ Experts say that the flow of wind is too **inconsistent** at the height of most roofs.		What things are consistent in your life? What things are inconsistent?

WORDS IN CONTEXT	DEFINITIONS	APPLY WORDS TO YOUR LIFE
⑧ Because they contain no liquids or moving parts, PV cells require very little **maintenance**.		What kinds of things require maintenance?
⑨ It is unfortunate that high-performing turbines remained switched off because **residents** complained about the noise.		What country and what type of building are you a resident of?
⑩ Solar systems and wind turbines are being installed on both homes and businesses at an **unprecedented** rate.		What products are selling at unprecedented rates these days?
⑪ **Utility**-scale turbines in the 3- to 5-megawatt (MW) range can be over 120 metres (400 feet) tall.		What is the name of the phone or electric utility in your area?

Before You Read

Can you imagine having solar panels or a wind turbine on your roof?

A. Working with two other classmates, hypothesize the possible advantages and challenges of installing solar panels or wind turbines where you live. Think about space, noise, and exposure to sun and wind. After, discuss your ideas with the class.

	SOLAR PANELS	WIND TURBINES
ADVANTAGES	• *generate your own heat and electricity to reduce your overall energy costs*	
DISADVANTAGES		

While You Read

B. Copy the reference for Reading 2 into the table on page 86. As you will later add information from Reading 1 (page 78), copy that reference as well.

C. While you read, write key information in the appropriate row. Use a separate page if you don't have enough space. You will use this information in your Warm-Up Assignment, so make sure to include enough details.

READING 1 REFERENCE READING 2 REFERENCE		
CHARACTERISTICS FOR COMPARISON OR CONTRAST	**SOLAR POWER**	**WIND POWER**
CONDITIONS FOR USE	• *south facing* • *sloped (or flat) roof* • *space* • *exposure (no trees, chimneys, dormers, vents to shade the panels)*	• *exposure to wind*
POSSIBLE USES		
DESCRIPTION OF ENERGY SOURCE AND HOW IT GENERATES POWER		
ADVANTAGES		
DISADVANTAGES		
WHERE EXCESS ENERGY IS STORED AND HOW		
EXAMPLES OF INNOVATIVE TECHNOLOGY		

Renewable energy is taking hold in cities and their suburbs, with solar systems and wind turbines being installed on both homes and businesses at an **unprecedented** rate. The **allure** is great: to save electricity and reduce dependence on fossil fuels, as well as to create a visible symbol that we are doing our part to go green.

5 There are some successful installations that have proven themselves over the years, and some exciting experiments happening, both on multi-unit buildings and individual homes. However, mounting a wind turbine or solar system on your roof isn't as simple—or often as beneficial—as it might seem. And there is a major upfront investment although the payback can be significant once the system is paid for. So 10 let's examine the possibilities and the pitfalls.

Solar

Since renewable energy relies on natural sources, your property has to be exposed to that source—in this case, the sun. So you'll need an area of south-facing sloped roof—or a flat roof where panels could be installed 15 facing south using a mounting mechanism to tilt them to the right angle—that measures at least 2 by 4 metres (or 6.5 by 13 feet). Ideally, the roof should receive full sun from 10 a.m. to 3 p.m. year-round. Keep in mind development possibilities or growing trees that could block the sun in the future. Even chimneys, dormers and vents can shade your panels and reduce 20 their efficiency. Your supplier will calculate the correct slope for your latitude.

There are two main ways to use the power of the sun to reduce energy costs in your home. You can use the heat from the sun's rays to heat your home or your domestic hot water, or to produce electricity to power lights and appliances …

25 In climates where temperatures rarely dip below freezing, a direct circulation system can be used, where pumps circulate household water through the collectors and into the home. In colder climates, an indirect circulation system is used, with pumps circulating a non-freezing, heat-transfer fluid through the collectors and a heat exchanger …

30 Most solar water heaters require a well-insulated storage tank. In two-tank systems, the solar water heater preheats water before it enters the conventional water heater. In one-tank systems, the backup heating system is combined with the solar storage in one tank.

Then, there is a solar electric system, using photovoltaic (PV) cells, which are 35 semiconductor devices, usually made of silicon. Photons in sunlight are absorbed by the silicon and electrons are knocked loose from their atoms, allowing them to flow through the silicon to produce electricity.

Because they contain no liquids, corrosive chemicals, or moving parts, PV cells require very little **maintenance**, don't pollute while in use, and operate silently. In a household 40 system, the cells are bundled together into solar panels, which have a sheet of glass on the front, allowing light to pass while protecting the cells from the elements. Panels are linked together in arrays to fit individual generation needs. You can add panels to your roof at any time after installation—given that you have the available space, of course—in order to increase power output …

45 The energy generated by solar panels can be stored in batteries. But in some jurisdictions, your roof-mounted PV system will probably be grid-tied, meaning that any excess electricity generated is sent to the transmission grid. Net metering programs give these systems a credit for the electricity they deliver to the grid. This credit offsets 50 electricity provided from the grid when the system cannot meet demand, effectively using the grid as a storage mechanism.

Due to the growing demand for solar energy, the manufacture of solar cells and PV arrays has been increasing by almost 50 percent a year recently. Technology has also been improving rapidly, 55 decreasing the cost and making the cells smaller and more **flexible**.

A Philadelphia company, SRS Energy, has even developed a dark blue roof tile made from a high-performance polymer used in car bumpers that has flexible solar technology embedded inside. The tiles are lightweight, unbreakable, and recyclable … Additionally, a 60 number of companies are introducing flexible, thin-film solar PV cells and modules that can be attached, via foil, directly to rooftops.

Wind

Wind power is the renewable energy technology that is growing most quickly, largely because it is one of the least expensive. Like solar, the cost of wind power has fallen 65 dramatically over the last decade or so. However, some wind energy experts feel that wind is not suited to rooftop installation. But more about that later.

The blades on a wind turbine use lift the same way airplanes do. The wind passes over the blades and the lift created causes them to move. The moving blades turn a shaft, which in turn rotates a series of large electromagnets inside a tightly wound 70 copper wire coil within the generator. The moving magnetic field between the coil and the magnets creates an electric current, which is drawn off and transmitted as electricity.

Wind turbines come in a variety of sizes and capacities from 300-watt (W) "mini" turbines that homeowners can install themselves, to **utility**-scale turbines in the 3- to 75 5-megawatt (MW) range that can be over 120 metres (400 feet) tall. In optimum circumstances, a 6 kW turbine **comprised of** a rotating blade and generator will produce around 15,000 kWh per year. This is enough to power a small office.

There are two main types of wind turbine: vertical axis and horizontal axis.

Home wind turbines that have a vertical axis are more suitable for rooftop mounting. 80 They are **impacted** less by winds that change directions, work at lower wind speeds, can be quieter than horizontal axis units, and can have a more pleasing **aesthetic** than other models. Some even look like roof vents …

Right now, the American Wind Energy Association (AWEA) estimates that just 1 percent of small wind turbines installed today are attached to roofs, and nearly 99 percent 85 to a tower.

And many small wind experts feel that towers are where wind turbines belong. They say that there is too much turbulence and **inconsistent** flow of wind from trees and other buildings at the height of most roofs, and the turbines create too much noise and vibration.

90 Typical advice is that for proper operation, the rotor of a wind turbine should be situated at least 10 metres (33 feet) above anything within 100 metres (328 feet). A tower is usually supplied when you purchase a wind turbine, but many municipalities will not allow towers to be installed. With trees, one needs to take into account the height to which they will grow during the turbine's lifespan …

95 The Warwick Wind Trials Project in the UK confirmed poor performance and noise issues with roof-mounted wind turbines. Its 2009 report summarizes the finding of a trial covering almost 200,000 hours of operation of twenty-six building-mounted wind turbines from five manufacturers across the UK during 2007 and 2008. Author and small wind expert Paul Gipe wrote on his blog that, "If further proof is needed 100 that mounting wind turbines on rooftops is a bad idea, the final report on the Warwick Wind Trials is it."

Gipe particularly referred readers to this part of the report: "Of particular note is that turbines on our high-rise sites … were able to generate as much energy in one month as other turbines in the trial did in one year. It is unfortunate that these high-performing 105 turbines had to remain switched off for the majority of the trial following complaints about noise from the building **residents**. The best-performing turbine in the trial generated an average of 2.382 kWh per day when in operation, equivalent to 869 kWh in a full year. The poorest site generated an average of 41 kWh per day when in operation or 15 kWh per year, *which is less than the energy it consumed to run the* 110 *turbine's electronics"* [emphasis added].

What everyone agrees on is that there are many companies and individuals happy to take advantage of a hot market for wind power and provide homeowners with what they want, rather than what will work. So buyer beware!

Fortunately, the challenges of rooftop wind have the inventor community hard at 115 work. Two wind turbines have recently won awards for their innovation in addressing the issues of efficiency, noise, and aesthetics.

Earlier this year, a Michigan-based company called WindTronics won a Gold Edison Award for its small rooftop Honeywell Wind Turbine. Designed by Imad Mahawili, a chemical engineer and long-time wind energy consultant, its gearless design 120 **eliminates** mechanical resistance and drag, allowing it to generate power in wind speeds as low as an unprecedented 2 miles per hour and as high as 45 miles per hour, without the typical noise, size, weight, and vibrations associated with traditional wind turbines. Weighing 170 pounds and 125 measuring 6 feet in diameter, the turbine can be mounted in several ways, including on a rooftop, a pole, or a commercial mount …

A UK company has taken a different approach to rooftop wind with its RidgeBlade system, which won 130 the Dutch Postcode's Green Challenge in 2009, providing its developers, The Power Collective, with funds to help bring the design to market. Designed by a former Rolls Royce turbine engineer, this elegantly simple micro-generation system employs 135 discreetly housed cylindrical turbines positioned horizontally along the apex of a sloping roof. The slope of the roof naturally channels wind into the turbine chamber, meaning RidgeBlade can produce electricity under low or variable wind conditions. The company claims that this high efficiency means that the system could pay for itself within a few years.

140 The lure is strong to reduce electricity bills, reduce greenhouse gases, and become more individually energy independent. And solar or wind can help in that regard. However, if your roof isn't suitable, remember that conservation can go a long way toward meeting those goals.

(1660 words)

_____

Priesnitz, W. (2010, September/October). Rooftop power. *Natural Life, 135,* 28–32.

After You Read

D. Review the information you wrote in your table in task C with another student. Answer the following questions.

1. Did you include as much information as possible from Reading 2? _____

2. Are there any blank spaces in the table? Why?

_____

_____

E. Using a different colour, add details on solar and wind energy from Reading 1 to the table to supplement the information from Reading 2 and fill in some of the blank spaces. Make sure the information in the table is as complete as possible. Why should you distinguish between information from Reading 1 and information from Reading 2 in the table?

MyBookshelf > My eLab >
Exercises > Chapter 3 >
Rooftop Power

_____

_____

FOCUS ON
ACCURACY

Varying Grammar and Vocabulary to Compare and Contrast

In English, there are many ways to compare and contrast items. Words and phrases that express similarities and differences can be categorized by grammatical function. You can choose from a wealth of compare and contrast expressions to find the best and most accurate ones to suit your needs.

Use these grammatical forms and vocabulary to express **similarity**.

GRAMMATICAL OR LEXICAL CATEGORY	WORDS/PHRASES	EXAMPLES
COORDINATE CONJUNCTION	and	Both solar **and** wind power are renewable sources of energy.
SUBORDINATE CONJUNCTIONS	as just as	Solar power is a renewable source of energy **as** is wind power. Solar power is a renewable source of energy **just as** wind power is.
ADVERBIAL CONJUNCTIONS	likewise similarly	Solar power is a renewable source of energy; **likewise**, wind power is a never-ending source of energy.

GRAMMATICAL OR LEXICAL CATEGORY	WORDS/PHRASES	EXAMPLES
EXPRESSIONS	is similar to is comparable to resembles	Solar power **is similar to** wind power because they are both sources of renewable energy.
	like	**Like** solar power, wind energy is renewable.
	as ... as	Solar power is **as** renewable a source of energy **as** wind power.
	equally	Solar and wind power are **equally** renewable.

The following forms and vocabulary express **dissimilarity**.

GRAMMATICAL OR LEXICAL CATEGORY	WORDS/PHRASES	EXAMPLES
COORDINATE CONJUNCTIONS	but yet	It is relatively easy to install solar panels on a home rooftop, **but** it is harder to install a wind turbine.
SUBORDINATE CONJUNCTIONS	although even if though whereas while	**Although** it is relatively easy to install solar panels on a home rooftop, it is harder to install a wind turbine.
ADVERBIAL CONJUNCTIONS	however in contrast nevertheless	It is relatively easy to install solar panels on a home rooftop; **however**, it is harder to install a wind turbine.
EXPRESSIONS	it is ... than it is	**It is** easier to install solar panels on a home rooftop **than it is** to install a wind turbine.
	unlike in contrast to	**Unlike** solar panels, wind turbines are difficult to install on a home rooftop.
	on the other hand	Solar panels are easy to install on a home rooftop. **On the other hand**, it is more difficult to install a wind turbine.
	differs from is different from	Solar power **differs from** wind power because it is easier to install solar panels than a wind turbine.

A. Work with the information from the table you completed in Reading 2, task C (page 86). On a separate page, write at least five compare and contrast sentences. Use a variety of conjunctions and expressions to make them interesting. After, check your sentences with a classmate and write your best one(s) on the board. You can use these sentences in your Warm-Up Assignment.

MyBookshelf > My eLab > Exercises > Chapter 3 > Accuracy Review

Selecting the Optimal Organization for Your Compare/Contrast Essay

Compare and contrast essays are organized so the reader can easily see the similarities and differences between items. There are two standard methods of displaying information: block style and point-by-point style. The two tables below demonstrate the differences in these patterns for a simple compare and contrast essay that contains three main points.

BLOCK STYLE ORGANIZATION
Introduction with Thesis
Item 1: • Point 1 • Point 2 • Point 3
Item 2: • Point 1 • Point 2 • Point 3
Conclusion with concluding statement

POINT-BY-POINT ORGANIZATION
Introduction with Thesis
Point 1: • Item 1 • Item 2
Point 2: • Item 1 • Item 2
Point 3: • Item 1 • Item 2
Conclusion with concluding statement

A. Which organizational pattern do the readings follow?

  ❶ Reading 1? _____

  ❷ Reading 2? _____

General advice to writers developing compare and contrast essays is to use the block style for simpler, less technical information, and the point-by-point style for complex, more technical information.

B. Why do you think block style organization is better for simpler topics and point-by-point organization is better for complex topics?

  _____

  _____

C. Based on the complexity of these topics, what organizational pattern might work best for compare and contrast essays?

  ❶ two holidays *Block* _____

  ❷ two cars with detailed performance information _____

③ two approaches to peace negotiations between two warring countries

_____

④ two mobile phone plans _____

⑤ two courses _____

D. Now provide an example of a topic that would work well with each of the two methods.

block style: _____

point-by-point style: _____

MyBookshelf > My eLab >
Exercises > Chapter 3 >
Focus on Writing

WARM-UP ASSIGNMENT
Write a Short Compare and Contrast Essay

Write a short compare and contrast essay on the topic of solar and wind power. Use the information from the table you completed in Reading 2, task C (page 86).

A. Select the characteristics of solar and wind power that will give you the most to write about. (You do not need to compare and contrast every characteristic.)

B. Choose the organizational style you think will most clearly illustrate the similarities and differences between solar and wind power.

C. Use a variety of conjunctions and expressions.

D. Use the citation style appropriate to your discipline to cite information from Reading 1 or Reading 2, where required.

Refer to the Models Chapter (page 278) to see an example of a compare and contrast essay and to learn more about how to write one.

> **!** When you receive feedback from your instructor or your classmates on this Warm-Up Assignment, you will have information that you can use to improve your writing on the Final Assignment.

Academic
Survival Skill

Building Your Knowledge of Discipline-Specific Vocabulary

As a language learner, you understand the importance of developing a strong vocabulary base. But are you aware that the more words you know, the easier it is to acquire new vocabulary? When you learn new words, chances are you will remember them more easily because they remind you of other words, sounds, or rhythms you already know.

Although it can be hard to know where to start, there are a few good techniques that can help you maximize your vocabulary acquisition.

To learn words that will be useful across a wide variety of disciplines, study the Academic Word List (AWL).

There are similar lists for specific disciplines, and researchers are continually working on new ones. If you are studying in any of the following fields, you could learn the words on these lists.

• Engineering Word List (Ward, 2009)
• Medical Academic Word List (Lei & Liu, 2016)
• Newspaper Word List (useful if you like to read or listen to the news) (Chung, 2007)
• Nursing Academic Word List (Yang, 2015)
• Science Word List (Coxhead & Hirsh, 2007)

You may be interested to know that, according to research, English-language students who keep their own vocabulary lists and notebooks learn more new words and are better at using them in their writing than students who don't (Walters & Bozkurt, 2009).

Begin your own discipline-specific vocabulary notebook. If your discipline already has an established vocabulary list, look for it in your library (using the reference information below). Each time you study the list, review twenty to thirty words, checking those you already know and writing and learning definitions for those you don't. Review the words every two days for a week, then once every week, and finally, once a month.

If there is no current vocabulary list for your discipline, start your own by reading a textbook in your field and looking for discipline-specific words that occur frequently. Follow the same procedure mentioned above for learning the new words. Learning twenty to thirty words a session is a good target.

Bring your early lists to class to compare with those of your classmates. You can double your vocabulary acquisition by learning each other's words.

References

Chung, T. (2009). The newspaper word list: A specialized vocabulary for reading newspapers. *JALT Journal, 31*(2), 159–182.

Coxhead, A., & Hirsh, D. (2007). A pilot science word list for EAP. *Revue Française de Linguistique Appliquée, XII*(2), 65–78.

Lei, L. & Liu, D. (2016). A new medical academic word list: A corpus-based study with enhanced methodology. *Journal of English for Academic Purposes, 22*, 42–53. doi.org/10.1016/j.jeap.2016.01.008

Walters, J., & Bozkurt, N. (2009). The effect of keeping vocabulary notebooks on vocabulary acquisition. *Language Teaching Research, 13*, 403–423. doi:10.1177/13621168809341509

Ward, J. (2009). A basic engineering English word list for less proficient foundation engineering undergraduates. *English for Specific Purposes, 28*, 170–182. doi:10.1016/j.esp.2009.04.001

Yang, M. (2015). A nursing academic word list. *English for Specific Purposes, 37*, 27–38. doi.org/10.1016/j.esp.2014.05.003

Geothermal Energy: An Introduction

Geothermal energy is another form of renewable energy. As you might guess from the word itself (*geo*, relating to the Earth, and *thermal*, relating to heat), geothermal energy is generated below the Earth's surface (or crust). Read this text to understand how geothermal energy is both similar to and different from solar and wind energy.

VOCABULARY BUILD

A. Complete each sentence in a way that demonstrates you understand the meaning of the word in bold. When you have finished, compare your sentences with two other classmates. Can you agree on the definitions of the words?

① One significant upside of geothermal energy is that it is **accessible** everywhere on Earth because ...

it is generated from the heat below the surface of the Earth.

② Another strength of geothermal energy is that it is **available** all day ...

③ Geothermal heat is generated deep in the Earth's **core,** which is located ...

④ The Earth's **crust** is located ...

⑤ **Despite** the advantages of geothermal energy ...

⑥ While conventional geothermal heating systems are useful, the next generation of **Enhanced** Geothermal Systems (or EGS) ...

⑦ There are geothermal **installations** all over the world; the largest ones are in ...

⑧ Although the costs of geothermal energy may seem **prohibitive** ...

⑨ The heat beneath the surface of the Earth **ranges** from ...

⑩ Geothermal energy is **reliable** because ...

⑪ The heat from the Earth is considered a **resource** because it is ...

⑫ Whether people adopt geothermal energy **ultimately** depends on ...

B. In this reading, the author uses multiple words to convey how vast the supply of geothermal energy is. Locate the following lines in the reading and list the three adjectives that are synonyms for *extremely large*.

Line 17: _____

Line 32: _____

Line 38: _____

MyBookshelf > My eLab >
Exercises > Chapter 3 >
Vocabulary Review

Before You Read

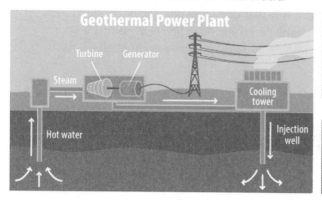
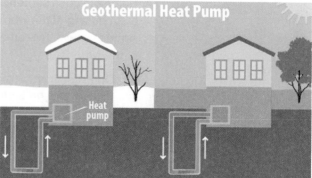

A. Look at the diagrams showing a geothermal power plant and a geothermal heat pump installation. With a partner, discuss what you can learn about geothermal power from these diagrams.

B. On a separate page, recreate a table similar to the one in Reading 2, task C (page 86), but with only two columns. In the first column, copy the characteristics for comparison and contrast (e.g., conditions for use, possible uses, description of energy source, advantages, etc.). In the second column, leave space to note information from Reading 3 in the appropriate rows. Completing this table will help you organize the information you need to write your Final Assignment.

C. Skim the reading. In the margins, write the headings from column 1 of the table next to the paragraphs that contain the points you need to include in the table. After, verify your margin notes with another student.

While You Read

D. Now read the text carefully and transfer information (in point form) to the table you created in Before You Read.

Geothermal Energy: An Introduction

Humans have a long history of tapping the Earth's heat. It warmed the waters of the spa towns in Britain where the Romans came to bathe. Today, natural hot-water spas around the world attract millions of visitors seeking the soothing comfort of that healing heat. Its fury has **bewildered** humans throughout history, with violent
5 **eruptions spewing** hot ash and lava from giant pores in the Earth's surface. Less dangerous—but no less impressive—are its displays of contained energy, such as those that entertain tourists in Wyoming's Yellowstone Park, where geysers spout with startling regularity and force. It **ranges** in temperature from the extreme heat of the Earth's **core** to the constant (and much more comfortable) temperatures found
10 just a few feet beneath the planet's surface.

bewildered (adj.): completely confused

eruptions (n.): sudden explosions

spewing (v.): discharging something quickly and in large quantities

Geothermal energy is one of the only[1] meaningful sources of renewable energy **available** to us that is not **ultimately** reliant on the sun.

Although the Earth's core is about 7000°C (12,000°F), the heat near the surface—the upper **crust** of rock that's about 100 kilometres (60 miles) thick, and below which
15 has never been explored[2]—has a nearby, nuclear source. Radioactive elements like thorium and uranium are spread throughout the upper crust, and are constantly decaying and releasing heat. Thus, the heat in the ground comes from a massive, but very weak, nuclear furnace.

Generally, [the temperature increases along with the depth]. There are exceptions,
20 like geysers, hot springs, and volcanoes—all examples of the Earth's extreme inner heat poking through to the surface via ruptures in the Earth's crust.

Think of geothermal energy as mining the heat in the ground. Today, that energy comes from two kinds of mining operations: high-temperature heat, from volcanic activity and hot springs that are easy to find along the Earth's fault lines; and low-
25 temperature heat,[3] which is located just a few metres beneath our feet. Think of the high-temperature mining as digging up a rich vein of gold, and the low-temperature mining as panning for gold flakes.

The first kind of mining is called hot geothermal. It's limited to places where the high-temperature [material] is close to the surface, near volcanoes or along cracks in
30 the Earth's crust—where the Romans built their baths. The second kind is often called geo-exchange, or ground-source heating. Although it's nowhere near as dramatic as the high-temperature [mining], it has enormous potential for carbon-free energy production. Best of all, [this kind of mining is **accessible** everywhere.]

[The next generation of] mining will be a hybrid of the two. It's called **Enhanced**
35 **Geothermal Systems (EGS)**, and it revolves around the simple idea that high-temperature heat can be found almost anywhere if [we search] deep enough. The potential of geothermal energy, once EGS is brought into commercial operation, cannot be overstated. It is simply colossal.

A recent study[4] by the Massachusetts Institute of
40 Technology (MIT) noted that the total geothermal energy available within 10 kilometres (6 miles) of the Earth's surface is 130,000 times the entire energy needs of the United States. Obviously, not all of it can be tapped, but even conservative
45 estimates of recoverable energy indicate that between 3000 and 30,000 times the total energy needs of the US are just sitting down there, waiting to be captured. This isn't intermittent power that depends on the sun or the wind; this
50 heat is available all day, every day, year-round.

So EGS could provide for all our … energy needs, all over the world, and it is both constant and **reliable**. At first glance, geothermal seems to be a bit of a **magic bullet**. Let's see if that's really
55 the case.

magic bullet (exp.): an easy solution that will solve complex problems

Geo-exchange: Mining the Heat in Your Own Backyard

Whether we're walking down a city street, strolling through a park, or sitting in our own backyard, there's a reliable, clean, and renewable energy **resource** just a few feet below us. Although we've known about it for decades, it's a resource that's scarcely
60 been tapped.

The temperature of the Earth just beneath the surface, starting at about 3 metres (10 feet) and continuing for hundreds of metres, is roughly constant, year-round. It stays somewhere between 8° to 16°C (46° to 60°F), depending on geography, depth, and time of year.[5] Geo-exchange is the art of using that energy to heat and cool buildings
65 throughout the year. Think of the ground as a "heat battery," and think of a "heat pump" as a way to get the heat in and out of that battery.

How Does It Work?

Let's look at an example for heating. First, you pump liquid—normally a glycol solution—through the
70 length of a pipe[6] (called the "geo-loop") that's buried or drilled into the ground.[7] The liquid absorbs heat from the surrounding earth as it travels through the pipe. Let's say the glycol goes in at 8°C (46°F) and comes out at 11°C (52°F). The heart of the system
75 is the heat pump,[8] which acts like a refrigerator in reverse. It takes heat out of the liquid and transfers it to the building. The liquid returns to its original temperature, and the process repeats. The net effect is to mine the heat from the ground and transfer it
80 to the building. [The same process in reverse can be used to cool a building.]

Here's the key to energy production: the heat pump can get three to five times more energy out of the ground than it consumes. That means it runs at 300 to 500 percent efficiency and
85 can lower a building's energy use by up to 75 percent. Depending on the source of the electricity, the carbon footprint can be almost completely eliminated.[9]

holy grail (exp.): something that people want very much, but is very difficult to achieve

Simply put, geo-exchange is the **holy grail** of heating and cooling—no other technology can touch it. High-efficiency furnaces, modern air conditioners, baseboard heaters—none of these come close. As a bonus, the entire heating system gets pushed to the
90 electrical grid, which will one day be powered by clean, carbon-free, renewable energy. There's no way a natural-gas furnace can ever go carbon-free.

So why isn't a geo-exchange system installed in every building? Mostly, [the cost is **prohibitive**]. A typical house would face about $10,000 in additional costs above and beyond the price of a furnace and air conditioner. You've got all those pipes to bury
95 in the ground, and maybe some holes to drill. Why go to all that bother and expense? It does pay for itself over time,[10] but we don't always think long-term.

Plus, there's often a disconnect between paying for the geo-exchange system and getting the savings. A typical condominium or housing developer doesn't pay the ongoing energy bills, and they're motivated to minimize construction costs. Again—why pay
100 for the extra expense?

Despite these hurdles, geo-exchange is catching on. There are more than a million **installations** in North America alone, and we've barely scratched the surface. The easy installations are in buildings with a big yard where you can bury the pipes, but now, [geothermal heating is being used in more urban settings.]

105 A building development called Planet Traveler, a hotel in a dense part of downtown Toronto, has been designed to be the greenest[11] hotel in North America. This hotel proves that buildings in dense urban cores, with little or no land for the geo-loop, could still use geothermal energy. The developer made an agreement with Toronto City Council that allowed 1200 metres (4000 feet) of pipe to be buried and ten holes
110 to be drilled into the publicly owned laneway that runs alongside the building. Not only did the city give approval, but it's now considering opening up all public lands—parks, laneways, everything—to geo-exchange. That would make Toronto the first city in the world to formalize this kind of relationship, allowing its citizens to be their own geo-exchange utility.

115 The technology may not be new, but as Paul Mertes, CEO of Canadian geo-exchange provider Clean Energy Developments, states, "Geo-exchange makes existing heating and cooling technologies look like an eight-track player."

(1338 words)

Endnotes

1. Tidal power is the other exception.
2. The deepest exploratory holes dug in the Earth's surface are only about 12 kilometres (7.5 miles) deep.
3. Heat and temperature are two different, but related, things. Temperature is not energy, but is a measure of the intensity of the energy. Heat is energy—a measure of the total kinetic energy of the molecules of a substance. Generally speaking, the higher the temperature, the higher the heat content. But here's an important difference: a lot of something at a low temperature can contain as much heat as a little bit of something at a high temperature. So heat can be "high-quality" (or high-temperature), and it can be "low-quality" (or low-temperature). Just because something has a low temperature doesn't mean it doesn't contain heat.
4. Massachusetts Institute of Technology, MIT-led interdisciplinary panel. (2006). *The future of geothermal energy: Impact of enhanced geothermal systems (EGS) on the United States in the 21st century.* Retrieved from https://www1.eere.energy.gov/geothermal/pdfs/future_geo_energy.pdf
5. Strictly speaking, there's an equilibrium of sorts near the surface (less than 20 metres or 60 feet) in which a small degree of solar energy is present as well. Beneath that point, however, almost all of the heat comes from that inner nuclear battery.
6. How long depends on two factors. The first is how much heating or cooling that's needed—the load, type, and size of building, insulation, where it's located, etc. The second is what's called the "thermal conductivity" of the ground; that is, how fast heat is transferred to and from the pipe. If the pipes hit an underground aquifer, for example, much less pipe is needed, since water has a very high thermal conductivity. A typical 278-square-metre (3000-square-foot) home might need 365 to 425 metres (1200–1400 feet) of buried pipe.
7. The loop can be horizontal, laid along a trench, or it can be installed in vertically drilled holes. Horizontal loops are cheaper, but need more area and must be at least 3 metres (10 feet) below ground. Vertical loops are normally installed to save space in dense areas.
8. The heat pump uses compressors, just like a refrigerator, to remove heat from the glycol solution through a heat exchanger. A refrigerator moves heat from the inside of the fridge to the room; the heat pump moves heat from the glycol solution to the building.
9. Since all of the energy the building uses is now electricity, if the grid is supplying renewable, zero-carbon electrons, the building has essentially eliminated any carbon footprint. While this may be unlikely for existing grids, it is possible.
10. Two to five years for a commercial installation, a few more for a house.
11. By "greenest," we mean something specific: an 80 percent reduction in carbon emissions from business as usual. Without geo-exchange, there was absolutely no possibility of reaching that target, since it was—by far—the lion's share of the carbon-reduction target.

Rand, T. (2010). *Kick the fossil fuel habit: 10 clean technologies to save our world* (pp. 61–66). Toronto: Eco Ten Publishing Inc.

After You Read

E. Answer the following questions to check your comprehension. When you have finished, verify your answers with your class.

1 What makes geothermal energy unique among forms of renewable energy?

_____

_____

_____

2 What heats the Earth near the surface?

_____

_____

3 Where can examples of high-temperature geothermal mining be found?

_____

_____

4 What are the benefits of geo-exchange, or ground-source heating?

_____

_____

_____

5 What are the disadvantages of geo-exchange or ground-source heating?

_____

_____

_____

6 The author writes about an innovative geothermal installation in a hotel in Toronto, Canada. Do you know of, or can you find, any geothermal installations near where you live?

_____

_____

_____

MyBookshelf > My eLab >
Exercises > Chapter 3 >
Geothermal Energy

**FOCUS ON
CRITICAL
THINKING**

Inquiring Further

Inquiring further about how things you read or learn about affect your life and environment is a form of critical thinking. In Reading 3, you read about geothermal energy. Do you think it might affect you? How? For example, do you know how (or whether) it is used in your country or city?

A. Work with a partner to research reliable information about geothermal energy in the city or country where you live, or a neighbouring one. Gather all the information you can and share it with your class.

B. Next, consider the relevance of this information to your life and environment. As a class, discuss what kind of impact geothermal energy might have on you in the future in terms of the

- buildings you may live in;
- transportation you may use;
- purchases you may make;
- places you may travel;
- employment you may find.

FINAL ASSIGNMENT

Write an Extended Compare and Contrast Essay

Write an extended compare and contrast essay presenting the similarities and differences between geothermal energy and either solar or wind power.

A. Use the information from the two tables you completed in While You Read for Readings 2 (pages 85–86) and 3 (page 96).

B. Select the organizational style that will make the comparisons and contrasts most obvious to your reader.

C. Use conjunctions and expressions to express your ideas accurately. Remember to cite sources as appropriate.

Refer to the Models Chapter (page 278) to see an example of a compare and contrast essay and to learn more about how to write one.

Critical Connections

In Focus on Critical Thinking (page 100), you inquired further about the impact geothermal energy might have on your future. In this section, inquire further about how the global transition to renewable energy will influence your life and environment.

A. Find and read material from reliable sources on wind and solar power, as well as other forms of renewable energy that may be used in your city or country.

B. Consider the areas of your life that might be affected by renewable energy in the future, such as habitation, transportation, shopping habits, travel, and employment.

Share your findings with a group of students.

CHAPTER 4

Sustainable Buildings

In 1987, the United Nations published the now famous *Report of the World Commission on Environment and Development: Our Common Future*, also called the *Brundtland Report* after the chair of the Commission, Gro Brundtland. The report defines sustainable development as development that "meets the needs of the present without compromising the ability of future generations to meet their own needs." This definition is now being applied to the building industry, which, in the past, destroyed vast expanses of land, used large amounts of materials, and consumed huge quantities of energy. With a growing awareness that these building practices cannot be sustained, present-day architects, engineers, and designers are utilizing exciting new technology to create sustainable (or green) buildings. How will these high-tech buildings influence the environment, our lives, and the economy?

In this chapter, you will

- learn vocabulary related to sustainable building practices;
- apply old knowledge to new information;
- use direct quotations and indirect speech and learn how to integrate these elements in your writing;
- observe text features to learn about the English language;
- identify writer perspective in a text;
- write short and extended reports on sustainable buildings.

GEARING UP

A. With a small group of classmates, look at the infographic of an environmentally friendly home. Discuss what features make it a sustainable building.

B. Next, with your class, discuss the building you are presently in. Is it sustainable? Which features have a positive impact on the environment? Which features have a negative impact? To help you with this task, consider the following questions.

- How do you get to the building? Is it near bus and bike routes or accessible by foot?

- Is there a parking lot that was built by destroying natural habitat?

- Is energy used to heat and/or cool the building?

- Where does the water in the building come from and where does the wastewater go?

- Can you open the windows?

- What is the orientation of the building? Do the windows in the room you are in face toward or away from the sun?

- What is the building made of? Are the materials local? How much energy would it have taken to get the materials on-site?

C. After the discussion, rate the building on a scale from 1 (not sustainable) to 5 (very sustainable) and then explain your reasons.

Below are the key words you will practise in this chapter. Check the words you understand, then underline the words you use. Highlight the words you need to learn.

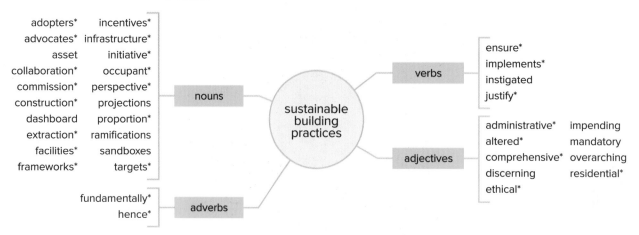

nouns

adopters*
advocates*
asset
collaboration*
commission*
construction*
dashboard
extraction*
facilities*
frameworks*

incentives*
infrastructure*
initiative*
occupant*
perspective*
projections
proportion*
ramifications
sandboxes
targets*

adverbs

fundamentally*
hence*

sustainable building practices

verbs

ensure*
implements*
instigated
justify*

adjectives

administrative*
altered*
comprehensive*
discerning
ethical*

impending
mandatory
overarching
residential*

*Appears on the Academic Word List

READING ❶ Dr. Sustainability: Environmental Scientist of the Year

A sustainable building reflects concern for the environment and a commitment to a better future. This is why the Centre for Interactive Research on Sustainability (CIRS) at the University of British Columbia (UBC) in Vancouver, Canada, is such an important symbol of hope. John Robinson, the professor who initiated the establishment of the Centre, believes that people can be encouraged to commit to a sustainable future when they see how green buildings can save energy and increase happiness.

A. Read the definitions of the key words (or quiz yourself on the definitions if you think you know them already). Locate the key words in Reading 1 using the line numbers indicated, then identify other words that form collocations with them. List the collocations in the last column.

KEY WORDS	DEFINITIONS	COLLOCATIONS
administrative (adj.) LINE 133	related to management of a company or organization	*administrative staff*
altered (adj.) LINE 50	changed	
commission (n.) LINE 71	group of people who have been given the official job of finding out about something	

KEY WORDS	DEFINITIONS	COLLOCATIONS
ethical (adj.) LINE 155	related to the principles of right and wrong	
extraction (n.) LINE 24	process of removal	
frameworks (n.) LINES 64, 108	sets of ideas upon which decisions are based	
fundamentally (adv.) LINE 85	in a way that is basic and important	
impending (adj.) LINE 89	anticipated in the future (especially unpleasant events)	
projections (n.) LINE 81	statements about what will happen in the future	

B. Now read the general definitions in the second column and find the key words in Reading 1. In the last column, write the meaning of each word as it is used in this context. Discuss with your class how the meanings of words can change depending on their contexts.

KEY WORDS	DEFINITIONS	MEANINGS IN CONTEXT
dashboard (n.) LINE 6	part of a car facing the driver, containing the instruments and controls	
sandboxes (n.) LINE 104	boxes filled with sand for children to play in	

Before You Read

Use reading strategies (see Chapter 1, page 4) to help you understand this text.

A. Skim Reading 1 to answer the questions. When you have finished, verify your answers with the class.

1 What is the topic of the reading?

_____

_____

2 How long is it? _____

3 What type of text is it? _____

4 What do you already know about the topic? Your discussion from Gearing Up may help you answer this question.

_____

_____

5 Based on the text type, how will the content most likely be organized?

_____

_____

While You Read

B. This reading can be divided into seven sections. Suggested headings are given below. Skim the reading and fill in the paragraph numbers corresponding to each section.

SECTION 1: Introduction to CIRS   PARAGRAPHS: _____1 to 3_____

SECTION 2: Introduction to John Robinson   PARAGRAPHS: _____

SECTION 3: John Robinson's Background   PARAGRAPHS: _____

SECTION 4: Harm Reduction versus
Regenerative Sustainability   PARAGRAPHS: _____

SECTION 5: The Role of Universities in Promoting
Sustainability   PARAGRAPHS: _____

SECTION 6: The Impact of CIRS   PARAGRAPHS: _____

SECTION 7: The Future of Sustainability   PARAGRAPHS: _____

Dr. Sustainability: Environmental Scientist of the Year

*It's a bold claim, but Vancouver might just be home to the greenest building in the world. Meet the geography professor who brought it to life—*Canadian Geographic's *environmental scientist of the year.*

1. The first thing you'll notice upon entering the University of British Columbia's Centre for Interactive Research on Sustainability on the school's Point Grey campus is that the building has a **dashboard**. You will also notice the building is referred to as "the greenest building in the world." Almost every interior space, for instance, is bathed in natural light. The corridors seem to breathe with unconditioned air, pleasantly scented with the pine that is the structure's most obvious material. It also has a lecture hall covered by a mounded green roof, which forms a hill of grass and shrubs between the two main wings of the building. But that dashboard—a wall-mounted flat-screen display showing the state of various building functions—just might capture and hold your attention the longest because of the crowd gathered around it.

Centre for Interactive Research on Sustainability

2. That's all in a normal day at the Centre for Interactive Research on Sustainability (CIRS), which has been a magnet for attention since it opened. At any given hour, even when one of the ongoing tours is not in progress, you'll find people standing in the lobby discussing the data on that dashboard, which shows, among other things, how much water has been recycled that day, the kilojoules count of harvested solar energy, and the rate of thermal-heat **extraction** from the soil on which the building sits.

3. CIRS is more than a workspace for living things, as the dashboard and the animated conversation attest. It's a living thing itself. People engage with it as if it were of an order higher than architecture.

4. If that's your reaction, then John Robinson will be pleased. The man who almost single-handedly brought this building to life is committed not only to making structures green in the ecological sense … but also to making them more humanly engaging. "CIRS is designed to be net positive in seven ways," says Robinson.
35 "Ecologically net positive in energy, operational carbon, water, and structural carbon. And also net positive for three human factors: health, productivity, and happiness."

5. Robinson is executive director of the UBC sustainability initiative, an ambitious academic and operational approach to sustainability, and CIRS is its public face … The $37-million, four-storey, 5400-square-metre "living laboratory" offers a
40 multidisciplinary space on campus for sustainability education and research and a physical structure in which sustainability ideas can be deployed and evaluated at scale …

6. In addition to being a symbol of UBC's sustainability efforts, the building can also be looked at as a culminating statement about Robinson's influential career to
45 date. Embedded in those pine timbers, and in details such as the skylight-mounted solar cells that double as energy collectors and providers of dappled shade, is a carefully built world view on sustainability that owes a lot to the route Robinson has taken through his professional life.

7. Originally interested in law (his father was a judge), Robinson found his vision of
50 the future irrevocably **altered** when Monte Hummel—then head of Pollution Probe, later president of World Wildlife Fund Canada—came to speak to his … [secondary school] classroom in Port Hope, Ontario. "It was the first time I heard the word *environment* used as a field or an issue," says Robinson …

8. Robinson remembers the defining moment of Hummel's address to the students.
55 "He showed us these cards. They ranged in colour from very light grey to very dark. He said, 'When you see smoke coming from an industrial smokestack, hold up these cards. If the smoke is darker than number three, phone the air management branch and report a violation.'" Robinson chuckles. "Such was the state of citizen science in those days." Still, he was hooked.

60 9. Robinson went on to work on the committee opposing the Mackenzie Valley pipeline, which led to an interest in energy issues, which led to a geography degree from the University of Toronto, a master's in geography from Toronto's York University, and a PhD in the same field (thesis subtitle: *An Investigation of Energy Policy and Conceptual* **Frameworks**) from the University of Toronto in 1981. A
65 professor in the University of Waterloo's Department of Environment and Resource Studies before moving on to UBC's Geography Department twenty years ago, Robinson has won several prestigious awards, including a share of the Nobel Peace Prize in 2007 for being a lead author in the last three assessments of the Intergovernmental Panel on Climate Change and a major award from BC Hydro
70 in 2010 for advancing energy conservation in the province …

10. … [In 1987, the Brundtland **Commission** … helped create the understanding of "harm reduction" in relation to the environment.] "It's basically the concept of limits," he [Robinson] says. "It leads to strategies of harm reduction and mitigation. Reducing the bad things. That becomes the largest frame." And for two reasons,
75 he passionately argues, this doesn't work. First, it's not enough. You can reduce emissions to zero, you can participate in Buy Nothing Day and other acts of

personal constraint, but this won't address the social aspects of sustainability, such as poverty. "You can't ignore development," says Robinson, "because the two greatest causes of environmental damage are great wealth and great poverty."

80 11. Perhaps more important, he argues that approaches to sustainability based on limits and harm reduction—warnings and dire **projections** calling for constraint—simply don't create behavioural change. "The literature on motivation is very clear," says Robinson. "The information-deficit model doesn't work. The idea that we change our behaviour because we change our attitudes, because we

85   change our values, because we get new information is just **fundamentally** wrong." Research has borne this out in multiple fields, which Robinson counts off on his fingers: health promotion, social psychology, energy efficiency, applied cultural anthropology, community-based social marketing …

12. If telling people about an **impending** climate-change disaster won't alter behaviour,
90   then what will? Here is where the most recent evolution in Robinson's thinking, and the CIRS building of which it is an emblem, take shape. What we need, insists Robinson, is a program of "regenerative sustainability." We need to start living in a way that eliminates the damage we cause going forward—across ecological, social, and economic lines—and also begins to improve the physical and social
95   environments around us. Not only does this approach necessarily go further than mitigation, it more reliably attracts participation.

13. "It's exciting, and it's way more motivating. I've given talks on this a couple of dozen times. I've never had a point that resonates more, that people get more interested in, because it's positive. Can we have regenerative buildings?" Robinson
100   eyes are alight with curiosity and enthusiasm. "How about transportation systems, cities, industrial processes? Could we be regenerative in steelmaking? I don't think we know, because we haven't examined those questions. And I think it's the job of universities and academics to really engage these questions."

14. Universities are the perfect "**sandboxes**," as Robinson puts it, for this kind of
105   experiment and exploration. They are organically suited to the role. They're scaled to the size of neighbourhoods. They're owner-occupied. They're mandated to teach and do research. Bring on the policy-makers, he says, to consider the regulatory frameworks required. Bring on the private companies with ideas they'd like to test with a view to future commercialization. Bring on the public to tour the
110   projects being tested and to get excited. And, perhaps most innovative of all, bring on the students, who within a couple of years should be able to get undergraduate minors in sustainability while working toward degrees in virtually every department at UBC, from engineering and computer sciences to dance and English.

15. There should be no specifically "green" jobs in Robinson's regenerative approach.
115   Sustainability should be part of everybody's job. "We're training sustainability ambassadors," affirms Alberto Cayuela, associate director of the UBC sustainability initiative, as he tours a group of engineering students through the constructed wetland water-filtration system at the front of CIRS.

16. On clear days in Vancouver, the glass flanks of CIRS rise sparkling in the sun; on
120   the city's frequent rainy days, its inner works rustle pleasantly with harvested water. One hundred percent of the building's water demand is satisfied by rain. Five hundred tonnes of carbon are **sequestered in** its building materials, more than were expended in its **construction**. Two hundred and seventy-five megawatt

sequestered in (phrasal verb): removed from the environment and hidden in

hours per year of surplus energy are produced from scavenged sources, including the energy harvested from a heat-leaky building next door. And as for the human factors, Cayuela says that the UBC Psychology Department currently has six different experiments under way to test the building's ability to change attitudes.

17. "Does being here make a person more likely to recycle?" he asks. "Do you learn better with skylights and displacement ventilation in the lecture hall?" The questions are open. And as if to immediately punctuate the confidence Cayuela projects, we are approached just then by one of his **administrative** staff, who apologizes for interjecting but feels she just has to share her own experience. A long-time sufferer of respiratory problems, she explains that her move across campus from one of the older library buildings six months ago has changed her life, literally. "The air in this building is clear," she says. "I can breathe."

18. It seems almost imaginary, the idea of buildings as net contributors to the environment in the ecological and human ways that comprise Robinson's "regenerative sustainability." ... "We don't want this world!" Robinson says, gesturing widely. "We want a different world that doesn't yet exist."

...

19. Robinson has to go. He has meetings to attend. He has projects under way. CIRS is a pinnacle accomplishment, but one suspects he has much more to come. Converting all of UBC to the regenerative model is a real objective for him. But then so, too, is "proselytizing" to other universities around the world, which should all, in Robinson's view, be embracing the same challenge.

20. In parting, he provides a working definition of sustainability that captures a long journey to this moment, to CIRS, to the strange combination of its practical and symbolic functions, to all that it represents. "Sustainability," says Robinson, "is the emergent property of a conversation about the kind of world we want to live in that's informed by some understanding of the ecological, social, and economic consequences of different choices. It's not a scientific concept we can just give people. It's a normative, **ethical** judgment that people need to make."

21. He pauses. In other words, people have choices in this matter. They can embrace a regenerative vision of the future ...

22. Then he finishes: "I'm very optimistic about our ability to make radical changes. That's why we built CIRS, to show people that it's possible. People have no idea it's even possible!"

23. Which is exactly what's going on among the people watching the CIRS dashboard: looking up with fascinated engagement at evidence of the building's inner workings. They're seeing what's possible.

(1837 words)

Taylor, T. (2012, June 1). Dr. Sustainability: Environmental scientist of the year. *Canadian Geographic, 132*(3), 60–64. Retrieved from http://www.canadiangeographic.ca/

After You Read

C. Answer these questions to demonstrate your comprehension. After, verify your answers with your class.

1. Review the first three paragraphs and list the sustainable features of the Centre for Interactive Research on Sustainability (CIRS).

   _____

   _____

2. a) What are the seven ecological and personal ways in which CIRS is designed to be net positive?

   _____

   _____

   b) Do you believe that a building, even a sustainable building, can influence people in terms of these personal factors?

   _____

3. What does the CIRS building offer students and researchers?

   _____

   _____

4. Robinson states that he became interested in the environment when Monte Hummel came to speak to his high school class. What "technology" did Hummel demonstrate that interested the young Robinson? Why does this seem funny today?

   _____

   _____

5. Does Robinson believe that warning people about environmental damage will encourage them to change their behaviour or live in a more sustainable way? Why or why not?

   _____

   _____

   _____

6. Why does Robinson believe that a "regenerative sustainability" approach to the environment will motivate more people to live sustainably?

   _____

   _____

7. Why does Robinson believe universities are "the perfect sandboxes" for sustainability efforts?

   _____

   _____

8 What are the sustainable features of CIRS, described in paragraph 16?

_____

_____

_____

_____

Watch a short video about the building's sustainable features and note the features that match the ones described in this article. In your Internet browser, search Centre for Interactive Research on Sustainability at UBC.

9 What are some of the research questions being explored at CIRS, as described in paragraph 17?

_____

_____

10 What evidence is there that CIRS improves people's health?

_____

_____

_____

11 Robinson states that regenerative sustainability is an idea that will encourage people to work toward a world "that doesn't yet exist." He believes people need to consider the "ecological, social, and economic consequences" of the choices they make. Do you find these ideas exciting and motivational? Why or why not?

_____

_____

MyBookshelf > My eLab > Exercises > Chapter 4 > Dr. Sustainability

FOCUS ON CRITICAL THINKING

Applying Old Knowledge to New Information

The goal of most academic work is to discover new information, or new ways of thinking about *old* (already known) knowledge. This section will describe two approaches that can help you achieve this goal.

One way to help you develop new ways of thinking is to apply old knowledge to new information. For example, you may already know about renewable sources of energy. In this chapter, you will learn about sustainable building practices—this may be new information for you.

A. Work with a partner to discuss how your previous knowledge about renewable energy connects to the new information you learned in Reading 1. Take point-form notes on a separate page.

Another way to develop a new perspective is to apply a familiar structure to new information. For example, you may already know about compare and contrast structures. In this chapter, you have just gained new information about Robinson's belief in regenerative sustainability, which refers to an innovative way to encourage people to behave sustainably.

B. Working with a partner, discuss how Robinson's ideas about regenerative sustainability compare and contrast with older ideas about the best ways to encourage sustainable behaviour. Use the compare/contrast table below to help organize your point-form notes.

	OLDER IDEAS ABOUT WAYS TO ENCOURAGE SUSTAINABLE BEHAVIOUR	REGENERATIVE SUSTAINABILITY IDEAL
Points of contrast	• *scientists scare people with negative evidence*	
Points of comparison	• *scientists are the source of information about the environment*	

C. When you have finished, discuss with your class which kind of encouragement would most motivate you to behave in environmentally friendly ways.

Would it be possible to develop an incentive that doesn't rely on the expertise of scientists? This is a "new" thought that is stimulated by the application of the compare/contrast framework to familiar knowledge.

READING ② China's Green Building Future

Reading 2 comes from the *China Business Review* magazine, which contains articles of interest to American and Chinese business markets. In this reading, you will learn about the growing green building trend in China.

VOCABULARY BUILD

A. Key words from Reading 2 are listed in column one of the table. Match them to the definitions in the second column.

KEY WORDS		DEFINITIONS
❶ adopters (n.)	_____	a) takes action to put something into effect
❷ advocates (n.)	_____	b) part of town that consists of private homes, not offices or stores
❸ collaboration (n.)	_____	c) people who try new things
❹ comprehensive (adj.)	_____	d) important new plan or project
❺ construction (n.)	_____	e) act of working together with other people
❻ facilities (n.)	_____	f) process of building
❼ implements (v.)	_____	g) required
❽ incentives (n.)	_____	h) amount in relation to a larger whole

KEY WORDS		DEFINITIONS
9 infrastructure (n.)	_____	i) people who publicly support a way of doing something
10 initiative (n.)	_____	j) including all details (thorough)
11 mandatory (adj.)	_____	k) rooms, buildings, or equipment provided for a purpose
12 proportion (n.)	_____	l) things that encourage or motivate you to do something
13 residential (adj.)	_____	m) basic systems and structures a country or organization needs to function, for example, roads, buildings, banks, etc.

B. Find collocations in Reading 2 that include key words from the table above.

1 Which noun collocates with the adjective *early*?

early _____

2 Which noun collocates with the adverbs *between* or *among*?

_____ between   _____ among

3 Which word forms collocations with nouns such as *industry, market,* and *project*?

_____ industry   _____ market   _____ project

4 Which verb collocates with the nouns *practices, policies,* and *programs*?

_____ practices   _____ policies   _____ programs

5 Which adjective collocates with the noun *buildings*?

_____ buildings

6 Which noun collocates with the adjective *small*?

small _____

C. On a separate page, answer the following questions to explain how key words from Reading 2 apply to you.

1 Name a cause or an issue for which you are an *advocate*.

2 Name a subject about which you have a *comprehensive* understanding.

3 Name a *facility* that you have seen or visited.

4 Name an *incentive* that would encourage you to study harder.

5 Name an *initiative* that you would like to be a part of.

6 Name something that is *mandatory* in your family.

Before You Read

A. There are four headings in this reading. Scan the headings and predict whether the article will present a positive or negative view of the green building industry in China. Why?

_____

_____

B. Skim the first paragraph of the article. Why does the author start by giving an example of a green building in Hangzhou, China?

_____

_____

C. Scan the second paragraph and answer the following questions in a few words. After, check your answers with a classmate.

① When did a building in China first receive a gold rating from the international LEED sustainable building rating system? _____

② Since then, what has happened in terms of the popularity of green building in China? _____

③ In the past (and often still now), what concerns have been more important than the environment in construction? _____

④ Who are the most likely green builders in China?

_____

⑤ What other factors may influence the future of green building in China?

_____

While You Read

D. Notes highlighting the main points of the reading are listed below, out of order. As you read, copy the notes in the appropriate places in the margins. Then, with a classmate, compare where you have written each note. Do you agree?

- Characteristics of green neighbourhoods
- PRC also promotes green communities
- Building costs seem more important than environment
- PRC government policies can influence green building
- LEED and Three Star rating systems
- China's five-year plans set targets for green building
- How the PRC government can encourage green building
- China's green building becoming more popular
- However, green buildings can pay for themselves
- Definition of green building
- Builders don't always benefit from long-term cost savings

China's Green Building Future

Green building makes up a small **proportion** of China's construction industry, but government targets may give sustainable building a boost over the next five years.

About 60 kilometres outside Hangzhou, the capital of Zhejiang province, is a luxury
5 resort surrounded by the bamboo forest and tea plantations of Moganshan. The owners of Naked Stables Private Reserve—named for its stripped-down, natural environment—aimed to make as minimal an impact on the surrounding environment

as possible by reducing water and energy use and growing their own food on site. "[The owners] did all these things because they thought it was the right thing to do,"
10 says Alessandro Bisagni, founder and managing director of BEE Inc., a sustainable building consulting firm that works on projects in China and the United States.

Since the first building in China was awarded a gold rating by the internationally recognized Leadership in Energy and Environmental Design (LEED) rating system in 2005, green building's popularity has grown in China. Green building still makes up
15 a small proportion of building in the world's largest construction market, where maximizing profits and lowering building costs often **trump** sustainable design and energy efficiency considerations. Multinational companies, large Chinese companies, and an increasing number of hotels and resorts are currently the most likely green builders in China, but increasing environmental awareness and central government
20 policies that set ambitious targets to reduce China's overall energy use may make green building practices more widespread in the coming years.

trump (v.): surpass in importance

Green Building on the Rise

In 2011, developers in China started constructing 1.9 billion square metres of
25 floor space and invested ¥6.2 trillion ($983 billion) in property development, according to the People's Republic of China [PRC] National Bureau of Statistics. At the same time, China's Twelfth Five-
30 Year Plan (FYP, 2011–15) aimed to reduce overall energy use by 16 percent per unit of gross domestic product (GDP) and

reduce carbon dioxide emissions by 17 percent per unit of GDP by 2015. Because buildings account for roughly 25 percent of all energy consumed in China, regulators
35 have focused on implementing green and energy-efficient practices in both new and established buildings …

In general, green building incorporates design, construction, and operations practices that use sustainable materials in construction, achieve energy efficiency and water savings, and improve indoor air quality, among other measurable targets. Green
40 building developers also consider a building or project's location, selecting sites with exposure to sunlight and sites that are close to public transportation, grocery stores, and other amenities.

Evaluating all buildings and development projects in China that take these strategies into account is difficult, but developers are increasingly applying for green building
45 labels, such as LEED certification and China's own green building certification, the Green Building Design Label, also known as Three Star. (The system assigns buildings one to three stars, with three stars being the highest rating.) In 2005, a PRC Ministry of Science and Technology office building in Beijing was awarded a LEED gold rating, the first building in China to receive LEED certification. The Beijing Olympic Village
50 and other **facilities** for the 2008 Olympics followed, and by the end of 2011, more than eight hundred construction projects had been registered for certification while nearly two hundred had been LEED certified. The Three Star system is newer and has fewer projects, but it has seen similar growth, increasing from ten projects certified in 2008 to eighty-three in 2010.

55 Challenges

Regardless of the certification system used, the green building concept does not always translate to the China market. According to a 2011 report by the China Greentech **Initiative**—a **collaboration** between more than one hundred organizations 60 that focuses on identifying and developing green tech solutions in China—lack of understanding of green building and misaligned **incentives** have slowed the adoption of green building in China. Experts say construction decisions are often made based on short-term costs, such as material and labour 65 costs, instead of considering the long-term savings from energy efficiency or green building techniques.

Bisagni says working on green building projects in the United States and China is like night and day because Chinese builders still prefer to cut costs in the short term. "The extent of solutions that you can propose in a project [in China] is limited in a 70 way because of that payback and cost mentality," he says. "In China, there's still a large knowledge gap. In order to cross that, it takes a lot of effort."

Green building experts say that it is a myth that sustainable buildings are expensive to build. "A green building can pay for itself," says Yingchu Qian, head of sustainability business in Asia for Faithful+Gould, a construction consulting firm. Qian, who has 75 worked on roughly 120 green building projects in China, says that the savings from energy-efficient practices and the premium developers can charge for green buildings help investors make back any additional money spent on construction. He said it usually takes five to ten years for a developer to make back the initial investment in a green building, but that in some cases it can take as little as two years.

80 Companies that chose to build green in China early on were not necessarily focused on cost. The early **adopters** in China have tended to be large, multinational corporations with a "sustainability vision" and those that see green building as a good marketing tool, says Jennivine Kwan, vice president of international operations at the US Green Building Council (USGBC), the organization that developed the LEED rating system. 85 But now, more companies are considering operation costs, return on investment, higher tenant occupancy rates, and a premium on rents. "Those things are real **tangible** financial reasons as to why people are building green buildings from an owner-developer point of view," she says.

tangible (adj.): easily seen or noticed

Because developers in China may not see immediate cost savings, they often overlook 90 the green features—such as better insulation and sealed windows—that could help the government meet its energy targets. This is especially true in the multi-family **residential** buildings that most people in urban China live in, say researchers at the US Department of Energy's Lawrence Berkeley National Laboratory (LBNL). "I think it also gets complicated because the tenants that live in the building didn't build it. 95 The builder doesn't operate the building, so they are not motivated to invest in better insulation," says Nan Zhou, a scientist at LBNL's China Energy Group.

LBNL researchers have been working with the PRC government to improve energy efficiency initiatives and labelling standards, including the PRC Ministry of Housing and Urban-Rural Development's building energy efficiency label. This rating system 100 ranks buildings from one to five stars. A building that receives a five-star rating is the most energy efficient—requiring an 85 percent reduction in energy use compared to buildings constructed in the 1980s. (Current building codes require that new buildings achieve a 50 percent reduction in energy use compared to the 1980s.) The energy efficiency label is still voluntary for most residential and non-residential buildings, but the government requires that certain buildings receive a star rating, including new government-owned and large public buildings, existing government-owned office buildings and large public buildings that apply for government energy **retrofit** subsidies.

retrofit (n.): addition of new or updated component to a building or system

Zhou says that because the green building and energy efficiency labels are still voluntary for the majority of buildings, such programs are not likely to reduce energy consumption in China on a large scale. "If there's a **mandatory** program … then that can definitely reduce energy use," Zhou says.

Eco-Cities

While the PRC government **implements** energy labelling programs, provides subsidies for energy-efficient technologies, and releases policies to support carbon and energy reduction goals, China's push to develop more sustainable communities, or "eco-cities," may also influence green building's future in the country.

According to the Asian Development Bank, the PRC government began encouraging development of sustainable communities as early as the mid-1990s. Dozens of eco-cities are currently being developed, according to some estimates, but arguably the most high-profile is the Sino-Singapore Tianjin Eco-City. The project is a collaboration between the governments of Singapore and Tianjin and promotes water and energy conservation, mixed-use development, and **comprehensive** public transport for the city's expected 350,000 residents … The entire project is expected to be complete by 2020.

The PRC government's eco-cities initiative may be one reason China has the largest number of LEED certifications for neighbourhood development projects outside the United States, says USGBC's Kwan. These projects help local governments and developers design "communities that are a little more human scale, that are linked better to the outside environment, and that provide that type of safe and healthy environment for all the people who live there," says Kwan. Like LEED for buildings, the LEED for neighbourhood development rating system evaluates an entire community. The rating system looks at whether the community has walkable streets and reduces residents' dependence on cars, and whether buildings and **infrastructure** are energy efficient, use renewable energy sources, and reduce water use.

Compared to the United States or other developed countries, mixed-use development is already common in China, where many neighbourhoods feature all the services most people need within walking distance. The government's role in urban planning also makes it easier to create sustainable communities, Kwan says. "China is one of the few places in the world that actually decides where a city is going to happen. They actually build the city."

Green Building's Future in China

An analysis by LBNL researchers shows that China made the largest energy efficiency improvements in new construction and hit targets in energy management in government and large-scale public buildings during the Eleventh FYP (2006–10) period. However, China has not been as successful during the first year of the Twelfth FYP, says LBNL's Zhou, and she expects the PRC government to continue including

milestone (n.): significant event in the development of something

energy and carbon reduction goals in future five-year plans. "This period will be very challenging because the first year has already ended and they did not meet the first-150 year **milestone**," she says.

mainstream (adj.): accepted by most people; conventional

Whether green building will play a large role in meeting these goals remains to be seen, but **advocates** remain optimistic that the green building market will continue to grow in China. Still, some think the PRC government will have to implement stronger policies before **mainstream** developers build green projects on a larger scale. 155 "The only way that can happen is from the top down," says Bisagni. "The government has to give direction about what green building has to be."

(1739 words)

Nelson, C. (2012, April–June). China's green building future. *China Business Review*, 32–35.

After You Read

E. Demonstrate your understanding by indicating whether the following statements are true or false. For any false statements, write a true one on a separate page.

STATEMENTS	TRUE	FALSE
❶ According to Bisagni, the owners of the Naked Stables Private Reserve (a luxury hotel) used a green building approach because they felt a sense of moral responsibility to reduce environmental damage.		
❷ One of the biggest challenges to adopting a green building approach in the construction of new buildings is the belief that they are more expensive to build.		
❸ Green buildings save money in the long term through reduced energy usage.		
❹ Owners of green buildings must charge lower rents because people don't want to live in green buildings.		
❺ Green building practices are useful, but they don't reduce energy use enough to help China meet its energy reduction goals.		
❻ Green building certification systems (like LEED and Three Star) make the public aware of sustainable building standards.		
❼ Most builders who have to choose between green building practices and lower labour and material costs choose lower costs.		
❽ An owner who builds a green building will never recover the costs.		
❾ Because builders don't live in the apartment complexes they build, they often don't see any value in using better insulation and windows.		
❿ The Chinese (PRC) government's own rating system for energy efficiency is mandatory for all new buildings.		
⓫ While it is possible to rate the energy efficiency of a building, rating communities on the same basis is too complicated.		
⓬ According to some experts, green building is going to succeed in China whether the government supports it or not.		

F. What did you learn that was new, interesting, or important? What would you like to learn more about?

_____

_____

_____

_____

_____

_____

MyBookshelf > My eLab >
Exercises > Chapter 4 >
China's Green Building Future

FOCUS ON WRITING

Using Direct Quotations and Indirect Speech

Readings 1 and 2 are both magazine articles that display characteristics of this text type, including direct quotations and indirect speech. These elements integrate the viewpoints of the speakers (the people quoted) to present information and lend authority to the text.

You will notice that there are no references for the quotations in these articles as there would be in a textbook or an academic journal. Instead of citing references, magazines provide background information about the people quoted, either before or right after the quotation.

A. In the following two examples from Reading 1 and Reading 2, highlight the background information provided about the speaker and underline the quotation.

> If that's your reaction, then John Robinson will be pleased. The man who almost single-handedly brought this building to life is committed not only to making structures green in the ecological sense ... but also to making them more humanly engaging. "CIRS is designed to be net positive in seven ways," says Robinson. "Ecologically net positive in energy, operational carbon, water, and structural carbon. And also net positive for three human factors: health, productivity, and happiness."

> "[The owners] did all these things because they thought it was the right thing to do," says Alessandro Bisagni, founder and managing director of BEE Inc., a sustainable building consulting firm that works on projects in China and the United States.

B. Skim Readings 1 and 2 and underline the first direct quotations from the following speakers. Then, highlight the background information that is provided about them.

FROM READING 1: John Robinson, Alberto Cayuela

FROM READING 2: Alessandro Bisagni, Yingchu Qian, Jennivine Kwan, Nan Zhou

C. On a separate page, following the models in Readings 1 and 2, combine the information below into a direct quotation. Present the information once with the speaker's background information before, and once with the information after, the quotation.

QUOTATION: In just a few short years, the topic of sustainable development has moved from the sidelines to centre stage in discussions about climate change, social equity, and economic prosperity—issues that will shape the very future of our planet.

SPEAKER: Richard Moe

BACKGROUND INFORMATION ABOUT THE SPEAKER: past president, National Trust for Historic Preservation

MyBookshelf > My eLab > Exercises > Chapter 4 > Focus on Writing

FOCUS ON ACCURACY

Integrating Quotations in a Text

The following examples from Readings 1 and 2 show the mechanics of how to integrate quotations in a text.

a) "The air in this building is clear," she says. "I can breathe."

b) "We don't want this world!" Robinson says, gesturing widely. "We want a different world that doesn't yet exist."

c) "A green building can pay for itself," says Yingchu Qian, ...

d) Then he finishes: "I'm very optimistic about our ability to make radical changes ..."

e) "Sustainability," says Robinson, "is the emergent property of a conversation about the kind of world we want to live in ..."

f) "We're training sustainability ambassadors," affirms Alberto Cayuela, ...

g) Robinson chuckles. "Such was the state of citizen science in 1970."

h) "It's exciting, and it's way more motivating. I've given talks on this a couple of dozen times. I've never had a point that resonates more ..."

A. Answer the questions referring to the examples above.

1 Quotation marks show the start and end of a quotation. Is the end punctuation located inside or outside the quotation marks?

_____

_____

2 Where is the speech tag (e.g., *she says*) located in the examples?

_____

_____

3 If the speech tag is located in the middle of a quotation, where is it inserted?

_____

_____

4 What other verbs can writers use besides *say* to integrate quotations in texts?

_____

_____

5 Can a writer integrate a quotation without using one of these verbs? If so, when?

_____

_____

6 Once a speaker has been identified with background information and an initial quotation has been introduced, how does a writer usually present a subsequent quotation?

_____

_____

B. To practise, add the correct punctuation and capitalization to the quotations in this paragraph. When you have finished, check your answers with a classmate.

Scott Parker, director of the North American Sustainable Building Innovation Association (NASBIA), states much more could be done to mitigate climate change in large cities. Green roofs and walls have been largely overlooked as an effective method to moderate internal building temperature and absorb CO_2 emissions. He points to projects in Europe and Japan, and emerging initiatives in Australia and New Zealand. Green roofs and walls he says are not the only solution to climate change challenges, but they can be implemented within the existing cityscape. He believes that green roofs and walls could be used to strategically alter city microclimates, creating spaces that are healthier for humans, plants, and animals.

C. An indirect quotation, called *indirect* or *reported speech*, is often used to provide context for a direct quotation. Look at the following example from Reading 2. Underline the direct quotation. Consider the purpose of the first sentence and answer the questions that follow.

> Bisagni says working on green building projects in the United States and China is like night and day because Chinese builders still prefer to cut costs in the short term. "The extent of solutions that you can propose in a project [in China] is limited in a way because of that payback and cost mentality," he says. "In China, there's still a large knowledge gap. In order to cross that, it takes a lot of effort."

① The first two lines of the paragraph are an example of indirect speech. How is this similar to a direct quotation? How is it different?

_____

_____

② What is the purpose of the indirect speech that comes before the direct quotation?

_____

_____

③ Why would a writer use indirect speech first and not a single, longer direct quotation?

_____

_____

D. Skim Readings 1 and 2 and highlight the indirect speech segments that precede direct quotations. (Use a different colour from the one used for Focus on Writing, task B.) Underline the direct quotations that follow the indirect speech segments.

① In the segments that you highlighted, what verbs (other than *says*) do the writers use to introduce indirect speech?

_____

_____

② On a separate page, following the models in Readings 1 and 2, combine the information below into an indirect speech segment followed by a direct quotation.

INDIRECT SPEECH: Zero net energy buildings operate with only energy generated on-site.

DIRECT QUOTATION: "This approach only addresses operating energy, not the energy required to construct the building."

SPEAKER: Jean Carroon

WARM-UP ASSIGNMENT
Write a Short Report

Write a report for a community group that would like to build an activity centre. The members are interested in green design but are worried that the costs will be too high.

A. In your report, include an example of a sustainable (green) building that you know about (or find an example online or in the library).

B. Integrate at least three quotations about the building from experts, possibly from the owners, architects, or users. Be sure to provide sufficient background information about the speaker when you introduce his or her initial quotation. For at least one of the speakers, include a second quotation that is preceded by indirect speech.

C. Your report should contain

- an introduction, with a definition of green building;
- body paragraphs including an example of a green building, integrated quotations, and data on how much energy, water, and carbon dioxide (CO_2) are saved (if available);
- a conclusion, with your recommendation on whether or not to use green design.

Refer to the Models Chapter (page 282) to see an example of a report and to learn more about how to write one.

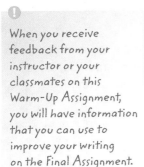

When you receive feedback from your instructor or your classmates on this Warm-Up Assignment, you will have information that you can use to improve your writing on the Final Assignment.

Academic Survival Skill

Observing Text Features to Learn about Language

You can learn even more about the English language by observing the features of English texts closely as you have done in this chapter. Observation can teach you about grammar points, vocabulary selection, text organization, and content development. Also, it is something you can do on your own; you do not need your instructor to guide you.

It is best to start with two similar texts. They could be the same type of text (for example, excerpts from economics textbooks), or different types of text on the same topic (for example, an Internet article and an academic essay on global unemployment). Read the texts closely; look for common characteristics that reveal written conventions in English. You might have your own questions about how the language works, so look for evidence of those features. Alternatively, you can look specifically for the following features.

GRAMMAR POINTS: Use of specific verb tenses, punctuation, articles, word forms, and noun, adjective, or adverb clauses

VOCABULARY SELECTION: Use of specific words, collocations, phrases, and expressions; word frequency; words that appear to be discipline-specific; words that appear to have broader use outside a discipline

TEXT ORGANIZATION: Topic and concluding sentences in paragraphs; location of thesis statement; expressions used to draw the reader's attention to a new point; level of detail in introduction and conclusion sections; placement of main points

CONTENT DEVELOPMENT: Examples used to support points; how writers accomplish elaboration; presentation of divergent viewpoints; use of references; use of paraphrases and summaries

A. To practise, use two texts from this chapter or two that you are reading for your academic work. Take notes on some of their common characteristics. What have you learned about English by noticing these common features?

B. When you have finished, work with a small group to share your new understanding of how the English language works.

READING ❸ How Do Green Buildings Pay?

While the author of Reading 2 indicates that costs still drive decisions about green building in China, the authors of Reading 3 make the case that green buildings actually return money to developers and owners in unanticipated ways.

VOCABULARY BUILD

A. Read the sentences with key words from Reading 3 in bold. From the context, guess the definition of each key word and choose the answer that best corresponds to the meaning.

❶ An additional reason to build green buildings is that green design enhances the building's **asset** value.
   a) something that you hope to achieve
   b) something that can be sold to pay debts
   c) plan that you must follow to achieve your goal

❷ **Discerning** tenants are drawn to green buildings, believing that it is good for their staff recruitment and their image with customers.
   a) showing the ability to make good decisions
   b) having confidence in the correctness of your opinions
   c) holding diverse perspectives on issues

❸ The key is to **ensure** that energy design strategies, building fabric and material choices, and building controls work to serve user expectations.
   a) begin to work toward a goal
   b) be sure that the goal will not conflict with other goals
   c) make certain something will happen properly

④ A zero carbon office is not of much value unless the workers occupying the building are healthy, alert, satisfied, motivated, and **hence** productive.

    a) therefore   b) in addition   c) however

⑤ More studies need to be undertaken before widespread changes are **instigated**.

    a) motivated   b) adjusted   c) implemented

⑥ Personal control of temperature is normally limited by a building management system, which sets **overarching** temperature standards.

    a) overall   b) controlling   c) customized

⑦ There should be good integration of the ecological and energy approaches, and these should recognize that performance means designing with user **perspectives** in mind.

    a) assets   b) viewpoints   c) connections

⑧ There are two important **ramifications** of green building design.

    a) initiatives   b) consequences   c) incentives

⑨ Good levels of insulation, air tightness, high daylight levels, and all the other **initiatives** behind low energy design lead to less resource use.

    a) development of other frameworks

    b) efforts to make further projections

    c) plans or processes to solve problems

⑩ New evidence has emerged that there are many secondary benefits to low energy design which help **justify** what is often an additional cost of sustainable solutions.

    a) provide an acceptable explanation

    b) develop a new goal

    c) reach a final conclusion

⑪ The concept of health should include physical and psychological factors, including the interface between building management systems and **occupants**.

    a) ramifications   b) residents   c) assets

⑫ Companies increasingly have environmental policies that lead to the setting of carbon emission **targets** related to all company activities from transport to building operations.

    a) goals   b) tariff   c) infrastructure

B. For this topic (and many other topics), it will be useful to write about how green building initiatives have an influence or an impact on the building's asset value, appeal to occupants, and attractiveness to customers. There are rules about the use of prepositions with the words *influence* and *impact*; these can change depending on the word form.

Read the example sentences on the next page (in two separate groups). Then answer the questions.

First Set of Examples:

    a) A green office building has <u>an impact on</u> how customers perceive the company.

    b) A green office building <u>impacts</u> its occupants in healthy ways.

    c) Government regulations have <u>an influence on</u> the development of new green initiatives.

    d) Government regulations <u>influence</u> the development of new green initiatives.

Rules about preposition use:

❶ When *impact* and *influence* are used as nouns, what preposition follows them? _____

❷ When *impact* and *influence* are used as verbs, what preposition follows them? _____

Second Set of Examples:

    e) Green builders <u>are influenced by</u> government regulations.

    f) The <u>impact</u> of light <u>on</u> productivity is well known.

More rules about preposition use (choose the best answer):

❸ In the passive voice, *is/are influenced* and *is/are impacted* are often followed by

    i) the preposition *by* + phrase.   ii) an adjective clause.

❹ *Influence + on* and *impact + on*

    i) can be separated by a noun or prepositional phrase.

    ii) can never be separated by a noun or prepositional phrase.

C. Once you have verified the rules on preposition use with the class, fill in the blanks below. Write *X* if no word is needed. Then, check your answers with a classmate.

❶ Performance factors range from individual measures of output and productivity to the broader impact _____ company targets.

❷ Both are influenced _____ conditions found in the workplace and in other common indoor environments such as schools, universities, and hospitals.

❸ The influence of company policy _____ green initiatives is significant.

❹ Lighting influences _____ performance and cognitive ability; in addition, it impacts _____ attitudes and motivation.

❺ The study of chronobiology (the impact of light _____ health) is an emerging discipline that may impact _____ design in the next decade.

❻ There is growing evidence that light has an influence _____ performance.

Nanyang Technological
University, Singapore

Before You Read

A. Skim Reading 3 to answer the questions. Then check your answers with
the class.

1 What is the topic of the reading?

_____

_____

_____

2 How long is it? _____

3 What type of text is it? _____

4 What do you already know about the topic?

_____

_____

5 Based on the text type, how will the content most likely be organized?

_____

_____

B. Write the four main headings from the reading in the top row of the table.
Working in a small group, brainstorm the advantages of green buildings in each
of these areas. Take notes as you discuss, then share your ideas with the class.

Life-Cycle Costing Advantages			
• _as energy prices rise, green buildings seem more cost-effective_			

While You Read

C. Reproduce the table above on a separate page. As you read, take point-form
notes about the advantages in each area. You will use these notes to answer
the questions in After You Read (page 133).

How Do Green Buildings Pay?

New evidence has emerged that there are many secondary benefits to low energy
design which help **justify** what is often an additional cost of sustainable solutions.
Both in the US and Europe, researchers have discovered that buildings based on more
ecological approaches lead to social and economic benefits for the developer. These
5 benefits can be grouped under four headings:

- better life cycle costing;
- improved productivity or performance in functional terms;
- better social relationships at a building and community level;
- enhanced image for the building and the organization responsible for its inception.

10 Taking the framework of social, economic, and environmental sustainability as a starting point, investigators have been able to identify wide and often interconnected advantages of green buildings. These apply across building types but are most readily determined within the realm of offices, schools, and hospitals. In the case of offices, data from market sources such as rents, value enhancement in real estate terms, 15 staff productivity, and company share prices provide growing evidence that there are measurable benefits of green design. In the case of schools, data on pupil learning performance (particularly the speed of learning to read), teacher satisfaction and turnover rates, antisocial behaviour, and community use of school buildings provides evidence that sustainable approaches to school design lead to many benefits (Edwards, 20 2006). In the case of hospitals, data on recovery rates and wider issues of patient and staff well-being support patterns are found (Lawson & Wells-Thorpe, 2002) … As with much real world and more practice-based research, there are patterns emerging within **disparate** data that increasingly point toward social and economic advantages of design and construction based upon environmental and ecological 25 principles (BCO, 2009).

disparate (adj.): unrelated

Life-Cycle Costing Advantages

As energy and other resource prices rise, the costing models of sustainability become more attractive. Good levels of insulation, air tightness, high daylight levels and all the other **initiatives** behind low energy design lead to less resource use (assuming 30 behaviour patterns match technical characteristics) and better long-term economics. These can be measured through building monitoring and are related to rises in fossil fuel prices. However, in the case of many developments …, the initiative to create a green office stemmed from wider corporate goals. Companies increasingly have environmental policies which lead to the setting of carbon emission **targets** related 35 to all company activities from transport to building operations. So, in many cases the starting point is company environmental policy that is sometimes influenced by **shareholder lobbying**. Corporate social and environmental responsibility drives the energy objectives, which in time justify the commissioning of a green building. Although the initial target is cost savings, the ethics of money companies are translated 40 into either constructing a green building or in preference to occupying one (as tenant), and this brings about financial benefits as energy prices rise.

shareholder (n.): someone who holds a financial interest in a company

lobbying (v.): efforts to convince the government

… What is important is to consider all the potential benefits, to put financial value on them, and to compare performance of green buildings with their less than green counterparts. Then a 45 picture emerges that can carry weight within the business world. There are two important **ramifications**. The first is that since energy efficiency does not provide financial justification on its own, the building should be designed from many sustainable **perspectives**—not just energy ones. The business model is 50 supported by the secondary benefits to energy-efficient design. **Hence**, there should be good integration of the ecological and energy approaches, and these should recognize that performance means designing with user perspectives in mind.

The second ramification stems from **asset** value enhancement. 55 Many business models recognize the economic advantages of sustainable architecture. Increasingly, companies such as British

Land in the UK carry out development from a green perspective, believing that potential tenants or owners will be attracted by the ethos of sustainability found in the building. This is one reason why the Building Research Establishment Environmental
60 Assessment Method (BREEAM), in the UK, and the Leadership in Energy and Environmental Design (LEED), in the US, have assumed such importance—certification is a brand that developers seek. **Discerning** tenants are drawn to green buildings, believing that it is good for their staff recruitment and their image with customers. However, the BREEAM or LEED certificate displayed in the foyer is only part of the
65 picture. More importantly, in terms of image, is what the workplace environment is like in areas of comfort, climate, and the degree of control over temperature, lighting, and ventilation. Buildings that offer tenants green choices improve their attractiveness in market terms. What the building looks like, particularly how sustainable it appears inside and out, is part of the complex equation. Green buildings need to display their
70 greenness to maximize the asset value premium. This is one reason why the double **facade**, solar shading, and renewable energy systems have grown in popularity—they signal sustainability.

facade (n.): front or visible part of a building

Improved Productivity and Performance

Evidence is growing that workplaces designed on green principles lead to increased
75 output and better performance standards. This applies to new building and ecological retrofits. The argument is based on comparative data between sustainable workplaces and non-sustainable ones in environmental terms. Performance factors range from individual measures of output and productivity to the broader impact on company targets. Both are influenced by conditions found in the workplace and in other
80 common indoor environments such as schools, universities, and hospitals.

The quality of the indoor environment where we spend nearly 90 percent of our lives has a big impact on health, well-being, quality of life, and our social relationships. In terms of the workplace and other institutional interiors, such as schools, we spend about a third of a typical day there. Hence, there are huge impacts which are direct
85 and less direct, short-term and long-term. One key argument of green approaches to design is that the interior is healthier as a consequence of the adoption of energy efficiency. Health and sustainability are closely related, many advocates argue. It is this relationship that allows advocates to argue that sustainable architecture improves productivity and performance whatever the building type. However, it is in the area
90 of green offices that evidence is most convincing.

fraught (adj.): full of problems

The linkages between health, productivity, and building design are complex and **fraught** with methodological difficulty. Estimates of the added value of ecological design vary considerably, and the cost and benefits are sometimes hard to sustain across the property industry as a whole. However, a pattern is emerging based on
95 four main assessments. The first is related to health, and this breaks down into physical dimensions (colds, infections, flu, allergies) and psychological ones (depression, fatigue). Both are directly influenced by the degree of daylight, noise, ventilation rates, proximity to windows and views, and importantly, the degree of personal control over the workplace environment. To be productive, it appears from many data sources
100 that the workplace should be designed with health as well as energy efficiency in mind. And health here should include physical and psychological factors, particularly the behavioural aspects of the interface between building management systems and **occupants**. Users of the workplace need to feel healthy and valued by the architectural context, not alienated by abstract and remote controls.

105 A healthy indoor climate improves personal performance and hence company productivity. Unhealthy conditions lead to absenteeism and sickness whose costs are borne by the company and also the state ... In technical terms, poor air quality impacts health and also concentration levels. High CO_2 concentrations and poor daylight distribution reduce output in the workplace even when temperatures are within
110 accepted standards. In areas such as financial services and creative industries, the workplace should promote imagination and in-depth thinking. Creativity is supported by workplace quality issues. One consequence of these arguments is that in supporting sustainable design approaches, architects should be aware that clients are more impressed by the debate about the workplace environment and its impact on
115 productivity than more abstract notions of global warming.

The Importance of Lighting to Health

Daylight levels, energy efficiency, health, and productivity are linked. However, there is growing evidence that the impact of light on performance in the workplace is greater than previously thought (Race, Venning, & Yarandipour, 2010). The discovery of non-
120 imaging ganglion cells in the eye in 2004 has led to new interest in the relationship between light and mental health. In particular, new research has highlighted the potential impact the blue spectrum of light has on alertness, concentration, and mental well-being. There are big implications for the office environment in particular since there appear to be benefits in maximizing the blue-white spectrum of artificial
125 lighting at the expense of the "warm" lighting normally provided. There are implications here for those who design and manage the workplace environment. However, more studies need to be undertaken before wholesale changes are **instigated**.

Lighting impacts several areas of job satisfaction. It influences performance and cognitive ability; it impacts attitudes and motivation; and it has a bearing on physical
130 and mental health. Hence lighting, whether artificial or natural, automatic or under user control, influences not only the level of energy use but the level of workplace productivity. There are four **overarching** considerations:

- maximize natural light over artificial light;
- allow for some sunlight penetration into the workplace environment
135   to **ensure** good contact with the white-blue light spectrum;
- provide for good levels of blue light in the artificial light sources employed;
- ensure there is a degree of user control over the provision of light at the workplace desk.

The study of chronobiology (the impact of light on health) is an emerging discipline
140 that may impact design over the next decade. In the meantime, the drive for energy efficiency in the workplace should be balanced by equal attention to human factors. After all, a zero carbon office is not of much value unless the workers occupying the building are healthy, alert, satisfied, motivated, and hence productive. Although low levels of **kWh/m²** for lighting may be desirable from the perspective of building
145 performance, in terms of the balance sheet it is the type, level, and design of lighting that most impact performance and company productivity.

Learning from Other Building Types

Although offices and educational buildings are the centre of attention in this reading, other sectors have developed new knowledge and new approaches to the design of
150 their interior environments. Hospitals have been the subject of a study involving Bryan Lawson and his team at Sheffield University (Lawson & Wells-Thorpe, 2002)

kWh/m²: total radiation in kilowatts per square metre of surface per hour

and Phil Nedin at Arup in London (Nedin, 2010). Hospital research aims to develop new understanding at the interface of environment and well-being, just as school research explores that between environment and learning, and offices between that
155 of environment and productivity. In each case, the interior environment, and in particular issues of comfort, well-being, and human performance, form the basis for evaluation. In hospitals, the prime concern is that of staff and patients, making an obvious parallel to the relationship between teachers and students in schools.

The research stemming from health-care environments provides food for thought.
160 Although each person's interaction with the interior environment is different, cases examined suggest that a balance is needed between sustainability, health, and well-being of both health-care workers and patients. Ensuring that the drive for efficiency of provision (including levels of carbon emission) is compatible with wider social and health targets has led Arup to propose a list of desirable elements in the design of
165 new hospitals (Nedin, 2010). The aim is to produce a therapeutic environment with interiors that provide patients, staff, and visitors with the following:

- natural daylight;
- artificial lighting;
- environmental control;
170 - thermal comfort;
- privacy and dignity;
- responsive acoustics;
- interesting/relaxing views;
- art.

175 Other points are noted by Nedin, but these are the most relevant across sectors. What is worth observing is the fine detail required and the different needs of different groups. This detail refers to elements within the traditional realm of environmental engineering and those things (which patients in particular value) which are usually ignored by designers and are outside normal checklists. Transferring the concept of
180 the therapeutic environment to the office workplace poses methodological difficulties, but there may be parallels between a therapeutic environment and a productive environment which are yet to be appreciated.

If office design has adopted lessons from health-care architecture, offices themselves have influenced other building types. There have been transfer of design approaches
185 and facade engineering from corporate offices to offices for rent, from offices to university teaching and research facilities, and from offices to libraries and schools. These have concerned the design of interior spaces (particularly open plans and use of **atria**), the use of solar technologies, and the understanding of social and creative spaces. The latter has involved awareness of socializing as a means of knowledge transfer and
190 places where communication occurs often as a consequence of low energy design.

atria (n., plural of *atrium*): high open spaces in a tall building

Better Social Relationships

Green buildings generally help to bring neighbourhoods together and encourage healthy lifestyles. Hence, there are benefits to companies, to individuals, and to communities. Evidence is more **anecdotal** the more one addresses the urban level of sustainability,
195 but the impact a green building has on neighbourhood attitudes to the environment can be measured … in terms of raised property values, increase in mortgage confidence from lenders, and lower cost of vandalism and neglected infrastructure (Kats, 2010).

anecdotal (adj.): subjective; based on personal experience

At the building level, green buildings provide increased opportunity for social exchange where atria are provided. Such spaces lead to social cohesion and the exchange of
200 ideas, which can be beneficial to companies. In workplace settings, giving users more choice over building controls (such as lighting levels, temperature settings, and ventilation rates) also encourages better interpersonal relationships and a shared culture of environmental respect. Green offices normally provide greater freedom to determine the environment of the workplace than air-conditioned buildings and this
205 in turn is good for constructing teams of cooperating individuals. However, the social benefits should not be exaggerated and can undermine the ecological balances of a well-functioning green workplace. For example, an individual who requires very high or very cold temperature settings can alienate neighbouring workers and upset finely tuned building control balances. Hence, personal control is normally limited by a
210 building management system (BMS), which sets overarching environmental standards.

Enhanced Image for Buildings and Organizations

Industry groups such as the British Council for Offices (BCO) and the British Property Federation (BPF) in the UK and their counterparts elsewhere increasingly advocate for the application of sustainable approaches, not least because of the overwhelming
215 business case in an age of rising energy prices, stricter legislation, and consumer choice. The same is true of universities, which are motivated by slightly different priorities. Here it is often international competitiveness and an eagerness to build green examples on campus that are the main drivers. However, it is important to recognize that the environmental argument alone is not sufficient to sway boardrooms;
220 there has to be a supporting economic and social case.

When businesses build, they are conscious of the messages their buildings send (Øvlisen, 2011). These messages are intended for audiences as diverse as board members, employees, clients, and customers. Hence the building of an office for rent or a headquarters building for self-occupation is rich in coded signals. One of the
225 most important of these is directed to neighbours. Green buildings demonstrate respect for both the local environment and global problems such as climate change. Hence, buildings are a useful way of communicating business concerns to an audience: a green image is a good image in many eyes.

(2576 words)

References

British Council for Offices (BCO). (2009). *Guide to specification* (pp. 14–42, 98–112).

Edwards, B. (2006, November). Environmental design and educational performance. *Research in Education, 77*, 14–32.

Kats, G. (2010). *Greening our built world: Costs, benefits and strategies* (pp. 187–188). Washington, DC: Island Press.

Lawson, B., & Wells-Thorpe, J. (2002, March). The effect of the hospital environment on the patient experience and health outcomes. *The Journal of Healthcare Design and Development*, 27–32.

Nedin, P. (2010). Design of the hospital environment to promote staff and patient wellbeing. *The Arup Journal, 1*, 14–17.

Øvlisen, M. (2011). Trade and industry. *New Architecture in Copenhagen DAC*, 68.

Race, M.-C. Venning, B., & Yarandipour, R. (2010). Lighting and health: A longitudinal study. *The Arup Journal, 1*, 41–43.

Edwards, B. W., & Naboni, E. (2013). *Green buildings pay: Design, productivity and ecology* (pp. 4–9). London: Routledge Taylor Francis Group.

After You Read

D. Answer the following questions from your own knowledge and your notes in the table from While You Read (page 127). After, verify your answers with a classmate.

1. Why do the costs of green buildings seem less expensive as the price of fossil fuels rise?

_____

_____

_____

_____

2. What features of green buildings do people find so attractive?

_____

_____

_____

_____

3. What aspects of employee health are improved in green buildings? What other ways do green buildings increase employee productivity and creativity?

_____

_____

_____

_____

4. How do green buildings promote better social relationships?

_____

_____

_____

5. How do green building practices enhance the building's image and reflect well on organizations?

_____

_____

_____

_____

MyBookshelf > My eLab >
Exercises > Chapter 4 >
How Do Green Buildings Pay?

FOCUS ON READING

Identifying Writer Perspective in a Text

Now that you have read the three texts in this chapter, you are in a good position to consider the differences in the writers' perspectives. Being aware of writer perspective helps you understand why information is presented in a certain way and if it contains any bias.

Often, a discussion of writer perspective is related to bias, for example, whether the writer is trying to persuade the reader to adopt his or her point of view. However, in this chapter, you also see that writer perspective is related to the positioning of the writer as an expert or an informed reader.

A. Answer the following questions.

1. In Reading 1 and Reading 2, how do you know that the writers are not experts on the subject of green building?

   _____

   _____

2. In Reading 3, do the writers position themselves as experts or as informed readers?

   _____

   _____

   _____

   _____

3. In Reading 3, the writers use the pronoun *we* twice (lines 81 and 83). Who does *we* refer to?

   _____

4. Why is this use of *we* (and *us*) unusual for a writer?

   _____

B. Your instructor will provide you with several short texts to read; you can also use readings from other chapters in this book or from other texts to complete this task. Read the texts and consider these questions.

1. Are the writers experts or informed readers, using the voices of other experts to give authority to the text?

2. Is there evidence of writer bias in any of the texts? Is the writer trying to convince the reader of a specific viewpoint?

3. Do any of the writers use the first person (*I*, *we*, or *us*) to associate themselves with a group of people?

C. Discuss the differences you find as a class.

FINAL ASSIGNMENT

Write an Extended Report

Write a report explaining the driving forces behind green building (or the lack of it) in the country or city in which you live or have lived.

A. Use your description from the Warm-Up Assignment as the core of this longer report. Show how that building was the result of (or the exception to) the drivers of sustainable building. Finish with a projection about the future of green building in the country or city you write about.

B. Position yourself as an informed reader and let the experts' quotations lend authority to your writing. For this report, include references for the quotations.

C. Your report should contain
- an introduction, with a definition of green building;
- a section on the forces driving green building in your country or city;
- an example of a sustainable building and its features;
- data on how much energy, water, and carbon are saved (if available);
- information about the social benefits of the building (if available);
- a conclusion with your projections about the future of green building in your country or city.

Refer to the Models Chapter (page 282) to see an example of a report and to learn more about how to write one.

Critical Connections

In Focus on Critical Thinking (page 111), you learned how applying old knowledge or structures to new information can help you achieve the academic goal of generating new ideas or new ways of thinking.

In this chapter, you read about three different systems for assessing the sustainability of a building or a community. Clearly, builders are motivated to design and build more sustainably if their buildings will be rated according to one of these systems. Now, apply your knowledge of how these systems work to other fields or industries.

A. With a partner, brainstorm other fields or industries that could benefit from incentives to be more sustainable. Select one of these and consider how you could design a system to encourage sustainability. Who would develop it? How could the ratings be distributed? Could companies (or people) win awards for sustainable work? How would this system change the field or industry?

B. Write a paragraph about your ideas or develop a short presentation for your class.

CHAPTER 5

Self-Driving Cars

It seems that everybody is talking about self-driving cars these days. These high-tech vehicles offer the potential to solve many of the world's transportation problems. Researchers and scientists suggest autonomous cars could reduce traffic congestion, air pollution, and accident rates. Nevertheless, these benefits are not easily achieved; there are a host of challenges to overcome before driverless vehicles are a reality for the average person. We can certainly anticipate the complex technical challenges required to make autonomous vehicles safe. However, other types of challenges might surprise us. What technical, ethical, and social challenges must be addressed before we can benefit from self-driving cars?

In this chapter,
you will

- learn vocabulary related to self-driving cars;

- identify paraphrases and summaries;

- use techniques to paraphrase and summarize;

- express uncertainty in a variety of ways;

- write conditionally to express what might happen;

- identify causes and effects;

- write a summary and a cause and effect essay.

GEARING UP

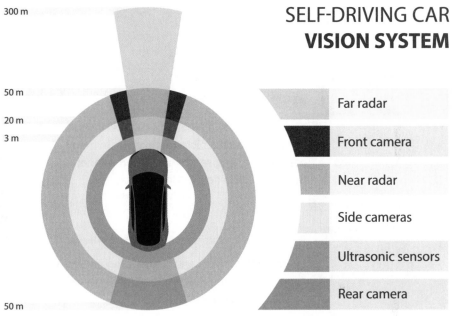

SELF-DRIVING CAR VISION SYSTEM

300 m

50 m

20 m

3 m

50 m

- Far radar
- Front camera
- Near radar
- Side cameras
- Ultrasonic sensors
- Rear camera

A. Survey your class to determine attitudes about self-driving cars.

1. How many of you have driven in an autonomous car?

2. How many of you would like to ride in an autonomous car? Why or why not?

3. How many of you are worried about the possible dangers of riding in self-driving cars? Why or why not?

B. In the table below, list the reasons why some people might be excited, and others might be concerned about autonomous vehicles. Use a separate page if you need more space.

EXCITING POSSIBILITIES OF AUTONOMOUS VEHICLES	CONCERNS ABOUT AUTONOMOUS VEHICLES
• *High-tech cool factor*	• *Loss of control over driving*

Below are the key words you will practise in this chapter. Check the words you understand, then underline the words you use. Highlight the words you need to learn.

nouns

algorithms   policy*
authorities*   regulators*
circumstances*   revelation*
corpus   sensors
functions*   simulation*
legislators*   spectrum
manipulation*   trolley
pedestrian

self-driving cars

verbs

adapting*   hacking
alleviate   interpret*
cease*   pose*
detect*   predict*
emerge*   resolve*

adjectives

apparent*   inevitable*
crucial*   insufficient*
hypothetical* precise*
inadequate*

adverb

presumably*

*Appears on the Academic Word List

READING ❶   Moving Forward

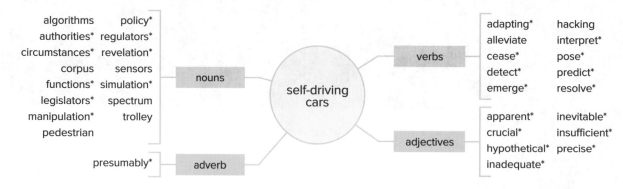

The author of this article discusses progress in autonomous vehicle technology in many countries, giving readers an international perspective on self-driving cars.

Learning synonyms and developing an awareness of word forms (how words change when they are used as different parts of speech) will help you paraphrase and summarize successfully.

A. Review the introductory paragraph to this chapter (page 136) and list all the synonyms for self-driving cars used in that paragraph.

_____

_____

B. Working with a partner, complete the following table by changing the form of each word to match the part of speech in the column heading.

VERB	NOUN	ADJECTIVE	ADVERB
automate		*automatic / automated*	*automatically*
	benefit		
regulate			
		congested / congestive	
navigate			

C. Write definitions for the key words from Reading 1. Look up the ones you do not know. Then answer the questions that follow.

WORDS	DEFINITIONS	WORDS	DEFINITIONS
1 algorithms (n.)	*set of instructions to be followed in strict order in problem-solving operations, especially by computers*	**8** policy (n.)	
2 alleviate (v.)		**9** pose (v.)	
3 circumstances (n.)		**10** precise (adj.)	
4 crucial (adj.)		**11** resolve (v.)	
5 hacking (v.)		**12** sensors (n.)	
6 inadequate (adj.)		**13** spectrum (n.)	
7 manipulation (n.)			

1 Which verb is a synonym of *cause*, and forms collocations with the nouns *problems* and *challenges*? _____

2 Which verb is a synonym of *find a solution to*, and forms collocations with the nouns *problems*, *concerns*, *conflicts*, and *disputes*? _____

3 Which verb is a synonym of *improve*, and forms collocations with the nouns *problems*, *situations*, and *suffering*? _____

4 What do these three verbs (answers 1, 2, and 3) reveal about Reading 1?

_____

5 Which adjective starts with a prefix that negates the root word? _____

6 Which noun refers to equipment that has human abilities? _____

7 Which word almost always follows the adjective *crucial*? _____

8 Which noun can have a negative connotation? _____

9 Which words might you associate with computer technology?

_____

Before You Read

A. For greater reading comprehension, consider the technology required
by autonomous vehicles before reading this text. Working in a small group,
answer the following questions.

1 Return to the infographic of the autonomous car in Gearing Up (page 137).
List the kinds of technology shown in the infographic.

Far and near radar, _____

2 This technology allows self-driving cars to "see" what is around them. List
the things that autonomous vehicles need to be aware of as they move.

_____

_____

3 Ultrasonic sensors are not the only technological features autonomous
vehicles require. What in-car (or on-board) technology is needed to
coordinate information from all the cars' sensors? What external
technology is required?

_____

_____

4 As well as technology, what other controls or regulatory systems are
needed to ensure autonomous vehicles are safe?

_____

_____

You now have an idea of the complexities related to self-driving vehicles.
This will help you as you read the following report.

While You Read

B. The following headings were removed from this report and randomized.
Read the headings and think about why some are in regular font and some
are *italicized*. What is the difference between the two types of headings?

_____

– ~~Introduction~~	– *Bad Weather*
– *Public Acceptance*	– *Alleviating Traffic Congestion*
– *Poor Highway Infrastructure*	– The Importance of Artificial Intelligence, High-Definition Maps, and Deep Learning to Autonomous Vehicles
– *Digital Hacking*	
– *Reducing Air Pollution*	
– Obstacles to Adoption and Utilization	– *Improving Highway Safety*
– Benefits of Autonomous Vehicles	– *Inadequate Spectrum*
	– Conclusion

C. As you read, insert the headings in the appropriate positions in the report. When you have finished, verify your heading placement with a classmate.

Moving Forward: Self-Driving Vehicles in China, Europe, Japan, Korea, and the United States

Introduction

Vehicles equipped with **sensors** and cameras navigate the streets of Mountain View, California; Austin, Texas; Kirkland, Washington; Dearborn, Michigan; Pittsburgh, Pennsylvania; Beijing, China; Wuhu, China; Gothenburg, Sweden; Rotterdam,
5 Netherlands; Suzu, Japan; Fujisawa, Japan; and Seoul, South Korea, among other places. Sophisticated on-board software integrates data from dozens of sources, analyzes this information in real time, and automatically guides the car using high-definition maps around possible dangers.

... The World Economic Forum estimates that the digital transformation of the
10 automotive industry will generate $67 billion in value for that sector and $3.1 trillion in societal benefits (Weinelt, 2016). That includes improvements from autonomous vehicles, connected travellers, and the transportation enterprise ecosystem as a whole.

This paper ... argues that connected vehicles are likely to improve highway safety, **alleviate** traffic congestion, and reduce air pollution. However, to do that, designers
15 must overcome obstacles such as poor infrastructure, bad weather, **inadequate spectrum**, **hacking** threats, and public acceptance.

The technology to meet these barriers has advanced rapidly and is poised for commercial deployment. But to make progress, each country needs to address particular issues. There are budgetary, **policy**, legal, and regulatory concerns to **resolve**.

20 In China, for example, the key is to develop a national policy framework for autonomous vehicles. It has multiple ministries which are responsible for the supervision of automatic driving (some with overlapping jurisdictions) and there needs to be greater clarity regarding who regulates and how they regulate. In addition, the government needs to invest in highway infrastructure for autonomous vehicles, eliminate the
25 current national prohibition on road testing, and reduce restrictions on road map development so that car makers and software designers can devise the most accurate navigational guides.

In Europe, the challenge is strengthening the artificial intelligence capability that is **crucial** to autonomous vehicles. One of the reasons why large technology firms such as Google
30 in the United States and Baidu in China have moved into transportation is the opportunity to apply the processing insights and rapid learning capacity developed through search engine technology to a new sector. To be
35 competitive in driverless vehicles, European auto manufacturers such as Audi, BMW (in collaboration with Intel), Volkswagen, Daimler, Mercedes-Benz, and Volvo need people with strong artificial intelligence skills
40 and high-performance computing aptitude

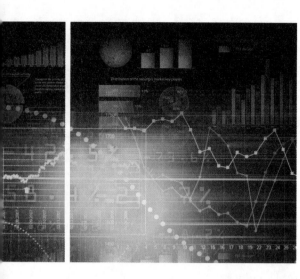

because car manufacturing no longer is about physical design as much as it is about software development and real-time data analytics ...

In Japan and Korea, governments and car manufacturers have
45 been cautious about autonomous vehicles. Firms such as Toyota, Honda, Nissan, Kia, and Hyundai are investing major resources. They are keeping track of what is happening in other countries and undertaking pilot projects. Yet they have to decide whether autonomous vehicles represent a high priority for them. If so, they
50 should invest resources in artificial intelligence, high-definition mapping, and data analytics, which are key to the future of this sector. Failure to do so means they will be left behind as the industry embraces autonomous vehicles in the coming years.

In the United States, the major difficulty is overcoming the regulatory fragmentation
55 caused by fifty states having differing preferences on licensing, car standards, regulation, and privacy protection. Right now, car manufacturers (such as Ford and General Motors) and software developers face conflicting rules and regulations in various states (G. Ivanov of Google, personal communication, June 21, 2016). This complicates innovation because makers want to build cars and trucks for a national
60 or international market. There also needs to be greater clarity in regard to legal liability and data protection, and legislation to penalize the malicious disruption of autonomous vehicles.

In each nation, government officials and business leaders have to resolve these matters because within a foreseeable period, the technology will have advanced to the point
65 where intelligent vehicles will spread into key niches such as ride-sharing, taxis, delivery truck, industrial applications, and transport for senior citizens and the disabled ... It is important for leaders to provide reasonable guidance on how to commercialize advanced technologies in transportation.

---

70 Autonomous vehicles involve the application of advanced technological capabilities to cars, trucks, and buses. These include automated vehicle guidance and braking, lane-changing systems, use of cameras and sensors for collision avoidance, artificial intelligence to analyze information in real time, and high-performance computing and deep learning systems to adapt to new **circumstances** through 3-D high-
75 definition maps ...

Without sophisticated artificial intelligence models and high-definition maps to analyze information and the capacity to learn from changing circumstances, autonomous vehicles would be difficult to operate safely. They simply would not be able to handle the complex conditions that exist on roads and highways around the world ...

80 ---

Many benefits are expected of autonomous vehicles. These include improving highway safety, alleviating traffic congestion, and reducing air pollution. Research studies have found there are major gains likely in each of these areas.

85 Highway deaths are a major problem around the world. In the United States, an estimated 35,000 people die in auto accidents each year, while in China, around 260,000 people die in vehicle accidents (Buckley, 2016; "Lessons," 2016). Japan experiences around 4000 highway deaths each year (Bloomberg, 2015).

Worldwide, according to the World Health Organization, 1.24 million people die 90 annually due to highway accidents (2010). It is estimated that traffic fatalities cost $260 billion each year and that accident injuries account for another $365 billion. This represents a total of $625 billion annually from highway fatalities and injuries (Morgan Stanley Research, 2014).

According to a RAND study, "39 percent of the crash fatalities in 2011 involved 95 alcohol use by one of the drivers" (Anderson et al., 2016, p. xiv). This is an area where autonomous vehicles almost certainly will produce major gains in terms of lives saved and injuries avoided …

Traffic congestion is a problem in virtually every large metropolitan area. In the United 100 States, for example, drivers spend an average of forty hours stuck in traffic, at an annual cost of $121 billion (U.S. DOT, 2015). For Moscow, Istanbul, Mexico City, or Rio de Janeiro, the wasted time is even higher. There, drivers can spend "more than a hundred hours a year in congested traffic" (Weinelt, 2016, p. 4) …

Once autonomous vehicles are phased in and represent a large part of the traffic, car-105 mounted sensors will be able to operate in conjunction with an Intelligent Traffic System to optimize intersection traffic flow. Time intervals for green or red lights will be dynamic and vary in real time, depending on the amount of traffic flowing along certain streets. That will ease congestion by improving the efficiency of vehicular flows.

110 Automobiles are major contributors to poor quality air. According to a RAND study, "Autonomous vehicle (AV) technology can improve fuel economy, improving it by 4 to 10 percent by accelerating and decelerating more smoothly than a human driver" (Anderson et al., 2016, p. xvi). Since smog in industrial areas is linked to the number of vehicles, having more autonomous cars is likely to reduce air pollution. A 2016 115 research study estimated that "pollution levels inside cars at red lights or in traffic jams are up to 40 percent higher than when traffic is moving" (Schlossberg, para. 4).

A shared autonomous vehicle system (SAV) also offers benefits in terms of emissions and energy. Researchers at the University of Texas at Austin examined pollutants such as sulfur dioxide, carbon monoxide, oxides of nitrogen, volatile organic compounds, 120 greenhouse gas, and particulate matter with small diameters. Their findings show "beneficial energy use and emissions outcomes for all emissions [types] when shifting to a system of SAVs" (Fagnant & Kockelman, 2014, p. 9) …

There are several key challenges as intelligent cars emerge. This includes technical
125 challenges arising from bad weather and digital hacking threats as well as obstacles
that require institutional or societal action such as road infrastructure improvements,
spectrum allocation, and public acceptance. Each of these matters **poses** problems
for autonomous vehicles and their success in the marketplace.

130 Bad weather represents an area where driverless cars do not perform very well. Heavy
rain, large amounts of snow, or atmospheric smog obscure road signs and lane
markings, and therefore raise the risk of driving accidents. It is difficult in these kinds
of situations for autonomous vehicles to make good decisions. According to Rob Grant
of Lyft, autonomous cars "don't behave well in certain weather conditions or poor
135 road conditions" (personal communication, July 5, 2016) …

Security is an important consideration in this sector. There have been reports of
vehicles hacked and systems disrupted. Autonomous cars depend on vehicle-to-vehicle
(V2V) communications and vehicle-to-infrastructure (V2I) connections. It is crucial to
140 maintain security in each of these pathways as well as in the personal electronic
communications that passengers transmit via email, phone calls, texting, Internet
surfing, and location data (Greenberg, 2015).

Researchers Jonathan Petit and Steven Shladover outline a number of security threats
to connected cars. These include hacking, jamming, data theft, ghost vehicles, or
145 malicious actions such as using bright lights to blind cameras, radar interference,
or sensor **manipulation** (2015) … Manipulating this type of information puts passengers
at risk and can potentially lead to serious accidents …

Infrastructure problems plague many countries. In India, for example, highways and
150 roads represent a major challenge. Nearly 38 percent of the country's roads are
unpaved, compared to about 16 percent in China. For these reasons, the World
Economic Forum ranks India eighty-seventh in infrastructure in the world, well below
the number 6 ranking for Japan, 7 in Germany, 46 in China, 48 in Thailand, and 76 in
Brazil (Bhattacharaya, Bruce, & Mukherjee, 2014).

155 Poor highways pose challenges for autonomous vehicles. Cars need predictable
surfaces and clearly defined traffic lanes. In a cross-country pilot drive, Delphi
engineers found substantial variations in lane markings. According to Glen De Vos,
"the automated vehicle encountered some roadways with wide white stripes, while
others had narrow yellow markings. Some lane markings were new, others were
160 faded, and some were marked with raised bumps" (*Hands off: The future of self-
driving cars,* 2016, pp. 22–23).

To the extent that roads are poorly marked or engineered, it is hard for either semi-autonomous or fully autonomous vehicles to traverse those routes. The risk of accidents goes up and there is a grave danger that computerized **algorithms** will lead to
165 poor decisions. Unless addressed, this will limit the ability of autonomous vehicles to thrive …

Inadequate spectrum is a major barrier in many countries. Finding dedicated frequency ranges is key to supporting autonomous vehicles. They need specific bands that
170 perform well regardless of weather or traffic conditions. Autonomous vehicles and industrial applications need mid-range spectrum below 6 GHz due to the need to balance connection speed and radio link reliability. In a number of places, these frequencies are in high demand and it is difficult to guarantee the reliable service that autonomous vehicles require. A dropped phone call is annoying to consumers, but a
175 lost connection for a driverless car could be deadly.

American manufacturers generally support a dedicated short-range communication (DSRC) system. According to Sandy Lobenstein of Toyota, "DSRC is a two-way, short- to medium-range
180 wireless communication protocol that allows vehicles to communicate with each other to detect and avoid hazards. DSRC-equipped vehicles broadcast **precise** information—such as their location, speed, and acceleration—several times
185 per second over a range of a few hundred metres. Other vehicles outfitted with DSRC technology receive these "messages" and use them to compute the trajectory of each neighbouring vehicle, compare these with their own predicted
190 path, and determine if any of the neighbouring vehicles pose a collision threat" (*The Internet of cars,* 2015).

Ultimately, the public must feel comfortable with autonomous vehicles for this
195 market to develop. As with any emerging technologies, it takes a while for individuals to accept new models and different ways of navigating. Just as the shift from horses to cars and cars to mass transit was controversial, so too is the looming transition to autonomous vehicles.

According to an American public opinion survey undertaken at the University of
200 Michigan, many people still prefer traditional approaches to vehicle operations. When asked about their preferences, 46 percent of Americans said they prefer no self-driving vehicles, followed by 39 percent who like partial self-driving [semi-autonomous] and 16 percent who support complete self-driving [fully autonomous] cars (Schoettle & Sivak, 2016).

205 The same survey revealed that there were interesting variations in attitudes by gender and age. Men (19 percent) were more likely to prefer full self-driving vehicles compared to women (12 percent). Young people aged eighteen to twenty-nine years

210 old (19 percent) and those between thirty and forty-four (22 percent) were the most likely to want self-driving vehicles, compared to those sixty and older (only 10 percent support self-driving) and those forty-five to fifty-nine (12 percent) …

215 Chinese drivers appear more open to vehicular experimentation. A World Economic Forum survey found that "75 percent of Chinese say they are willing to ride in a self-driving car" (Spring, 2016; Hao, 2016) This view was echoed in a separate

220 survey undertaken by the Roland Berger consulting firm. It found that "96 percent of Chinese would consider an autonomous vehicle for almost all everyday driving, compared with 58 percent of Americans and Germans" (Girault, 2016). People in China do not have the same

225 positive emotional relationship with driving and their own cars, and therefore are more amenable to self-driving cars …

The technology underlying autonomous vehicles is well developed and poised for commercial deployment. Major automotive companies and software developers have

230 made considerable progress in navigation, collision avoidance, and street mapping.

But in each country, there are budgetary, policy, and regulatory issues that need to be addressed in order to gain the full benefits of autonomous vehicles … From an outside standpoint, work needs to be done to overcome obstacles such as poor infrastructure, bad weather, spectrum limitations, hacking, and public acceptance. If

235 car developers can overcome these barriers, there will be substantial advances for transportation and society.

There remain broader societal and ethical considerations, though, that must be considered as we move closer to commercialization. How should programmers build ethical choices into automated features and advanced algorithms? For example, if an

240 automated car is facing the outcome between hitting one child or a group of ten kids, how does it make that choice? What are the factors in the algorithm that would lead its system to veer one way or another? One can imagine a wide variety of ethical issues and software designers have to make choices regarding how to deal with them (Bonnefon, Shariff, & Rahwan, 2016). Learning how to navigate these complicated

245 issues is a major challenge facing the world.

(2405 words)

References

Anderson, J., Kaira, N., Stanley, K., Sorensen, P., Samaras, C., & Oluwatola, O. (2016). *Autonomous vehicle technology: A guide for policymakers* (Rep.). Santa Monica, CA: RAND Corporation. Retrieved from https://www.rand.org/pubs/research_reports/RR443-2.html

Bhattacharaya, A., Bruce, A., & Mukherjee, A. (2014, November). *Make in India: Turning vision into reality* (p. 20, Rep.). Boston Consulting Group. Retrieved from http://www.manufacturingchampions.in/Document/NewsLetter/CII-BCG%20Report%20on%20Make%20In%20India%20-%2013th%20Manufacturing%20Summit%202014.pdf

Bloomberg. (2015, October 28). Japan's carmakers proceed with caution on self-driving cars. *Business Times*. Retrieved from https://www.businesstimes.com.sg/transport/japans-carmakers-proceed-with-caution-on-self-driving-cars

Bonnefon, J-F., Shariff, A., & Rahwan, I. (2016, June 24). The social dilemma of autonomous vehicles. *Science, 352*(6293), 1573–1576. doi: 10.1126/science.aaf2654

Buckley, C. (May 30, 2016). Beijing's electric bikes, the wheels of e-commerce, face traffic backlash. *New York Times*. Retrieved from https://www.nytimes.com/2016/05/31/world/asia/beijing-traffic-electric-bikes.html

Fagnant, D. J., & Kockelman, K. M. (2014, January 1). The travel and environmental implications of shared autonomous vehicles, using agent-based model scenarios. *Transportation Research Part C: Emerging Technologies, (40)*, 1–13. doi: 10.1016/j.trc.2013.12.001

Girault, J. (2016, April 23). Chinese firms accelerate in race toward driverless future. *Phys.Org*. Retrieved from https://phys.org/news/2016-04-chinese-firms-driverless-future.html

Greenberg, A. (2015, July 21). Hackers remotely kill a Jeep on the highway—with me in it. *Wired*. Retrieved from https://www.wired.com/2015/07/hackers-remotely-kill-jeep-highway/

Hands off: The future of self-driving cars: Hearing before the Committee on Commerce, Science and Technology United States Senate, 114th Cong., 17 (2016, March 15) (testimony of Glen W. De Vos of Delphi).

Hao, Y. (2016, April 11). Officials want to open way for autonomous driving. *China Daily*. Retrieved from http://www.chinadaily.com.cn/business/motoring/2016-04/11/content_24429558.htm

The Internet of cars: Hearing before the House Committee on Oversight and Government Reform House of Representatives, 114th Cong., 10 (2015, November 18) (testimony of Sandy Lobenstein).

Lessons from the Tesla crash. (2016, July 11). *New York Times*. Retrieved from https://www.nytimes.com/2016/07/11/opinion/lessons-from-the-tesla-crash.html

Morgan Stanley Research. (2014, February 25). *Nikola's revenge: TSLA's new path of disruption*, (pp. 24–26).

Petit, J., & Shladover, S. E. (2015, April). Potential cyberattacks on automated vehicles. *IEEE Transactions on Intelligent Transportation Systems, 16*(2), 546–556. doi:10.1109/TITS.2014.2342271

Schlossberg, T. (2016, August 29). Stuck in traffic, polluting the inside of our cars. *New York Times*. Retrieved from https://www.nytimes.com/2016/08/30/science/traffic-air-pollution-inside-cars.html

Schoettle, B., & Sivak, M. (2016, May). *Motorists' preferences for different levels of vehicle automation: 2016* (Rep. No. SWT-2016-8). Ann Arbor, MI: University of Michigan Sustainable Worldwide Transportation.

Spring, J. (2016, April 22). Look Mao, no hands! China's roadmap to self-driving cars. *Reuters*. Retrieved from https://www.reuters.com/article/us-autoshow-beijing-china-selfdriving/look-mao-no-hands-chinas-roadmap-to-self-driving-cars-idUSKCN0XK021

U.S. Department of Transportation. (2015). *Beyond traffic, 2045: Trends and choices*, p. 11.

Weinelt, B. (2016, January). *Digital transformation of industries: Automotive industry*. World Economic Forum in collaboration with Accenture.

World Health Organization. (2010). *Global Health Observatory Data: Number of Road Traffic Deaths*.

_____

West, D. M. (2016, September). *Moving forward: Self-driving vehicles in China, Europe, Japan, Korea, and the United States*. Centre for Technology and Innovation at Brookings (pp. 1–4, 9–14, 24–25).

After You Read

D. Working with a partner, answer the following questions to demonstrate your comprehension.

1. Why does the author start the report by referring to a) the countries where research on self-driving cars is being conducted, and b) the amount of money the autonomous car sector will generate globally?

_____

2 What is the thesis of this report?

_____

_____

3 What are the major challenges the following countries and regions face concerning the adoption of self-driving cars?

China: _____

_____

Europe: _____

Japan and Korea: _____

_____

The United States: _____

_____

_____

4 What forms of technology support the development of autonomous vehicles?

_____

_____

_____

5 In the sections *Improving Highway Safety*, *Alleviating Traffic Congestion*, and *Reducing Air Pollution*, why does the author start by providing statistics?

_____

_____

_____

6 How will autonomous vehicles improve highway safety, alleviate traffic congestion, and reduce air pollution?

_____

_____

_____

_____

_____

7 How could bad weather, digital hacking, and poor highway infrastructure pose problems for autonomous vehicles?

_____

_____

8 How could inadequate Internet spectrum and public acceptance prevent the widespread use of self-driving cars?

_____

_____

_____

9 In one sentence, summarize the author's conclusion.

_____

_____

_____

10 In the final paragraph of the report, what new challenge does the author mention?

_____

_____

MyBookshelf > My eLab >
Exercises > Chapter 5 >
Moving Forward

FOCUS ON READING

Identifying Paraphrases and Summaries

One of the ways the author of Reading 1 (Darrell West) presents information about self-driving cars is by integrating information and points from other authors and researchers. In some cases, West uses quotes or indirect speech (see Chapter 4, Focus on Writing, page 119, and Focus on Accuracy, page 120). In other cases, he paraphrases and summarizes information from other sources.

In paraphrases and summaries, writers use their own words to present others' ideas. For each instance, the writer must provide an in-text citation with a complete reference at the end of the text. (See Chapter 2, Academic Survival Skill, on page 57.)

What is the difference between paraphrasing and summarizing?

A paraphrase is approximately the same length as the original text; a summary is shorter than the original text. A formal summary is approximately one-third to one-quarter the length of the original text although this is not an absolute rule. For both paraphrases and summaries, it is important for writers to use their own words, not the words of the original author.

Why paraphrase and summarize?

Writers paraphrase and summarize other authors for many reasons:
- To build arguments for and against their thesis
- To give credit to the authors who first wrote about these ideas
- To avoid constant use of quotations
- To avoid plagiarism
- To demonstrate their extensive knowledge of the field
- To establish their writing as academic

In general, writers must paraphrase or summarize and provide a citation and reference for specific ideas and research outcomes.

A. Skim the in-text citations in Reading 1 and complete the following tasks.

1 Underline the in-text citations that refer to direct quotations of the original authors' words.

2 Highlight those that are paraphrases and summaries of original authors.

3 Does anything about these in-text citations surprise you?

_____

4 When you look at an in-text citation, can you tell if the author has paraphrased or summarized the original authors' views? Why or why not?

_____

B. Look at two of the original sources (shown below) that West integrated into his writing. For each, find the corresponding citation in Reading 1 and identify whether he paraphrased or summarized the sources.

Example 1:

> More than 35,200 people were killed in car crashes in this country last year, up 7.7 percent from 2014. People caused most of those accidents. Driverless cars could help reduce that toll substantially, but those vehicles are still years away.
>
> _____
> Lessons from the Tesla crash. (2016, July 11). *New York Times*. Retrieved from https://www.nytimes.com/2016/07/11/opinion/lessons-from-the-tesla-crash.html

_____

Example 2:

> I was driving 70 mph on the edge of downtown St. Louis when the exploit began to take hold. Though I hadn't touched the dashboard, the vents in the Jeep Cherokee started blasting cold air at the maximum setting, chilling the sweat on my back through the in-seat climate control system. Next the radio switched to the local hip hop station ... at full volume. I spun the control knob left and hit the power button, [but nothing happened]. Then the windshield wipers turned on, and wiper fluid blurred the glass ...

> The Jeep's strange behaviour wasn't entirely unexpected. I'd come to St. Louis to be Charlie Miller and Chris Valasek's digital crash-test dummy, a willing subject on whom they could test the car-hacking research they'd been doing over the past year. The result of their work was a hacking technique ... that can target Jeep Cherokees and give the attacker wireless control, via the Internet, to any of thousands of vehicles. Their code is an automaker's nightmare: software that lets hackers send commands through the Jeep's entertainment system to its dashboard functions, steering, brakes, and transmission, all from a laptop that may be across the country ...
>
> _____
> Greenberg, A. (2015, July 21). Hacker's remotely kill a Jeep on the highway—with me in it. *Wired*. Retrieved from https://www.wired.com/2015/07/hackers-remotely-kill-jeep-highway/

C. The following examples show how West integrates paraphrases and summaries into his writing. The notes illustrate the methods he uses. Read the examples and the notes, then answer the questions.

PARAPHRASE OR SUMMARY	NOTES ON INTEGRATION
Researchers Jonathan Petit and Steven Shladover outline a number of security threats to connected cars. These include hacking, jamming, data theft, ghost vehicles, or malicious actions such as using bright lights to blind cameras, radar interference, or sensor manipulation (2015).	• Authors' names mentioned directly in the sentence • Use of verb *outline* • In-text citation at end (only year required as authors' names are in the text)
According to an American public opinion survey undertaken at the University of Michigan, many people still prefer traditional approaches to vehicle operations. When asked about their preferences, 46 percent of Americans said they prefer no self-driving vehicles, followed by 39 percent who like partial self-driving [semi-autonomous] and 16 percent who support complete self-driving [fully autonomous] cars (Schoettle & Sivak, 2016).	• Authors' names not mentioned directly in the sentence • No verb used to integrate summary • *According to* is a preposition to introduce information from a source. • Only the in-text citation at the end attributes the information to the original authors.
Right now, car manufacturers (such as Ford and General Motors) and software developers face conflicting rules and regulations in various states (G. Ivanov of Google, personal communication, June 21, 2016).	• This is a summary from an interview the author did with G. Ivanov of Google. • The in-text citation is the only indication of this information. As there is no paper (or electronic) document, there is no matching reference in the References section.

① Select one page of Reading 1 and review each in-text citation to determine which paraphrases and summaries are integrated with a direct inclusion of the author's name and a corresponding verb, and which are not.

② When West integrates a paraphrase or summary with a direct inclusion of the author's name, which verbs and phrases does he use?

_____

_____

_____

_____

Academic
Survival Skill

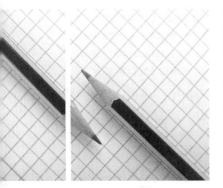

Using Techniques to Paraphrase and Summarize

Transferring another author's words into your own is not always simple. Fortunately, there are techniques that can help you paraphrase and summarize. You can apply these techniques to this excerpt from the conclusion of Reading 1.

> The technology underlying autonomous vehicles is well developed and poised for commercial deployment. Major automotive companies and software developers have made considerable progress in navigation, collision avoidance, and street mapping.

First, it's essential to understand the meaning of the original text. If you don't understand the meaning of the original, take the time to reread it and look up the meaning of words you don't know. Once you have a good understanding of the original text, there are several techniques you can use to arrive at your own wording, either in a paraphrase or a summary.

To start, cover up the original words and say or write what you understand them to mean. This is a step toward using your own words when paraphrasing. In addition, you can use the following techniques to paraphrase successfully.

Paraphrasing

Using the first sentence of the excerpt above as an example, here are some techniques you can use when paraphrasing.

USE SYNONYMS:	The equipment necessary for self-driving cars is established and ready for commercial use.	← *A good start, but the sentence structure is too similar to the original. This technique by itself does not produce a successful paraphrase.*
CHANGE WORD FORMS:	The technological developments that underlie autonomous vehicles are at the point of commercialization.	← *Good change in word forms, but the words and sentence structure are still too similar to the original. This technique by itself does not produce a successful paraphrase.*
CHANGE SENTENCE STRUCTURE:	As the technology underlying autonomous vehicles is well developed, it is now poised for commercial deployment.	← *Good move to a new sentence structure, but the words are too similar to the original. This technique by itself does not produce a successful paraphrase.*
MOVE FROM ACTIVE TO PASSIVE:	The technology underlying autonomous vehicles has been well developed and is ready to be commercially deployed.	← *Good move to passive voice, but the words are still too similar to the original. This technique by itself does not produce a successful paraphrase.*

These are all good techniques but on their own, none are sufficient to create a good paraphrase. A combination of methods yields the best results.

A. Which techniques were combined to create this paraphrase?

> The technological progress necessary for the commercialization of self-driving cars has been achieved.

_____

_____

It is also important to remember to introduce the paraphrase to give credit to the original author.

> West (2016) states that the technological progress necessary for the commercialization of self-driving cars has been achieved.

B. Paraphrasing one sentence at a time is a good way to analyze the different techniques, but you will probably want to paraphrase several sentences at once. In the following paraphrase, which techniques were used?

> West (2016) states that the technological progress necessary for the commercialization of self-driving cars has been achieved. Vehicle steering, accident prevention, and road mapping have all been significantly improved by the large car firms.

_____

_____

Summarizing

While paraphrasing is useful, it is more likely you will want to summarize large amounts of information into a few sentences that you can integrate in your writing. To write a summary, you first need to identify the main points of the original source.

C. In the excerpt below, underline the main points.

> The technology underlying autonomous vehicles is well developed and poised for commercial deployment. Major automotive companies and software developers have made considerable progress in navigation, collision avoidance, and street mapping.
>
> But in each country, there are budgetary, policy, and regulatory issues that need to be addressed in order to gain the full benefits of autonomous vehicles. Governments can accelerate or slow the movement toward self-driving vehicles by the manner in which they regulate. Addressing relevant issues and making sure regulatory rules are clear should be high priorities in all the countries considering autonomous vehicles ...
>
> From an outside standpoint, work needs to be done to overcome obstacles such as poor infrastructure, bad weather, spectrum limitations, hacking, and public acceptance. If car developers can overcome these barriers, there will be substantial advances for transportation and society.

D. Once you have identified the main points, paraphrase them to create a summary.

_____

_____

_____

_____

E. Practise paraphrasing and summarizing. On a separate page, choose one of paragraphs 5, 6, or 7 from Reading 1 and work through the process presented in this section.

- Paraphrase the first sentence using each of the four paraphrasing techniques, then combine the techniques into the "perfect" paraphrase.
- Paraphrase the rest of the paragraph.
- Summarize the whole paragraph, reducing it to approximately one-third of its current length.
- Don't forget to include the author's name and the date of publication in an appropriate way.

WARM-UP ASSIGNMENT

Write a Summary

Your goal is to write a summary of the introduction from Reading 1. You will use this summary in your Final Assignment.

A. Working on your own, underline the main points of the introduction. Then compare what you have underlined with a classmate. Close your books and tell each other the main points. This will help ensure you understand the meaning of the original text.

When you receive feedback from your instructor or your classmates on this Warm-Up Assignment, you will have information you can use to improve your writing on the Final Assignment.

B. Again working on your own, paraphrase the main points to create a summary that is approximately one-third the length of the original text. Combine techniques such as using synonyms, changing parts of speech, changing the sentence structure, and shifting from active to passive voice (or the reverse).

C. Be sure to cite the author and publication date either at the beginning or at the end. Finish with a complete reference to Reading 1. (To write an accurate reference, you will need to include page numbers. The introduction that you have just summarized is on pages 1–3 of West's original report.)

Refer to the Models Chapter (page 286) to see an example of a summary and to learn more about how to write one.

While there are many advantages to self-driving cars, we must think carefully about the decision-making algorithms that will allow autonomous vehicles to make value-based, life-changing decisions. Will the cars make better life and death decisions than human drivers?

VOCABULARY BUILD

A. In this reading, you will discover many expressions that refer to sudden movements by people or cars. Working with your class, on the board, draw a street with cars and a person walking along the sidewalk. Use a marker or an eraser to demonstrate the movements these expressions describe:

- Veers sharply
- Swerves sharply
- Performs a sharp evasive manoeuvre
- Darts out / darts into the road / darts into the path of
- Hurtles toward

B. Key words from Reading 2 are in bold in the sentences in the first column of the table. Write the meaning of each of the key words in the second column.

KEY WORDS IN CONTEXT	MEANINGS OF KEY WORDS
❶ Autonomous vehicles will sense danger long before it would become **apparent** to a human driver and slow down or stop.	*noticeable or obvious*
❷ Self-driving cars can **detect** objects with 360-degree sensory data in daylight or at night.	
❸ Most automakers and experts expect some sort of standard to **emerge**—even if it's not entirely clear what it will be.	
❹ The moral issue for self-driving cars is represented by a **hypothetical** autonomous vehicle with malfunctioning brakes, hurtling toward a school bus.	
❺ A recent study found that respondents generally agreed that a car should, in the case of an **inevitable** crash, kill the fewest number of people possible.	
❻ "Shouldn't we treat everyone the same way?" he asked. "Ultimately, it's a societal decision," meaning it may have to be settled by **legislators**, courts, and **regulators**.	

KEY WORDS IN CONTEXT	MEANINGS OF KEY WORDS
7 A certain number of occupants will die if the car swerves; a number of **pedestrians** will die if it continues.	
8 It's difficult to know what objects a self-driving car will "see" and **predict** what those objects will do next and what the car's reaction should be.	
9 **Presumably** then, there could be a circumstance in which the responsibility for someone darting into the path of an autonomous vehicle at the last minute rests with that person.	
10 Through millions of computer **simulations** and data from real self-driving cars being tested, the cars themselves can begin to learn the "best" way to respond to a given situation.	
11 Automakers largely downplay the risks of "the **trolley** problem"—named for a no-win hypothetical situation in which a person witnessing a runaway **trolley** could allow it to hit several people or, by pulling a lever, divert it, killing someone else.	

Before You Read

The author asks readers to consider this terrible hypothetical situation: what would happen if, in an emergency situation, an autonomous car had to choose between hitting a pedestrian directly ahead or swerving to avoid the pedestrian and likely injuring the occupants of the car? What choice should the car make?

A. Working in a small group, discuss the following hypothetical situations. Take point-form notes in the final column to indicate your group's optimal solutions.

HYPOTHETICAL SITUATIONS	FIRST OPTION	SECOND OPTION	OPTIMAL OUTCOME
1 Pedestrian darts out in front of autonomous car	Car hits pedestrian	Car swerves and hits brick wall	
2 School bus swerves in front of autonomous car	Car hits school bus	Car veers sharply to avoid bus and crashes	
3 Small animal runs across a road	Car hits animal	Car performs an evasive manoeuvre and goes into a ditch	

B. Who should make decisions about the optimal outcomes in these hypothetical situations: legislators, regulators, researchers, or drivers? Discuss your thoughts with your class.

While You Read

C. This reading is a newspaper article. While you read, take notes on its organizational and text features.

_____

_____

_____

D. One of the features of this article is the use of idiomatic language. As you read, write down the idioms you notice on a separate page. After, work with a classmate to define the idioms. Write your best definitions on the board to share with your class.

Morality, Ethics of a Self-Driving Car: Who Decides Who Lives, Dies?

Consider this hypothetical situation:

It's a bright, sunny day and you're alone in your [beautiful] new self-driving vehicle. You're sitting back, enjoying the view, moving along at the 70 km/h speed limit.

As you approach a rise in the road, heading south, a school bus appears, driving north,
5 one driven by a human, and it veers sharply toward you. There is no time to stop safely, and no time for you to take control of the car.

Does the car:

A. Swerve sharply into the trees, possibly killing you but possibly saving the bus
10 and its occupants?

B. Perform a sharp evasive manoeuvre around the bus and into the oncoming lane, possibly saving you, but sending the bus and its driver swerving into
15 the trees, killing her and some of the children on board?

C. Hit the bus, possibly killing you as well as the driver and kids on the bus?

In everyday driving, such no-win choices
20 may be exceedingly rare but, when they happen, what should a self-driving car—programmed in advance—do? Or in any situation—even a less **dire** one—where a moral snap judgment must be made?

dire (adj.): extremely serious or terrible

semi-autonomous vehicle (n.): vehicle that is controlled by computer algorithms, but can also be driven by a human

25 It's not just a theoretical question anymore, with predictions that in a few years, tens of thousands of **semi-autonomous vehicles** may be on the roads. Some $80 billion has been invested in the field. Tech companies are working feverishly on them, with Google-affiliated Waymo among those testing cars in Michigan, and mobility companies like Uber and Tesla racing to beat them. Detroit's automakers are placing a big bet
30 on them.

There's every reason for excitement: self-driving vehicles will ease commutes, returning lost time to workers; enhance mobility for seniors and those with physical challenges; and sharply reduce the more than 35,000 deaths on US highways each year.

But there are also a host of nagging questions to be sorted out as well, from what
35 happens to cab drivers to whether such vehicles will create sprawl.

And there is an existential question:

Who dies when the car is forced into a no-win situation?

"There will be crashes," said Van Lindberg, an attorney in the Dykema law firm's San Antonio office who specializes in autonomous vehicle issues. "Unusual things
40 will happen. Trees will fall. Animals, kids will dart out." Even as self-driving cars save thousands of lives, he said, "anyone who gets the short end of that stick is going to be pretty unhappy about it."

Whether the technology in self-driving cars is superhuman or not, there is evidence that people are worried about the choices self-driving cars will be programmed to take.

45 Last year, for instance, a Daimler executive set off a wave of criticism when he was quoted as saying its autonomous vehicles would prioritize the lives of its passengers over anyone outside the car. The company later insisted he'd been misquoted, since it would be illegal "to make a decision in favour of one person and against another."

Last month, Sebastian Thrun, who founded Google's self-driving car initiative, told
50 Bloomberg that the cars will be designed to avoid accidents, but that, "If it happens where there is a situation where a car couldn't escape, it'll go for the smaller thing."

But what if the smaller thing is a child?

How that question gets answered may be important to the development and
55 acceptance of self-driving cars.

Azim Shariff, an assistant professor of psychology and social behaviour at the University of California, Irvine, co-authored a study last year that found
60 that while respondents generally agreed that a car should, in the case of an **inevitable** crash, kill the fewest number of people possible regardless of whether they were passengers or people outside
65 of the car, they were less likely to buy any car "in which they and their family member would be sacrificed for the greater good."

Self-driving cars could save tens of thousands of lives each year, Shariff said. But
70 individual fears could slow down acceptance, leaving traditional cars and their human drivers on the road longer to battle it out with autonomous or semi-autonomous cars. Already, the American Automobile Association says three-quarters of US drivers are suspicious of self-driving vehicles.

"These ethical problems are not just theoretical," said Patrick Lin, director of
75 the Ethics and Emerging Sciences Group at California Polytechnic State University, who has worked with Ford, Tesla, and other autonomous vehicle makers on just such issues.

While he can't talk about specific discussions, Lin says some automakers "simply deny that ethics is a real problem, without realizing that they're making ethical
80 judgment calls all the time" in their development, determining what objects the car will "see," how it will **predict** what those objects will do next, and what the car's reaction should be.

The Trolley Problem

Automakers and suppliers largely downplay the risks of
85 what in philosophical circles is known as "the **trolley problem**"—named for a no-win **hypothetical** situation in which, in the original format, a person witnessing a runaway trolley could allow it to hit several people or, by pulling a lever, divert it, killing someone else.

90 In the circumstance of the self-driving car, it's often boiled down to a hypothetical vehicle hurtling toward a crowded crosswalk with malfunctioning brakes: a certain number of occupants will die if the car swerves; a number of **pedestrians** will die if it continues. The car
95 must be programmed to do one or the other.

Philosophical considerations aside, automakers argue it's all but bunk—it's so **contrived**.

contrived (adj.): seeming to be false

"I don't remember when I took my driver's licence test that this was one of the questions," said Manuela Papadopol, director of business development and
100 communications for Elektrobit, a leading automotive software maker and a subsidiary of German auto supplier Continental AG.

If anything, self-driving cars could almost eliminate such an occurrence. They will sense such a problem long before it would become **apparent** to a human driver and slow down or stop. Redundancies—for brakes, for sensors—will **detect** danger and react
105 more appropriately.

"The cars will be smart—I don't think there's a problem there. There are just solutions," Papadopol said.

Alan Hall, Ford's spokesperson for autonomous vehicles, described the self-driving car's capabilities—being able to detect objects with 360-degree sensory data in
110 daylight or at night—as "superhuman."

"The car sees you and is preparing different scenarios for how to respond," he said.

Lin said that, in general, many self-driving automakers believe the simple act of braking, of slowing to a stop, solves the trolley problem. But it doesn't, such as in a theoretical case where you're being tailgated by a speeding fuel tanker.

115 Some experts and analysts believe solving the trolley problem could be a simple matter of **regulators** or **legislators** deciding in advance what actions a self-driving car should take in a no-win situation. But others doubt that any set of rules can capture and adequately react to every such scenario.

The question doesn't need to be as dramatic as asking who dies in a crash, either. It
120 could be as simple as deciding what to do about jaywalkers or where a car places itself in a lane next to a large vehicle to make its passengers feel secure or whether to run over a squirrel that darts into a road.

Chris Gerdes, who as director of the Center for Automotive Research at Stanford University has been working with Ford, Daimler, and others on the issue, said the
125 question is ultimately not about deciding who dies. It's about how to keep no-win situations from happening in the first place and, when they do occur, setting up a system for deciding who is responsible.

For instance, he noted California law requires vehicles to yield the crosswalk to pedestrians but also says pedestrians have a duty not to suddenly enter a crosswalk against the light. Michigan and many other states have similar statutes.

Presumably, then, there could be a circumstance in which the responsibility for someone darting into the path of an autonomous vehicle at the last minute rests with that person—just as it does under California law.

But that "forks off into some really interesting questions," Gerdes said, such as whether the vehicle could potentially be programmed to react differently, say, for a child. "Shouldn't we treat everyone the same way?" he asked. "Ultimately, it's a societal decision," meaning it may have to be settled by legislators, courts, and regulators.

Researchers, automakers, academics, and others understand something else about self-driving cars and the risks they may still pose, namely that for all their promise to reduce accidents, they can't eliminate them.

"It comes back to whether you want to find ways to program in specifics or program in desired outcomes," said Gerdes. "At the end of the day, you're still required to come up with what you want the desired outcomes to be, and the desired outcome cannot be to avoid any accidents all the time.

"It becomes a little uncomfortable sometimes to look at that."

The Hard Questions

Automakers will have to decide what the car "sees" and what it doesn't. Seeing everything around it—and processing it—could be a waste of limited processing power. Which means another set of ethical and moral questions.

Then there is the question of how self-driving cars could be taught to learn and respond to the tasks they are given—the stuff of science fiction that seems about to come true.

While self-driving cars can be programmed—told what to do when that school bus comes hurtling toward them—there are other options. Through millions of computer **simulations** and data from real self-driving cars being tested, the cars themselves can begin to learn the "best" way to respond to a given situation.

For example, Waymo—Google's self-driving car arm—in a recent government filing said through trial and error in simulations, it's teaching its cars how to navigate a tricky left turn against a flashing yellow arrow at a real intersection in Mesa, Arizona. The simulations—not the programmers—determine when it's best to inch into the intersection and when it's best to accelerate through it. And the cars learn how to mimic real driving.

Ultimately, through such testing, the cars themselves could potentially learn how best to get from Point A to Point B, just by having programmed them to discern what "best" means—say the fastest, safest, most direct route. Through simulation and data shared with real-world conditions, the cars would "learn" and execute the request.

At the American Center for Mobility in Ypsilanti, Michigan, where a test ground is being completed for self-driving cars, CEO John Maddox said vehicles will be able to put to the test what he calls "edge" cases that vehicles will have to deal with regularly—such as not confusing the darkness of a tunnel with a wall or accurately predicting whether a person is about to step off a curb or not.

The facility will also play a role, through that testing, of getting the public used to the idea of what self-driving cars can do, how they will operate, how they can be
175 far safer than vehicles operated by humans, even if some questions remain about their functioning.

Most automakers and experts expect some sort of standard to **emerge**—even if it's not entirely clear what it will be.

At SAE International—a global standard-making group—chief product officer Frank
180 Menchaca said reaching a perfect standard is a daunting, if not impossible, task, with so many fluid factors involved in any accident. Speed. Situation. Weather conditions. Mechanical performance.

Even with that standard, there may be no good answer to the question of who dies in a no-win situation, he said. Especially if it's to be judged by a human.

185 "As human beings, we have hundreds of thousands of years of moral, ethical, religious, and social behaviours programmed inside of us," he added. "It's very hard to replicate that."

(1981 words)

Spangler, T. (2017, November 25). Morality, ethics of a self-driving car. *Waterloo Region Record*, p. D8.

After You Read

E. Complete the following sentences to demonstrate your comprehension. When you have finished, discuss your answers with the class.

1. The author starts the article with the description of the hypothetical

   situation because _____

2. The author states that the benefits of self-driving cars include

   _____

   _____

3. According to the author, the essential question about self-driving cars is

   _____

4. The author establishes authority by _____

5. According to Van Lindberg, situations that could cause problems for

   autonomous cars include _____

   _____

6. To demonstrate people's concerns about the choices autonomous vehicles

   will make, the author _____

   _____

7. The author includes a fact from the American Automobile Association

   to demonstrate that members of _____

   _____

8 Patrick Lin believes that some automakers _____

_____

9 The trolley problem is a hypothetical situation in which an observer, seeing

a runaway trolley, _____

_____

10 Ultimately, while autonomous cars will reduce the number of accidents,

they can't _____

11 Frank Menchaca believes that _____

_____

_____

MyBookshelf > My eLab >
Exercises > Chapter 5 >
Morality, Ethics of a Self-Driving Car

F. As a class, discuss the following question: If you had an autonomous vehicle waiting for you outside right now, would you use it to take a long trip? Why or why not?

FOCUS ON ACCURACY

Expressing Uncertainty

When we write about an evolving issue, like the development and adoption of self-driving cars, there will always be some uncertainty about the future. Writers can express this uncertainty in a variety of ways, for example, by strategically combining the use of modals (e.g. *could*, *should*, *may*) with other language elements. Here are some sentences from Readings 1 and 2 to analyze.

A. Read the sentences and underline the modals. When you finish, compare your answers with a classmate's.

1 A dropped phone call is annoying to consumers, but a lost connection for a driverless car <u>could</u> be deadly.

2 Addressing relevant issues and making sure regulatory rules are clear should be high priorities in all the countries considering autonomous vehicles.

3 How should programmers build ethical choices into automated features and advanced algorithms?

④ Self-driving cars could save tens of thousands of lives each year, Shariff said. But individual fears could slow down acceptance, leaving traditional cars and their human drivers on the road longer to battle it out with autonomous or semi-autonomous cars.

⑤ Automakers and suppliers largely downplay the risks of what in philosophical circles is known as "the trolley problem"—named for a no-win hypothetical situation in which, in the original format, a person witnessing a runaway trolley could allow it to hit several people or, by pulling a lever, divert it, killing someone else.

⑥ Some experts and analysts believe solving the trolley problem could be a simple matter of regulators or legislators deciding in advance what actions a self-driving car should take in a no-win situation.

⑦ The question doesn't need to be as dramatic as asking who dies in a crash, either. It could be as simple as deciding what to do about jaywalkers or where a car places itself in a lane next to a large vehicle to make its passengers feel secure or whether to run over a squirrel that darts into a road.

⑧ Presumably, then, there could be a circumstance in which the responsibility for someone darting into the path of an autonomous vehicle at the last-minute rests with that person—just as it does under California law.

⑨ Seeing everything around it—and processing it—could be a waste of limited processing power.

⑩ Then there is the question of how self-driving cars could be taught to learn and respond to the tasks they are given—the stuff of science fiction that seems about to come true.

⑪ Ultimately, through such testing, the cars themselves could potentially learn how best to get from Point A to Point B, just by having programmed them to discern what "best" means—say the fastest, safest, most direct route.

⑫ In everyday driving, such no-win choices may be exceedingly rare but, when they happen, what should a self-driving car—programmed in advance—do?

⑬ It's not just a theoretical question anymore, with predictions that in a few years, tens of thousands of semi-autonomous vehicles may be on the roads.

⑭ How that question gets answered may be important to the development and acceptance of self-driving cars.

B. Review the sentences in task A again, this time looking for evidence that the author is asking questions: either the sentence is a question, or it contains the word *question*. Put a star beside these sentences.

C. Review the following sentences from task A one more time, and circle specific words that suggest uncertainty. Write them next to the sentence numbers below. These words are often used to express an uncertainty.

Sentence 7 _whether_   Sentence 11 _____

Sentence 8 _____   Sentence 13 _____

Sentence 10 _____

D. Based on tasks A, B, and C above, list three techniques that writers can use to express uncertainty.

• _____

• _____

• _____

E. Using these techniques and the topics listed below, write sentences that express uncertainty about the future of self-driving cars. After, share your best sentences with your class.

1 Development of a national policy framework for self-driving cars in China

_____

_____

2 Greater investment in highway infrastructure in China

_____

_____

3 Improved capability in artificial intelligence in Europe

_____

_____

4 More development in high-definition mapping and data analytics in Japan and Korea

_____

_____

MyBookshelf > My eLab >
Exercises > Chapter 5 >
Accuracy Review

FOCUS ON WRITING

Writing Conditionally

In addition to the techniques described in Focus on Accuracy (page 162) to express uncertainty, writers can use conditional sentences (and variations on conditional sentences) to show that what happens next depends on certain conditions.

Conditional sentences often start with *if* in a subordinate clause to express a cause and effect relationship (e.g., If A, then B). You may be familiar with the standard patterns of verb tense use in conditional sentences. These patterns are summarized in the next table.

CONDITIONAL SENTENCE PATTERNS	VERB FORM IN THE *IF*-CLAUSE	VERB FORM IN THE RESULT CLAUSE	EXAMPLE
❶ Present time, true condition	Present	Present	If I <u>see</u> a self-driving car on the road these days, I <u>am</u> surprised.
❷ Future time, true condition	Present	Future	If a self-driving car <u>has</u> an accident, the driver of the car <u>will be</u> angry.
❸ Present time, untrue condition	Simple past	*Would* + base form *Could* + base form *Might* + base form	If self-driving cars always <u>made</u> the best driving decisions, humans <u>would be</u> happy to buy them. If a self-driving car <u>were</u>* for sale, people <u>would buy</u> it.
❹ Past time, untrue condition	Past perfect	*Would have* + past participle *Could have* + past participle *Might have* + past participle	If the development of self-driving cars <u>had been</u> simple, automakers <u>would have succeeded</u> before now.

*The verb *be* in this pattern is irregular, with both singular and plural subjects followed by *were*.

As is common in advanced texts, the cause and effect relationships expressed in the conditional sentences in Readings 1 and 2 follow variations of these standard patterns. The authors strategically use verb tenses to express uncertain circumstances. You will analyze some conditional sentences from these two readings in the following tasks.

A. Read the sentences and underline the *if-clauses* and the *verbs* in the results clauses. When you finish, compare your answers with a classmate's.

❶ Yet they [the governments and automakers in Japan and Korea] have to decide whether autonomous vehicles represent a high priority for them. If [this is] so, they <u>should invest</u> resources in artificial intelligence, high-definition mapping, and data analytics, which are key to the future of this sector.

❷ If car developers can overcome these barriers, there will be substantial advances for transportation and society.

❸ For example, if an automated car is facing the outcome between hitting one child or a group of ten kids, how does it make that choice?

❹ Last month, Sebastian Thrun, who founded Google's self-driving car initiative, told Bloomberg that the cars will be designed to avoid accidents, but that "If it happens where there is a situation where a car couldn't escape, it'll go for the smaller thing."

❺ A certain number of occupants will die if the car swerves; a number of pedestrians will die if it continues.

❻ If anything [were to happen], self-driving cars could almost eliminate such an occurrence.

❼ "Even with that standard, there may be no good answer to the question of who dies in a no-win situation," he said. "Especially if it's to be judged by a human."

B. Review the sentences in task A again. In the first column of the table below, write the number of the sentence that follows the pattern (and pattern variations) described in the second column.

SENTENCE	CONDITIONAL PATTERN AND VARIATION
1	Pattern 1, using modal *should* in the results clause
	Pattern 3, no variation
	Pattern 1, using present continuous in the *if*-clause, and present (in question form) in the result clause
	Pattern 1 using modal *may* in the results clause; *if*-clause is in a separate sentence that is not correctly punctuated, causing a sentence fragment
	Pattern 2, *if*-clauses and results clauses are reversed
	Pattern 2, using modal *can* in the *if*-clause
	Pattern 2, using present in the *if*-clause and future in the result clause (no variation although the *where* phrases are confusing)

C. Review the sentences in task A again and put a star beside the ones that are either questions or that contain the word *question*.

D. Working with a partner, write conditional sentences (using either standard verb tense patterns or variations) about self-driving cars based on the topics below. You will use conditional sentences when you write your Final Assignment.

① Simplified national-level regulations for self-driving cars in the United States

_____

_____

② More national-level laws about data protection in the United States

_____

_____

③ Greater public acceptance of autonomous vehicles

_____

_____

④ More clarity about how self-driving cars will make decisions in no-win situations

_____

_____

MyBookshelf > My eLab > Exercises > Chapter 5 > Focus on Writing

E. When you have finished, share your best sentences with your class.

The Social Life of Autonomous Cars

The author reports on observations made during a study based on video recordings of self-driving cars. The videos reveal that human drivers and autonomous vehicles don't always interpret traffic conditions in the same way.

VOCABULARY BUILD

A. Select the best words from the box to replace the bold key words in the sentences.

> ~~adapting~~   authorities   cease   corpus   functions   insufficient
>
> interpret   revelation

① These videos reveal some of the challenges of **modifying** _____adapting_____ autonomous cars to human social activity on the road.

② Although the Google car edges forward, the motion is **inadequate**

_____ to signal an urgency to proceed.

③ We collected a **group** _____ of ninety-three video clips—totalling 10.5 hours—recorded in the US, the UK, Germany, France, Sweden, Hong Kong, Iceland, and Canada.

④ Human drivers also **infer** _____ other drivers' inaction.

⑤ Hours after the video appeared on YouTube, California **regulators**

_____ forced Uber to **stop** _____ testing until it had obtained proper permits.

⑥ Perhaps the most interesting **surprise** _____ comes from interactions between such cars and other drivers.

⑦ Cars such as the Tesla Model S and the Volvo XC90 now feature advanced

self-driving **abilities** _____, with tens of thousands of these vehicles on roads worldwide and more appearing every year.

MyBookshelf > My eLab > Exercises > Chapter 5 > Vocabulary Review

Before You Read

When we think of autonomous cars, we envision a future where all cars are self-driving—where all vehicles will be programmed to understand when to stop or proceed, accelerate or decelerate, and maintain or change lanes. However, in reality, as we move toward this ideal future, human-driven cars will share the road for many decades with semi-autonomous and autonomous cars. Automakers and researchers anticipate that this transition phase will cause some challenges. Humans will not share the programmed understanding of self-driving cars, and the human drivers may not make predictable driving decisions.

A. Working in a small group, consider the following driving situations. Take point-form notes on your thoughts about possible problems.

SITUATIONS	HUMAN-DRIVEN VEHICLES	AUTONOMOUS VEHICLES	POSSIBLE PROBLEMS
1. Three cars: In car 1, the human driver sees car 3 entering the highway up ahead. Car 2 (self-driving) needs to change lanes to make room for car 3.	In car 1, the human driver politely leaves space for car 2 (self-driving) to move into.	Car 2 (self-driving) doesn't interpret the car 1 human behaviour as an opportunity to change lanes.	*Human driver will be frustrated by the lack of response from the autonomous car. If car 2 changes lanes after a hesitation, it might cut off car 1.*
2. Three cars: Cars 1 and 2 are self-driving and waiting at a stoplight. They leave a big space between them for safety. In car 3, the human driver wants to move into the same lane as cars 1 and 2.	The human in car 3 sees a big space between cars 1 and 2.	Cars 1 and 2 continue to leave a big space between them.	
3. Two cars: Cars are waiting at a stop sign. Car 1 is a self-driving vehicle and should move through the intersection first. Car 2 is human driven.	The car 2 driver is waiting for car 1 to move through the intersection.	Car 1 is programmed to roll forward cautiously to signal intention to move through the intersection.	
4. Two cars: There is an accident on the road ahead. Car 1 (self-driving) slows down for safety.	The human driver in car 2 wants to move more quickly to pass the accident.	Car 1 proceeds slowly.	

B. When you have finished, discuss the possible problems your group identified with the class.

C. Do you believe that autonomous cars should be identified in some way so that human drivers can recognize them? Why? Discuss your answer with a partner.

While You Read

D. As you read, you will come across three situations described above in task A and their outcomes. For each situation, write what actually happened.

SITUATION	ACTUAL OUTCOME
1	

SITUATION	ACTUAL OUTCOME
2	
3	

The Social Life of Autonomous Cars

Until the day comes when all vehicles are fully autonomous, self-driving cars must be more than safe and efficient—they must also understand and interact naturally 5 *with human drivers.*

Cars such as the Tesla Model S and the Volvo XC90 now feature advanced self-driving **functions**, with tens of thousands of these vehicles on roads worldwide and 10 more appearing every year. In addition, Tesla and other companies like Delphi and Google are testing fully autonomous cars, which have travelled millions of miles on American roads.

15 We're in the midst of a global field test of autonomous driving technology, yet results from these tests are proprietary, with little publicly available data. Occasionally, flaws in the technology are exposed by videos taken by in-car **dashcams** and passengers' mobile phones and uploaded to social media sites like YouTube, prompting media discussion and sometimes controversy. For example, in December 2016, on the 20 first day of a trial launch of a fleet of Uber self-driving cars with human monitors in San Francisco, a motorist's dashcam captured one such car driving through a red light and narrowly missing a pedestrian. Hours after the video appeared on YouTube, California **authorities** forced Uber to **cease** testing until it had obtained proper permits (Rodriquez, 2016).

25 At Stockholm University, we've developed a new method that provides a quick, partial view of self-driving systems using public videos (Brown & Laurier, 2017). These videos reveal some of the challenges of **adapting** autonomous cars to human social activity on the road.

Repurposing Online Videos

30 YouTube is the world's largest **repository** of **third-party** videos. For our first study, we used a range of terms to search this repository for clips involving both semi-autonomous cars with driver-assistance functionality and fully autonomous test cars. We mostly excluded promotional videos and instead focused on reviews and travelogues, many of which contain long stretches of silent driving and commentaries 35 on system actions.

dashcam (n.): camera placed on the dashboard of a car to record what happens on the road ahead

repository (n.): space in which large quantities of things are stored

third-party (n., used as adj.): someone who is not one of the main two people involved

We collected a **corpus** of ninety-three video clips—totalling 10.5 hours—recorded in the US, the UK, Germany, France, Sweden, Hong Kong, Iceland, and Canada. The average length is nine minutes, with seven of the clips over thirty minutes. Most illustrate Tesla's driver-assistance
40 system, Autopilot, and three show similar systems in the Volvo XC90 and a Honda Civic. Nine videos, totalling eleven minutes, recorded Google's self-driving cars. In addition, a South by Southwest (SXSW) presentation on the Google project shows several interesting incidents.

The Social Road

45 We drew upon well-established linguistic and sociological methods that analyze unobtrusive video recordings of humans to better understand driving behaviour and some of the potential problems posed by autonomous vehicles. Perhaps the most interesting **revelation** comes from interactions between such cars and other drivers …

50 In the YouTube videos we collected, most of the time Autopilot drives without incident. Yet, due to its simple mechanics, Autopilot sometimes misunderstands other drivers' actions. While people can often discern other drivers' intentions as well as mood or character—aggressive, hesitant, selfish, unpredictable, and so on—based on changes (or the absence of changes) in their car's speed, direction, and so on, Autopilot lacks
55 this ability.

Consider, for example, this fairly common situation. On a divided highway with two lanes in each direction, a Tesla driver is in the right lane in heavy traffic. Ahead on his right he sees a pickup truck merging onto the highway from a connector road. The Tesla driver activates his left-turn signal, indicating his desire to move to the left
60 lane to make room for the truck. A driver in a silver car approaching from behind in the left lane sees the signal and stops accelerating, offering a space for the Tesla driver to enter. Autopilot, however, doesn't recognize this polite "gesture" and continues to maintain the Tesla's position. The silver car's driver, concluding that the Tesla driver has rejected the offer, starts accelerating again. Autopilot, determining the lane change
65 to still be safe, directs the Tesla to move over.

The action produced by the Tesla's robotic coordination might not "bother" another autonomous driving system, but the silver car's driver understandably perceives this as doubly rude: the Tesla driver first apparently rejects his offer and then cuts in front of him at the last second. The Tesla driver acknowledges this rudeness in the video:
70 "Well, we pulled in ahead of that guy and from what I saw it wasn't something he was exactly encouraging."

This example demonstrates that, even if autonomous cars can be safe and reliable, they fail to recognize the social nature of the road. Human drivers aren't always "in tune" with one another, but they're not just algorithmic agents—in most cases they
75 can detect the same kind of subtle cues that we exhibit in personal interactions.

Seeing a Gap as Just a Gap

In addition to not understanding what others on the road are doing, autonomous driving systems have trouble recognizing what their own actions might communicate to human drivers. In this example, a human driver crosses a four-lane highway and
80 then enters a left-turn lane just before an intersection, squeezing his red vehicle in the narrow space between two self-driving cars …

Yet, while the human driver might not show the best judgment, his behaviour is understandable. As drivers, we learn the importance of maintaining a safe distance behind the car ahead. This principle is likewise incorporated into autonomous driving
85 systems. In this case, the second self-driving car slowly approaches the intersection and leaves a gap between itself and the first self-driving car. However, as the Tesla example shows, gaps in the road aren't just safe following distances—they can also be **interpreted** by other drivers as offers to enter the space. The human driver might have perceived the gap between the self-driving cars as such an offer.

90 The driver might also simply have tried to force his way in. People don't always drive sensibly or legally, especially in situations that can lead to anger or confusion such as in construction zones or heavy traffic. On busy roadways, some drivers will exploit any space they can find. In this case, the self-driving car approaching the intersection dealt with the human driver's action appropriately, slowing down and allowing the
95 red vehicle to enter the space.

Sometimes It's Good to Be a Creep

Human drivers also interpret other drivers' *inaction*. This too can cause problems for autonomous driving systems … In this example, a Google self-driving car arrives at a four-way stop just before a driver in a white car on the cross street. Research on
100 four-way stops underlines the importance of creeping into the intersection to let other drivers know that you're attentive to the situation and ready to take your turn. Although the Google car edges forward, the motion is **insufficient** to signal an urgency to proceed. The driver on the cross street interprets this as hesitation and accordingly moves into the intersection first. This causes the Google car to brake abruptly, much
105 like a novice driver, which in turn causes the driver behind to also stop quickly to avoid a rear-end collision.

Our videos also show drivers, apparently annoyed by the Google car's slowness, **tailgating** the vehicle to "urge" it forward through intersections.

tailgating (v.): driving too close to the back of the car in front

Conclusion

110 My goal here isn't to critique the current generation of self-driving cars, which are still in the early stages of development. Rather, it's to point out that driving isn't just a mechanical operation but also a complex social activity. Until the day comes when all vehicles are fully autonomous, self-driving cars must be more than safe and efficient—they must also understand and interact naturally with human drivers. So
115 long as most vehicles on the roadway continue to be operated by people, self-driving car designers must consider how their choices impact other drivers as well as their own vehicles' passengers. If not, the social road could get a lot bumpier.

(1300 words)

References

Brown, B., & Laurier, E. (2017). The trouble with autopilots: Assisted and autonomous driving on the social road. In *Proceedings of the 2017 CHI Conference on Human Factors in Computing Systems (CHI '17).* (pp. 416–429). New York, NY: ACM. doi: 10.1145/3025453.3025462

Rodriguez, J. F. (2016, December 14). Video appears to show Uber self-driving car running red light in SF. *San Francisco Examiner.* Retrieved from www.sfexaminer.com/uber-self-driving-vehicle-appears -launch-red-light-first-day-sf

Brown, B. (2017, February). The social life of autonomous cars. *Computer, 50*(2), 92–96.

After You Read

E. Indicate whether the following statements are true or false. For each false statement, write a true one on a separate page. Share your answers with the class.

STATEMENTS	TRUE	FALSE
1 There are many companies testing self-driving cars, and the results are easily accessible to the public.		
2 Sometimes people notice autonomous cars in test conditions and record the pilot test by dashcam.		
3 In a pilot test of Uber's self-driving cars, a dashcam (belonging to a human driver) recorded one of the autonomous vehicles nearly hitting a pedestrian.		
4 Authorities allowed Uber to continue with the pilot test.		
5 For this study, the author used ninety-three videos of autonomous and semi-autonomous cars uploaded to YouTube.		
6 The videos were recorded by drivers in other autonomous cars.		
7 Self-driving cars are very good at determining the mood of human drivers.		
8 Human drivers may interpret safe distances between autonomous cars as opportunities to move into a lane.		
9 Autonomous cars are programmed to be cautious at four-way stop intersections. Human drivers may misinterpret this caution.		
10 If human drivers knew that another car was autonomous, they would slow down and give the car plenty of room.		

MyBookshelf > My eLab >
Exercises > Chapter 5 >
The Social Life of Autonomous Cars

F. With the class, discuss the following question: Do you believe that driving is a simple mechanical operation or a complex social activity?

FOCUS ON CRITICAL THINKING

Identifying Causes and Effects

Now that you have read the three texts in this chapter, you have a good understanding of the technological and regulatory challenges (from Reading 1), the moral issues (from Reading 2), and the complex social interactions (from Reading 3) related to self-driving cars. As you prepare to write your Final Assignment, it will be useful for you to think critically about what it will take for people to adopt self-driving cars.

A. Work in a small group to brainstorm conditions that would have to exist for self-driving cars to replace conventional cars. On a separate page and using the table below as a model, list those conditions in the first column. In the third column, brainstorm conditions that would lead to self-driving cars not being successful.

CONDITIONS → (CAUSES)	POSITIVE EFFECT	CONDITIONS → (CAUSES)	NEGATIVE EFFECT
• *Fuel prices rise.*	Self-driving cars (which should use less gas) replace conventional cars.	• *A new technology is developed that is more appealing than self-driving cars.*	Self-driving cars are not successful.

FINAL ASSIGNMENT
Write an Extended Cause and Effect Essay

A cause and effect essay explains how conditions (or causes) influence outcomes (or effects). Like many essays, a cause and effect essay starts with an introduction (that includes a thesis statement) and ends with a conclusion. The body of the essay presents the various causes and their possible effects. You worked as a group to brainstorm possible causes and effects in Focus on Critical Thinking. Now, work on your own to write a cause and effect essay that responds to this question:

> What technological, moral, and social variables (causes) will influence the adoption (effect) of self-driving cars?

A. Integrate the summary you wrote in the Warm-Up Assignment (page 154). Include paraphrases and summaries (as appropriate) from the three readings. Write accurate in-text citations and references to document which information comes from which source.

B. As you write, use modals and specific vocabulary to help you express uncertainty. Write conditional sentences (using both standard verb patterns and variations) to show how what happens next depends on certain conditions.

Refer to the Models Chapter (page 287) to see an example of a cause and effect essay and to learn more about how to write one.

Critical Connections

Thinking critically about causes and effects can be a good way to generate new knowledge and deepen your understanding of issues. In this chapter, you carefully considered the causes that might affect the success of self-driving cars. Now apply this new way of thinking to other issues to gain new insights.

A. Work with a small group to identify the causes that will determine the success (or lack of success) of one or two of the following initiatives. For each initiative, replicate the table from Focus on Critical Thinking to record your ideas. When you have finished, share your ideas with your class.

Initiatives:
- Development of a global language such as Esperanto
- Widespread use of drones for agriculture
- Development of ultra-private smartphones
- Possibility of "smart" wind and solar power
- Development of a global curriculum
- Ability to print in 3-D using a material other than plastic
- Ability to transport vaccines without requiring cold storage
- Widespread adoption of instantaneous translation technology, making language learning obsolete

CHAPTER 6

High Technology in Higher Education

Technology is a powerful tool that influences many areas of our lives. We use it to connect with friends, accomplish our work, and pursue our hobbies. In addition, we can use technology to help us learn. However, the use of technology in higher education is not always successful. Effective use of educational technology must be premised on comprehensive knowledge of how people learn best. How can technology be used most effectively in college and university classrooms to support student learning?

In this chapter, you will

- learn vocabulary about technology and higher education;

- identify characteristics of different writing styles;

- recognize verb tense patterns in informal and academic writing;

- understand the importance of maintaining authentic voice;

- evaluate information for annotated bibliographies;

- learn to exploit your library's resources;

- write short and longer annotated bibliographies.

GEARING UP

A. Working with a partner, list the kinds of digital technology you use for the following purposes in your lives.

CONNECTING WITH FRIENDS	WORKING EFFICIENTLY	PURSUING HOBBIES	STUDYING

When you have finished, join another group and compare your answers.

B. With your new combined group, discuss the technologies you have used to help you study. Talk about your best and worst experiences with technology in a classroom or other educational setting. Then select the very best and worst of the stories to share with your class.

Below are the key words you will practise in this chapter. Check the words you understand, then underline the words you use. Highlight the words you need to learn.

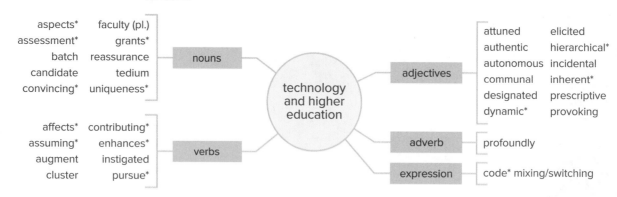

nouns		adjectives	
aspects*	faculty (pl.)	attuned	elicited
assessment*	grants*	authentic	hierarchical*
batch	reassurance	autonomous	incidental
candidate	tedium	communal	inherent*
convincing*	uniqueness*	designated	prescriptive
		dynamic*	provoking

technology and higher education

verbs		adverb	
affects*	contributing*	profoundly	
assuming*	enhances*		
augment	instigated	expression	
cluster	pursue*	code* mixing/switching	

*Appears on the Academic Word List

READING 1 — Using Technology as a Learning Tool

The author of this reading identifies himself as a "Net Gener," a person who is part of the Internet Generation who grew up using technology in all areas of his life. Here, he writes about how technology can only be used successfully in higher education if faculty members (professors) understand how Net Geners learn best.

A. Read the following sentences with key words from Reading 1 in bold. Choose the best synonym for each key word from the options given.

1 "Does this mean that interactive technology is bad for the classroom? No. It means that it should simply **augment** what is already there," Assa continued.

    a) assess   b) evaluate   c) strengthen

2 There were numerous computer labs all over campus, and professors actively used **assessment** tools like WebAssign and WebCT in their classes.

    a) evaluation   b) candidate   c) faculty

3 "Historically, **communal** learning has always been the most effective way for educating the student and generating thought-**provoking** discussion in class."

    a) dynamic   d) intense

    b) group   e) communal

    c) unique   f) stimulating

4 Arman Assa, MBA **candidate**, said that learning technology has not advanced enough to replace the social interaction in the classroom.

    a) faculty   b) student   c) employer

5 Patrick is a creative and **dynamic** designer, but he is not a design major—he's in computer engineering.

    a) active   b) argumentative   c) unique

© ERPI • Reproduction prohibited

6 Using technology only **enhances** the hands-on experience; it does not—and cannot—replace human interaction.

    a) pursues   b) delivers   c) improves

7 **Faculty** members can receive **grants** for using technology in the classroom and developing new learning technologies.

    a) staff   d) research money

    b) students   e) gifts

    c) professors   f) approval

8 Net Geners are not locked into one thing although all are highly motivated and **pursue** their interests with passion.

    a) find   b) follow   c) discover

9 Technology must be used for a practical purpose—that is, applied to a final project where creativity and **uniqueness** are required and rewarded.

    a) distinctiveness   b) selectiveness   c) reflectiveness

B. Use the key words from task A to answer these questions.

1 Which key words are associated with colleges or universities?

_____

2 Which two verbs have a similar meaning?   _____

3 Which noun (used as an adjective) can refer to a single professor, a group of professors, a university organizational unit, or a skill that someone has?   _____

4 Which adjective forms collocations with the nouns *learning, land, garden*, and *well*?   _____

5 What verb forms collocations with the nouns *career, interest, goal*, and *policy*?   _____

6 What adjective can have both positive and negative connotations (meanings)?   _____

7 Which key words from task A have not been used in task B?   _____

Before You Read

Skim the reading and complete the following tasks to help you read faster and with greater comprehension.

A. In this article, there are nine headings (not including the title). Although they are all in the same font, some are main headings and some are subheadings. Write the headings in the appropriate column to produce an outline of the article content. When you have finished, check your answers with the class.

HEADING NUMBER	MAIN HEADINGS	SUBHEADINGS
1	*How the Net Gen Learns*	
2		
3		
4		

HEADING NUMBER	MAIN HEADINGS	SUBHEADINGS
❺		
❻		
❼		
❽		
❾		

B. Based on your classification of the headings in the table, work with your class to answer the following questions.

❶ What characteristics does the author believe reflect how the Net Gen learns?

_____

❷ Do you believe that the author is correct? Do these characteristics reflect how you learn? Can you add characteristics that best reflect how the Net Gen learns?

_____

While You Read

C. As you read, list all the technology that is mentioned in the article on a separate page. After, review your list and place a check mark beside the technologies that you have also used. Then, compare your answers with another student. Add any technologies that you use for learning that were not mentioned in the article. You will use this list again as you plan your Warm-Up Assignment.

Using Technology as a Learning Tool, Not Just the Cool New Thing

As a member of the Net Generation, all my life I have been surrounded by advances in digital technology, almost to the point where I cannot do my work as a journalist without it. In university, I used **assessment** tools such as WebAssign and WebCT in classes as supplements to lectures and textbooks. But now technology is advancing at
5 such a rate that traditional ways of teaching and learning are not pushing students and teachers to their full potential … Before curricula can be created to challenge the Net Generation, though, **faculty** must know how Net Geners learn and interact with each other, with technology, and with life in general. Remember that word—*interact*.

How the Net Gen Learns

10 Are you interested in knowing how Net Geners learn? Let me illustrate by using [my experiences and those of my friends].

Learning by Doing

Patrick Clarke, graphics editor for a student newspaper, sits down at a computer and launches Adobe InDesign. He opens a template for the news page and pulls in graphics,
15 pictures, and text. He manipulates the blocks on the virtual newspaper page, moving back and forth between two other Adobe products, Photoshop, and Illustrator. By the time the page is sent to the printer for printing, the elements on the page have been manipulated, edited, and re-edited at least a dozen times. Patrick is a creative and **dynamic** designer, but he is not a design major—he's in computer engineering.

20 Chris Reynolds is a business major and wants to open a music store when he graduates. In his spare time, he is a DJ musician. He spins and mixes his own beats, using a computer, sound-editing software, turntables, and a keyboard. He teamed up with a friend to make a how-to video on spinning. They used digital video and professional editing software to create the video. Because he is a DJ, he worries about court cases
25 involving the music industry. A recent case where the use of "sampling" was ruled illegal hit him hard, as sampling is widely used by DJs when they create their music.

Jake Seaton is a big arts and entertainment fan. He lives and breathes for music, movies, and anything Hollywood. He can tell you about film and music history and can quote even the most obscure lines from zombie movies (his favourites). He also is
30 up-to-date on the latest in computer and console gaming. He chose a multidisciplinary degree in music journalism and has taken distance-education courses. In high school he won a state architecture award and has taught himself to use Photoshop and InDesign.

These are representatives of the Net Generation. They all use computers in their class
35 work and in their hobbies. They have a wide range of interests outside their chosen area of study. They are not locked into one thing, although all are highly motivated and **pursue** their interests with passion. They use the latest in technology, whether cellphones, computers, PDAs, MP3 players, or digital cameras. They expect things to work properly and work fast. They get bored if not challenged properly, but when
40 challenged, they excel in creative and innovative ways. They learn by doing, not by reading the instruction manual or listening to lectures. These are the learners that faculty must reach.

When I first [started university], I
45 came to a public university dedicated to technology. There were numerous computer labs all over campus, and professors actively used assessment tools like WebAssign and WebCT
50 in their classes. In an experimental psychology class, I used SAS statistical software to crunch data I had collected from experiments. I used online message boards to post ideas and
55 criticism in my opinion/editorial writing class.

In my technical document design class, I experienced the best use of technology in a class: hands-on,
60 experimental, and interactive. This course covered the fundamental designs of technical documents: instruction manuals, memos, resumés, and so forth. Taught in a computer lab, the class sat one student to a computer. We learned to use Adobe Pagemaker, the most popular desktop publishing program at the time. With basic exercises from the instructor and trial-
65 and-error assignments with broad guidelines, I learned not only how to use the program but also design fundamentals—by doing the actual design, not by reading it out of a book.

tinkering (v.): making small changes to improve something

This is how the Net Generation learns: by doing … And the same "**tinkering**" practice applies in the classroom: doing hands-on work and working in groups, students
70 get a better grasp of concepts the professor is trying to teach. Using technology only **enhances** the hands-on experience; it does not—and cannot—replace human interaction. There's that word again.

Interaction, not Isolation

Distance education is the popular option for nontraditional learners … In theory, the
75 Net Generation should learn better through Internet courses because they have been surrounded by computers all their lives and know how to use the technology already. [However,] just the opposite is true. Net Geners like the social interaction that comes with being in class with their peers. While they may use technology in their daily lives, relationships are a driving force in the learning process.

80 Jake Seaton, as a part of his multidisciplinary degree, took a video course through distance education—and didn't like it. "I needed the structure of going to class. I would go to my other classes and then come home and have another class to watch on TV," he said. "I didn't like it. At the end of the day,
85 I wanted to be done, not have to work at a class at home."

This is typical among Net Geners: learning through social interaction is important. Feedback from the professor is vital, and working in groups is the norm. Arman Assa, MBA **candidate** and president of PackMUG—the Mac Users' Group
90 at university—said that learning technology has not advanced enough to replace the social interaction in the classroom. "Historically, **communal** learning has always been the most effective way for educating the student and generating thought-**provoking** discussion in class. I don't believe technology has
95 reached a point where we can duplicate that effectively on a computer," Assa said. "Some instructors argue that chat rooms, message boards, and instant messaging are good substitutes, but they are by no means replacements for the exchange of knowledge [face-to-face].

100 "Does this mean that interactive technology is bad for the classroom? No. It means that it should simply **augment** what is already there," Assa continued. "For instance, one of my human resource classes in the MBA [program] has regular classroom discussion, but the instructor augments it with message board interaction. It was a very effective tool for helping introverts who don't talk in class to join the discussion."

…

105 ## Challenges for Higher Education

So what do Net Geners want from learning technology? Interactivity—whether it is with a computer, a professor, or a classmate. They want it; they **crave** it. Traditional lectures are not fulfilling the learning potential of typical students today. Distance education and online courses don't work well with Net Geners—the social component
110 of learning is required. As technology in the classroom progresses, more and more students are going to demand it be included. This will pose challenges, though.

crave (v.): strongly desire something

Funding

First, technology costs money. What else is new? Faculty members can receive **grants** for using technology in the classroom and developing new learning technologies.
115 This is fine on the department level, but for a university to implement learning technology on a massive scale will take [lots of money.]

Access and Skills

Second, students need to be able to use the technology … Colleges need to teach students computer skills beyond the fundamentals. Skills such as digital document
120 archiving, webpage design using Dreamweaver or Flash, setting up wireless networks, and using a firewall are quickly becoming the norm, where in the past they were considered advanced knowledge. Even basic upkeep and troubleshooting are still left up to tech-support hotlines, often located halfway around the world. These are the skills students need to know to be competitive. Many colleges offer introductory
125 courses in computer science that are available as electives in many disciplines. Updating the introductory course curricula—or even standardized tests—will go a

fostering (v.): encouraging

long way in **fostering** computer skills …

Interaction

Third, technology must be relevant and interactive to the coursework. A faculty
130 member who uses PowerPoint in a lecture is not using technology interactively. Students need a practical use for technology, whether to manipulate data or to explore the inner recesses of the human body without cutting up cadavers. Students need to communicate quickly with each other, but in a centralized manner. That is why message boards are great. Members-only message boards allow students and faculty
135 to communicate with each other. Plus, faculty members can use the course lockers during lectures and provide information outside lectures for students to explore at their own pace.

Relevance

Fourth, technology must be used for a practical purpose—that is, taking the
140 fundamentals and technology learned over a semester and applying them to a final project, where creativity and **uniqueness** are required and rewarded. In my technical document design class, we had to create a useful technical document: write the text and design a technical document using Pagemaker. My group designed an instruction booklet for a video game …

145 Using technology for some practical purpose, and not for the sake of using technology, must be the clear objective. "Students are often the guinea pigs in 'IT-enabled' classes as faculty test out whether the latest innovations actually help learning," Assa said. "Some faculty, in an effort to use the latest buzzword or receive the next big grant, are testing technology simply for the sake of technology, rather than using technology
150 as a tool for learning. When people focus too much on technology, they lose sight of the true purpose of technology, which is to facilitate learning in the classroom."

The Next Generation

The next generation of learners will meet and surpass the Net Generation's expectations of educational standards. Those standards will only be met if faculty and administrators
155 today establish the infrastructure of learning technology in the classroom. And this

means not just using PowerPoint in the lecture hall, but understanding how technology can be used to reach the most people in an effective way. It will take great effort on both sides—students and faculty alike—to learn and use technology effectively. But the benefits will be well worth the effort.

(1732 words)

McNeely, B. (n.d.). Using technology as a learning tool, not just the cool new thing. *Educause*. Retrieved from: https://www.educause.edu/research-and-publications/books/educating-net-generation/using-technology-learning-tool-not-just-cool-new-thing

After You Read

D. Write short answers to the following questions. When you have finished, verify your answers with a classmate.

1 Why is it important to understand how the Net Gen learns?

_____

_____

2 Why does the author describe his own and his friends' use of technology?

_____

_____

_____

3 What expectations do Net Geners have of their technology? How do they feel if they are not challenged? How do they respond if they are challenged? How do they learn?

_____

_____

_____

4 What rationale does the author use for discouraging the pursuit of distance (online only) education for Net Geners? Do you agree with the author?

_____

_____

5 What do the author and Arman Assa believe is the place of technology in the classroom?

_____

6 In the last section, the author outlines four challenges to the use of technology in higher education and makes four recommendations. What are his recommendations to encourage technology use?

• _____

• _____

• _____

• _____

7 Who will need to work to successfully integrate technology into higher education?

_____

_____

_____

8 What do you think are the author's criteria for successful technology use in higher education classrooms? Answer this question by completing the following sentence with as many options as possible. Then discuss the options with your class.

Successful technology use in higher education classrooms must ...

- _be interactive;_____

- _____

- _____

- _____

- _____

MyBookshelf > My eLab > Exercises > Chapter 6 > Using Technology as a Learning Tool

FOCUS ON CRITICAL THINKING

Identifying Characteristics of Different Writing Styles

You can learn a lot about writing by identifying features that are unique to different styles of writing. In this section, you will identify the various features that can be placed along the spectrum between academic (formal) and non-academic (informal) writing styles.

A. To focus your attention on the differences and similarities between the styles, begin by reading the introductions to the readings in this chapter. When you have finished, position the three readings on the spectrum between informal and academic (formal) writing. Can you explain your reasons for placing them where you did?

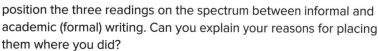

Verbs are in bold to help you answer question 6 in task B.

Reading 1 (page 178)

As a member of the Net Generation, all my life I **have been surrounded** by advances in digital technology, almost to the point where I **cannot do** my work as a journalist without it. In university, I **used** assessment tools such as WebAssign and WebCT in classes as supplements to lectures and textbooks. But now technology **is advancing** at such a rate that traditional ways of teaching and learning **are not pushing** students and teachers to their full potential ... Before curricula **can be created** to challenge the Net Generation, though, faculty **must know** how Net Geners **learn and interact** with each other, with technology, and with life in general. **Remember** that word—_interact_.

© ERPI • Reproduction prohibited

Reading 2 (page 190)
This case study, based on previous research (Bytheway, 2011), **was instigated** in response to informal reports of vocabulary gains of students at Victoria University of Wellington (New Zealand) and the University of Twente (The Netherlands) who **play** massively multiplayer online role-playing games (MMORPGs). This study **examines** and **explains** how in-game culture **affects** vocabulary learning strategies that **are used** by English second language learners in MMORPGs ...

Reading 3 (page 204)
Consumer products like Alexa and Google Home **can tell** us how **to prepare** a meal and **answer** dinner-party trivia questions about the Treaty of Paris. So how long before tools that **are powered** by artificial intelligence **start assuming** more of the classroom work that professors **handle** today?

Informal Writing   Academic (Formal) Writing

Reading 1

_____

_____

_____

_____

_____

B. Answer the following questions to increase your awareness of some key writing features.

1. What perspective (first, second, or third person) is used in each reading?

   Reading 1: _____

   Reading 2: _____

   Reading 3: _____

   What perspective is characteristic of more academic writing?

   _____

2. In which readings do the authors address the reader directly?

   Reading 1: ☐   Reading 2: ☐   Reading 3: ☐

   a) Highlight the sentences in the introductions above where the authors address the reader.

   b) What effect does this have? Is it characteristic of academic or informal writing?

   _____

   _____

③ Which reading(s) use(s) in-text citations (and references, not included here)?

Reading 1: _____

Reading 2: _____

Reading 3: _____

In-text citations are characteristic of what style of writing? _____

④ Which readings use short forms or informal vocabulary? List these indicators of informal writing style next to the appropriate readings below.

Reading 1: _____

Reading 2: _____

Reading 3: _____

⑤ In which reading(s) can you find very long sentences? Is this a characteristic of informal or academic writing?

_____

_____

_____

_____

_____

⑥ Examine the tenses of the verbs that are in bold in the three paragraphs.

a) In which paragraph(s) are the verb tenses most consistent?

_____

b) What pattern of verb tense use is characteristic of informal writing?

_____

c) What pattern of verb tense use is characteristic of academic writing?

_____

⑦ Which paragraphs do you find

a) the easiest to read; why?

_____

_____

b) the hardest to read; why?

_____

_____

c) the most engaging to read; why?

_____

_____

Recognizing Verb Tense Patterns in Informal and Academic Writing

Writers of academic documents are often correctly advised to keep verb tenses mostly consistent. The Introduction in Reading 2 provides an example of mostly consistent verb tense use. Writers of informal documents seem to use greater variety in their verb tenses, as demonstrated in the introductions in Readings 1 and 3.

In many cases, writers use words and short phrases that act as clues to help readers recognize shifts in verb tense and voice.

A. Read the introductions to Readings 1 and 2 again below; this time, the verbs are in bold and indicators that signal shifts in the verb forms are underlined. After, answer the questions that follow.

---

phrase signalling an ongoing state (past to present) described best by present perfect tense

use of simple modal can to show present time

We know the author is a journalist; we assume he went to university in the past; this phrase indicates a move to past tense.

signal that something must happen in order for something else to be possible

use of modal must to show necessity

use of present tense to show truth

Introduction of Reading 1:

As a member of the Net Generation, all my life I **have been surrounded** by advances in digital technology, almost to the point where I **cannot do** my work as a journalist without it. In university, I **used** assessment tools such as WebAssign and WebCT in classes as supplements to lectures and textbooks. But now technology **is advancing** at such a rate that traditional ways of teaching and learning **are not pushing** students and teachers to their full potential ... Before curricula **can be created** to challenge the Net Generation, though, faculty **must know** how Net Geners **learn and interact** with each other, with technology, and with life in general. **Remember** that word—*interact*.

by-phrase signalling passive voice (present perfect tense, passive voice)

This phrase often includes the word now. Although now is not included here, it is implied, and it signals a shift to the present tense

move to present time

use of present progressive to show continuous activity

use of modal can to show possibility, and unsignalled move to passive voice [because curricula are created by teachers]

imperative form to address reader directly

past tense, passive voice (not indicated with a by-phrase)

move to present tense to describe habitual actions

remain in present tense, shift to passive voice

Introduction of Reading 2:

This case study, based on previous research (Bytheway, 2011), **was instigated** in response to informal reports of vocabulary gains of students at Victoria University of Wellington (New Zealand) and the University of Twente (The Netherlands) who **play** massively multiplayer online role-playing games (MMORPGs). This study **examines** and **explains** how in-game culture **affects** vocabulary learning strategies that **are used** by ESL learners in MMORPGs ...

The author uses the past tense to explain why she started this research project.

remain in present tense to describe the study

shift to passive voice signalled by this by-phrase

B. Complete the following sentences based on your analysis of the introductory paragraphs.

1 In some cases, there is a word or phrase that _____ the appropriate verb tense and voice.

2 These indicators can come before or _____ the verb in a sentence.

3 Passive voice *may* be indicated with a _____.

4 Authors of _____ writing generally use a reduced range of verb tenses.

C. Working with a partner, choose either lines 13 to 19 or lines 153 to 159 from Reading 1 (page 178) and analyze the verb tense shifts. Underline the verbs and use arrows to point to the time indicators (if any). When you have finished, check your analysis with another pair of students who worked on the same paragraph. Then, verify your answers with your instructor.

D. On a separate page, write a paragraph (of at least seven sentences) in *informal style* about how technology use among your friends has changed in the last ten years. Use indicators to signal shifts in verb tense and voice. Write at least two sentences in the passive voice. When you have finished, exchange papers with a classmate and edit each other's paragraph. Revise the paragraphs as required, then submit them to your instructor. Write the best ones on the board or post them on a shared website.

MyBookshelf > My eLab > Exercises > Chapter 6 > Accuracy Review

In-Game Culture

Do you play MMORPGs? Massively multiplayer online role-playing games are a form of technology that language learners can use to learn English vocabulary. The author of this journal article examines the vocabulary learning strategies of people who use MMORPG technology.

VOCABULARY BUILD

A. Key words from Reading 2 are listed in the first column of the table. Working with a partner, use the line numbers in the second column to find the words in the reading and use the context to help you write definitions in the third column. Use a dictionary as required.

KEY WORDS	LINE NUMBERS	DEFINITIONS
❶ affects (v.)	12	
❷ aspects (n.)	231	
❸ authentic (adj.)	48	
❹ autonomous (adj.)	5	
❺ contributing (v.)	52	
❻ code switching/mixing (exp.)	123	
❼ elicited (adj.)	10	
❽ hierarchical (adj.)	233	
❾ inherent (adj.)	8	
❿ incidental (adj.)	44	
⓫ instigated (v.)	15	
⓬ prescriptive (adj.)	50	

Before You Read

In this study, students choose MMORPG technology for themselves, for use outside the classroom. Most often, they aren't using the technology to learn vocabulary; rather, language learning is a happy outcome of technology use.

A. In a group of three, discuss the following questions.

① Have you ever played MMORPGs? If so, which ones? Did you use English as your "playing language"? Do you think these games help you learn English vocabulary?

2 Have you ever used other kinds of technology to learn language on your own? For example, have you ever downloaded an application (app) designed to help you learn English? If so, which one(s)? Do you feel you learned some English by interacting with these apps?

3 List the apps you know of that are designed to help you learn languages.

B. Skim Reading 2 and, on a separate page, write all the article headings to create an outline (similar to the one you developed in Reading 1, Before You Read, page 177). When you have finished, compare outlines with a classmate. Based on your outline, what do you think the results of the case study will be? Write your prediction here.

_____

While You Read

C. As you read, complete the following tasks to help you identify the main points in this article.

1 In the abstract, highlight one sentence that explains what the author of this case study researched.

2 In the second paragraph of the Introduction, highlight the two sentences that explain why this research is important.

3 In the Introduction section, in the paragraph that starts with, "Strategies are activities …" highlight the sentence that indicates what the author hopes will happen in classrooms as a result of this research.

4 In the Methodology section, highlight the sentences that describe the data that was collected for this study.

5 In the Results section, highlight the sentence that previews the organization of the rest of the article.

6 Consider headings 4 through 11 that describe the characteristics of MMORPGs; put a star beside the two that you believe are the most helpful for learning new vocabulary. Be prepared to explain your choices.

7 In the Conclusion section, circle the sentence that acknowledges that the research has limitations.

8 In the Conclusion section, highlight the two sentences that summarize the results of this research.

9 In the Conclusion section, underline the sentences that suggest possible directions for further research.

10 Which two sections of the article contain in-text citations that refer to other research in this field? Explain why these citations are only found in those sections.

_____

_____

_____

D. When you have finished, compare answers with a classmate. Discuss your choices for question 6 and your explanation for question 10.

In-Game Culture Affects Learners' Use of Vocabulary Learning Strategies in Massively Multiplayer Online Role-Playing Games

Abstract

Millions of language learners use commercial off-the-shelf computer games as informal learning contexts. Massively multiplayer online role-playing games (MMORPGs) are rich meaningful vocabulary learning contexts with in-game cultures that encourage
5 creativity, decrease anxiety, force interaction, demand cooperative and **autonomous** learning, increase motivation, and reward curiosity. **This case study of World of Warcraft® players examined how the in-game culture affected participants' use of vocabulary learning strategies.** Using research processes **inherent** in Grounded Theory, rich data was collected from MMORPG texts and observations of, interviews
10 with, and **elicited** texts from a criterion sample of six English as a Second Language (ESL) experienced gamers … The results highlight the need to value how the MMORPG culture **affects** language learners' vocabulary learning strategies and argue for study into autonomous language learning in commercial off-the-shelf digital games.

1. Introduction

15 This case study, based on previous research (Bytheway, 2011), was **instigated** in response to informal reports of vocabulary gains of students at Victoria University of Wellington (New Zealand) and the University of Twente (The Netherlands) who play massively multiplayer online role-playing games (MMORPGs). This study examines and explains how in-game culture affects vocabulary learning strategies that are used
20 by ESL learners in MMORPGs …

Learning vocabulary is essential for second language acquisition and can be acquired explicitly and implicitly (Nation, 2001) in formal (in classrooms) and informal (outside classrooms) learning contexts (Ortega, 2009). Vocabulary learning opportunities in informal learning contexts, such as passive media (newspapers, television) are valued
25 by learners and teachers; however, the use of passive media is decreasing and use of interactive media (digital games) is increasing (Williams, Yee, & Caplan, 2008). Informal language learning contexts are changing, and therefore the vocabulary learning strategies that learners create, select, and use are also changing. Learners, teachers, and researchers need to examine how interactive media is affecting
30 learners' vocabulary learning strategies and processes to insure learning in formal contexts remains effective and relevant to language learners' experiences in the real and digital worlds around them.

Strategies are activities learners consciously choose to regulate their language learning (Griffiths, 2008), and language learning
35 strategies become language learning processes when learners use them unconsciously and automatically. Gu (2005) and Nation (2008) assert that vocabulary learning processes can to a considerable extent determine overall success or failure of second language acquisition. Vocabulary learning researchers are
40 increasingly examining "how" people learn. To date, many researchers have used artificial memory and recall tasks to examine psychological memory strategies, such as list learning, short-term recall tasks, initial learning, basic recognition, and

incidental learning. However, the … pedagogical authenticity of many of these
45 experiments is questionable (Gu, 2005). Research that examines learner-centred
contexts (rather than teacher-centred contexts) where learners select vocabulary
items and manage autonomous vocabulary learning is limited to date (Stockwell,
2011). Qualitative research conducted in **authentic** second language learning
environments adds valuable insight from another perspective. It is time that research
50 turned from a **prescriptive** and quantitative focus on how much is learned, what is
learned, and what should be learned, to examining how people learn in complex
learning contexts with multiple and incongruent **contributing** criteria. When we
know how people learn in realistic complex contexts, then we can discover ways to
improve teaching practices, learning strategies and processes, and learning outcomes.

55 MMORPGs are worth examining as language learning contexts because they are
positive learning environments (Steinkuehler, 2007), provide opportunities for
meaningful communication (Thorne, 2008), and are played by millions of people (Yu,
2009). MMORPGs are digital games that are played online by thousands of players
simultaneously in real time. MMORPGs are real-time strategy games where players
60 complete collaborative tasks (such as quests and battles) in teams and guilds, trade
virtual and real items, explore virtual worlds, and interact for social and in-game-
business purposes (Mayra, 2008). To play the game, players must communicate with
each other: meaning-focused written and spoken communication are essential to the
game experience … This study examines World of Warcraft® (Blizzard Entertainment,
65 2004), a commercial off-the-shelf MMORPG.

2. Methodology

A sample of six ESL expert gamers, recruited from Victoria University of Wellington,
volunteered. All participants used English as a second language, had an IELTS
[International English Language Testing System] overall band score of 6.0 to 7.5.
70 All participants were male and aged twenty to thirty. The participants were from
Germany, Malaysia, Ukraine, and Vietnam, and two of the participants were
from China. Their first languages were German, Hokkien, Russian and Ukrainian,
Vietnamese, and Mandarin. All of the participants had completed secondary
education and three of the participants had completed undergraduate qualifications.
75 Participants' fields of studies and professions included foundation studies, aviation
management, marketing, and electrical and mechanical engineering. The participants
had played MMORPGs for at least five hours every week for more than four years
and played several high-level characters (above level 75) in World of Warcraft®,
which is evidence of vast gaming experience and clear status as expert gamers.
80 Data was collected from approximately five hours of observations of gameplay,
approximately six hours of semi-structured interviews, three elicited email texts
and sixty-four World of Warcraft® texts. Observations and interviews were digitally
recorded. During interviews, participants were asked to express personal opinions,
explain ideas further, give specific examples, and share significant stories. [Codes
85 assigned to important information are represented in *italics*.]

3. Results and Discussion

Participants used a variety of vocabulary learning strategies that were affected by the
MMORPG culture, including *requesting/giving explanation, giving/receiving feedback,
observing players, interacting with players, reading in-game information/pop-ups, using
90 word to learn word use, guessing from context, equating image/action to word, recognizing*

incongruent (adj.):
unexpected or incompatible

knowledge gap, selecting words for attention, and looking up words in dictionaries/ Google … MMORPGs are rich informal vocabulary learning contexts with in-game cultures that encourage creativity, decrease anxiety, force interaction, demand cooperative and autonomous learning, and increase motivation.

95 *4. Informal Vocabulary Learning Context*

MMORPGs are rich vocabulary learning contexts. Players are surrounded with huge amounts of meaningful spoken and written English language. The in-game vocabulary includes specialized terms (e.g., *subtlety afflicting*), general service words (e.g., *return instead*) and **Leetspeak** (e.g., *18r nOOb*), which are able to be transferred to and used 100 in other digital and real-world contexts. Although MMORPGs can be played in a huge number of languages, all participants stressed that MMORPGs with an English interface on an English server present a huge variety of English language that they consider meaningful and valuable for vocabulary learning. Observations of participants' gameplay also showed a massive variety and amount of English language on players' 105 screens. Use of the strategy *playing/chatting* in English was continuously observed. Participants usually had multiple texts showing and were continually opening and closing tabs and pop-ups to access, show, and hide further information and settings, and they were also typing chat messages to several different groups of people.

Leetspeak (n.): informal spelling system that combines numbers and letters

5. MMORPG In-Game Culture

110 An in-game culture exists in MMORPGS. Participants were aware of in-game cultural norms and expectations and appeared to want to belong to the MMORPG community. The participants stated that they valued interaction with other players and also a feeling of belonging and being "not foreign": "but you can learn … how to talk to them and … how to be same to them and not act like maybe foreigners." … Participants 115 in this study never referred to native speakers and non-native speakers, but rather spoke about highly proficient (pro) and less proficient (beginner) English language users. MMORPGs are international and nationless virtual environments where "to play" is "to belong." MMORPGs are plurilingual contexts, where English … is used as a convenient language to communicate with other plurilingual members of the game 120 community. Players' vocabulary learning strategies are affected by this plurilingual culture. Standard English is not the participants' objective; instead, effective communication to enable gameplay is the participants' objective. The users of this plurilingual context appear to accept **code switching** and **code mixing** to enable effective communication … Language learners in MMORPGs appear to have a relaxed 125 attitude to language use and readily swap languages and accept non-standard forms of language to facilitate communication between a wide range of community members.

6. Encourage Creativity

Players are encouraged by the in-game cultural norms to try new creative language and learning strategies. The speed of the gameplay affects language use in MMORPGs. 130 All participants stressed how important fast communication was in MMORPGs, and how this need for speed resulted in accepting non-standard English, using in-game short forms, and valuing creating new words. Observations showed that gameplay was fast and required participants to swap quickly between tasks. Participants used the keyboard and mouse to control camera angle and character movement, select 135 and use various skills and weapons, access inventories and other pop-up tabs, and chat. Participants described accepting non-standard language: "I know that people will understand it 'cause they make a mistake when typing as well, 'cause it is really

fast. The game is going really fast," and "in the online games the most critical parts is the
140 speed. You have to keep everything short, simple, and you know, easy to communicate with short forms, and you create your own words out of nowhere. Your own type of spelling forms, for example later we put L8R
145 …" Participants are able to freely use nonstandard (or incorrect) language, and take risks. Participants used the strategy *using word to learn word use*, where they would readily use a word before they understood the meaning,

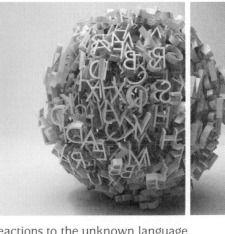
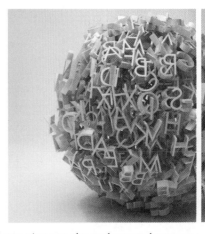

150 or use words in order to test out the use of and reactions to the unknown language. In addition, the need to communicate fast encourages participants to use the strategy *guessing from context* and *equating image/action to word* frequently so as not to interrupt gameplay. The in-game cultural norms relax language norms and increase creative use of language during the language learning process.

155 *7. Decrease Anxiety*

In-game culture also appears to lower learning anxiety and affect creation, selection, and use of vocabulary learning strategies. Participants described how they felt relaxed about language attempts during gameplay and how they experienced decreased learning anxiety. Participants overwhelmingly expressed a casual attitude toward
160 language use in MMORPGs. Participants reported using the vocabulary learning strategy *interacting with players* in a relaxed way: for example, "write more, so just type in and don't worry about the stuff. The more you use it, you will much better. It's more relaxing." Participants also sometimes focused only on receptive skills, and avoided productive skills, and used the strategy *observing players*.

165 *8. Force Interaction*

Interaction and communication are an inherent part of MMORPG gameplay and in-game culture. Participants described interacting with players as an inherent part of playing MMORPGs, an in-game cultural norm. Players complete collaborative tasks (quests and battles), trade virtual and real items, explore virtual worlds, and interact
170 for social and in-game business purposes: all of which require meaningful communication. Interaction is simply something players do to play the game, rather than to purposefully help learn words. The MMORPG cooperative and interactive culture affects participants' use of the vocabulary learning strategy *interacting with players*. Participants frequently used this strategy because of the in-game cultural
175 norm of cooperative play.

9. Demand Cooperative Learning

MMORPGs demand cooperative learning among players. The in-game culture encourages social groups to complete cooperative team tasks and uses both rules of the gameplay and rules of the in-game culture. Participants never used traditional
180 formal-education terms, such as teacher, student, pupil, or learner, to define people's roles when teaching or learning words or gameplay in MMORPGs. Participants appeared to value both learning from other players and teaching other players, and recognized both as valuable for their own vocabulary learning progress.

10. Demand Autonomous Learning

185 MMORPGs demand autonomous learning of both gameplay and language essential for gameplay. Participants took responsibility for their vocabulary learning: "You much more active in the game than in a classroom. You not as shy, so you can easily ask whatever, or say whatever! So you just take responsible." MMORPG culture affects vocabulary learning strategies because the in-game cultural expectation is that people
190 need to learn autonomously and independently ... Players appeared to be motivated to use vocabulary learning strategies because they want to play the game, and they need words to play the game, and also to become active members of the in-game community and culture.

11. Increase Motivation

195 MMORPGs are highly motivating contexts that affect how often and long participants play. A participant described how relevant the learning is in MMORPGs, how motivated he feels in MMORPGs, and the intense level of concentration he achieves in MMORPGs ... It appears that in MMORPGs learners do not need to use strategies to manage their motivation. Instead, the game and in-game culture provide motivation for learning
200 English words and remove responsibility from individual learners to manage their motivation. No participant suggested that they purposefully used a strategy to manage their motivation to learn vocabulary.

12. Conclusion

This study includes limitations such as the small sample size, unknown effect of
205 participants' first and second languages and original and assimilated cultures, possible behaviour change from observations, information change from interviews, and unreliable reporting. However, MMORPG culture affected how gamers used vocabulary learning strategies. Participants of this study purposefully used vocabulary learning strategies within MMORPGs to manage their learning autonomously, without teachers ...
210 directing their learning. [Teachers] need to remember to look outside classrooms, away from material prepared specifically for education, and also examine complex informal learning contexts that learners select themselves. The effects of digital games are often portrayed negatively by the media (Chatfield, 2010; Gee, 2007; Mayra, 2008; McGonigal, 2011; Williams et al., 2008). However, teachers need to **dispel** these negative myths
215 and inform learners about how vocabulary learning strategies can be used in MMORPGs to help the learning of English words. Teachers already encourage the use of passive media such as reading newspapers and watching TV for vocabulary learning, and this encouragement needs to be extended to interactive media such as MMORPGs.

dispel (v.): make something go away

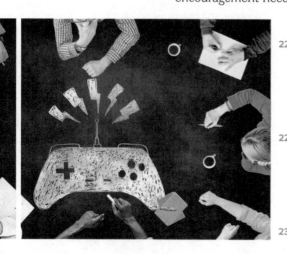

Teachers need to raise gamers' awareness of the vocabulary
220 learning strategies they use in MMORPGs and together explore learners' autonomous learning behaviour in digital game contexts. Gamers should be helped to transfer vocabulary learning strategies they develop and use within MMORPGs to other vocabulary learning contexts, both inside and outside
225 schools and educational institutes. Teachers could have gamers teach the vocabulary learning strategies they use in MMORPGs to other non-gaming learners for use in other vocabulary learning contexts. For many learners, information about how MMORPGs can be used to help vocabulary learning may be
230 valuable and empowering ...

This study skims the surface of many **aspects** of MMORPGs as contexts for vocabulary learning strategies. Ways in which MMORPG culture affects vocabulary learning strategies could be explored further. How do **hierarchical** structures between gamers affect vocabulary learning strategies? How does playing alone or playing
235 collaboratively affect vocabulary learning strategies? … These are just a few ideas for further research. The effects of MMORPG in-game culture and MMORPG contexts on language learning, vocabulary learning, and learning strategies and vocabulary learning strategies are yet to be explored.

(2469 words)

References

Blizzard Entertainment. (2004). *World of warcraft®* [Video game]. Irvine, CA.

Bytheway, J. A. (2011). *Vocabulary learning strategies in massively multiplayer online role-playing games.* (Master's thesis). Wellington, NZ: Victoria University of Wellington; Retrieved from http://researcharchive. vuw.ac.nz/xmlui/handle/10063/1727

Chatfield, T. (2010). *Fun inc.: Why games are the 21st century's most serious business.* London: Virgin Books.

Gee, J. P. (2007). *Good video games + good learning: Collected essays on video games, learning and literacy* (Vol. 27). New York, NY: Peter Lang.

Griffiths, C. (Ed.). (2008). *Lessons from good language learners.* Cambridge: Cambridge University Press. doi: I0.1017/CB09780511497667

Gu, P. Y. (2005). *Vocabulary learning strategies in the Chinese EFL context.* Singapore: Marshall Cavendish Academic.

Mayra, F. (2008). *An introduction to game studies: Games in culture.* Los Angeles, CA: Sage Publications.

McGonigal, J. (2011). *Reality is broken: Why games make us better and how they change the world.* London: Johnathan Cape.

Nation, P. (2001). *Learning vocabulary in another language.* Cambridge: Cambridge University Press. doi:10.1017/CB09781139524759

Nation, P. (2008). *Teaching vocabulary: Strategies and techniques.* Boston, MA: Heinle Cengage Learning.

Ortega, L. (2009). *Understanding second language acquisition.* London: Hodder Education.

Steinkuehler, C. (2007). Massively multiplayer online gaming as a constellation of literacy practices. *E-Learning and Digital Media, 4*(3), 297–318. doi:10.2304/elea.2007.4.3.297

Stockwell, G. (2011). Online approaches to learning vocabulary: Teacher-centred or learner-centred. *International Journal of Computer-Assisted Language Learning and Teaching, 1*(1), 33–44. doi:10.4018/ ijcallt.2011010103

Thorne, S. L. (2008). Transcultural communication in open Internet environments and massively multiplayer online games. In S. Magnan (Ed.), *Mediating discourse online* (pp. 305–327). Amsterdam: John Benjamins Publishing. doi: 10.1075/aals. 3.17tho

Williams, D., Yee, N., & Caplan, S. E. (2008). Who plays, how much, and why? Debunking the stereotypical gamer profile. *Journal of Computer-Mediated Communication, 13*(4), 993–1018. doi: 10.1111/j.1083-6101.2008.00428.x

Yu, T. W. (2009). Learning in the virtual world: The pedagogical potentials of massively multiplayer online role playing games. *International Education Studies, 2*(1), 32–38. doi:10.5539/ies.v2n1p32

———

Bytheway, J. (2014). In-game culture affects learners' use of vocabulary learning strategies in massively multiplayer online role-playing games. *International Journal of Computer-Assisted Language Learning and Teaching, 4*(4), 1–13. doi: 10.4018/ijcallt.2014100101

After You Read

After you have finished these tasks, verify your answers with your class.

E. Answer the following questions.

1 Why did the author instigate research on this topic?

_____

_____

2 How many game players (research participants) took part in this study? Do you think this is a sufficient sample size?

_____

_____

_____

3 In the second, third, and fourth paragraphs of the Introduction, the author uses several arguments to convince readers that this research is important. Put a check mark next to the arguments listed below that the author uses.

AUTHOR'S ARGUMENTS	
1 Vocabulary learning is essential for second language acquisition.	✓
2 Strategy use is an important field of research.	
3 Vocabulary learning strategies become part of language learning processes.	
4 Language learning processes determine (to a considerable extent) language acquisition success.	
5 MMORPGs were designed to enhance language learning opportunities.	
6 Many researchers have studied how people learn, but the research tasks in those studies are not authentic (based on how people really learn).	
7 Teachers should only be concerned with how students learn in classrooms.	
8 Researchers should study learning environments in which learners (rather than teachers) control what is to be learned.	
9 MMORPG players work hard to use accurate English grammar while they play.	
10 MMORPGs are worth studying because they are positive, interactive learning environments used by millions of people.	

4 How did the researcher determine that the participants were expert game players?

_____

_____

_____

5 What data did the researcher gather?

_____

_____

_____

6 List the strategies that the researcher observed the gamers using to learn English vocabulary.

_____

_____

_____

_____

F. Match each characteristic of MMORPGs (in column 1) to its best description (in column 2).

CHARACTERISTICS OF MMORPGS		DESCRIPTION OF THE CHARACTERISTIC
❶ Informal vocabulary learning context	_b_	a) A big part of the game is playing with others cooperatively. Learning from and "teaching" others is a valuable part of players' own language learning.
❷ MMORPG in-game culture		b) Game players use and are exposed to huge amounts of meaningful English language.
❸ Encourage creativity		c) There is no direct instruction on how to play the game. Players are expected to learn on their own as they play.
❹ Decrease anxiety		d) Players must interact with other players who may be high- or low-level English language users; players have a casual and easygoing attitude to in-game language use.
❺ Force interaction		e) When playing, players are intensely absorbed by the game; they do not need to force themselves to concentrate.
❻ Demand cooperative learning		f) Players report using language without worrying about correctness. Players learn by using language and observing other players.
❼ Demand autonomous learning		g) The game is fast and players must respond quickly to play collaboratively. Players use informal language and use language flexibly to communicate their ideas.
❽ Increase motivation		h) Players play collaboratively to accomplish tasks, not to learn language. Interaction is the normal condition in MMORPGs.

G. Although this research is about vocabulary learning strategies MMORPG players use outside of class, the researcher makes recommendations for teachers in the Conclusion. List five of these recommendations.

_____

_____

_____

_____

_____

_____

_____

MyBookshelf > My eLab >
Exercises > Chapter 6 >
In-Game Culture

FOCUS ON READING

Maintaining Authentic Voice

You probably noticed that the author of Reading 2 included quotes to support her points in some sections of the article. As you read, you can *hear* the voices of these expert MMORPG players—who are also intelligent, thoughtful language learners.

A. Return to the following sections of Reading 2 (page 190) and read the quotes indicated by the line numbers. Then work with your class to answer the questions.

- MMORPG In-Game Culture, lines 113–114
- Encourage Creativity, lines 136–144
- Decrease Anxiety, lines 161–163
- Demand Autonomous Learning, lines 186–188

① Why did the author include these quotes?

② We are often less formal when we speak than when we write. Review the quotes again and indicate how you can tell that the players were speaking informally when the author recorded them.

③ Why did the author keep the players' voices? Should she have tried to revise or correct their language?

FOCUS ON WRITING

Evaluating Information for Annotated Bibliographies

In the Warm-Up and Final Assignments, you will write an annotated bibliography to review research on a technology-related topic of your choice. An annotated bibliography is sometimes an assignment by itself; other times, it is the start of a longer report or essay writing process.

An annotated bibliography is a list of references (in the citation format of your discipline), each one followed by one or two short paragraphs. The list is often preceded by a short paragraph that describes the research you are reviewing and the research question that is guiding your search.

The short paragraphs under each reference include both a summary and an evaluation of the information in the original text. Evaluating information is usually more challenging, and perhaps more interesting, than summarizing. As you know, a summary reduces the length of the original text and restates the original author's main points. An evaluation, particularly in an annotated bibliography, is also short; it states your own thoughts about the original text.

The example below follows the format of an annotated bibliography (using APA citation format).

A. Read the paragraphs on the next page and label each one as either a summary or an evaluation. Check your labels with a partner and then work with your class to respond to the questions.

Example of an Annotated Bibliography Entry for Reading 2

Bytheway, J. (2014). In-game culture affects learners' use of vocabulary learning strategies in massively multiplayer online role-playing games. *International Journal of Computer-Assisted Language Learning and Teaching, 4*(4), 1–13.

Label: _____

The author of this research study demonstrates that players of massively multiplayer online role-playing games (MMORPGs) practise multiple vocabulary learning strategies as they play. The researcher suggests that the use of vocabulary learning strategies is a natural outcome of MMORPG in-game culture that encourages learner autonomy and creative, collaborative interaction. Although the participant sample size is small (n=6), the findings of the study are sufficiently encouraging that the researcher concludes with recommendations to teachers to recognize the value of playing MMORPGs.

Label: _____

This article is one of the first to consider the effect of MMORPG in-game culture on the use of vocabulary learning strategies. It would be helpful to know if players/learners actually learn more vocabulary (which words and how many) through their playing. As with any research on language learning, it would be useful to know if players are successful at transferring their new vocabulary and vocabulary learning strategies to other contexts. The researcher seems critical of teachers who, in the past, have undervalued the language learning outcomes of playing MMORPG in relation to passive media such as reading books and watching movies. In the Conclusion, the researcher uses strong language (*need to* and *should be*) to make her recommendations to teachers.

1 Could you simply use the article's abstract for the summary paragraph?

_____

_____

2 What is the difference between the content of the summary and the content of the evaluation?

_____

_____

3 What questions did the writer ask to develop ideas for the evaluation paragraph?

_____

_____

_____

_____

_____

_____

4 Skim both paragraphs and highlight the verbs. What verb tenses does the writer use? If there are shifts in the verb tenses, how are these signalled?

_____

_____

_____

B. To practise, work with a partner and write an annotated bibliography entry for Reading 1 on a separate page. Share your draft with another pair of students and revise it (if necessary) based on their comments. If possible, post your annotations on a shared website to receive further feedback from your classmates or your teacher.

MyBookshelf > My eLab >
Exercises > Chapter 6 >
Focus on Writing

Academic
Survival Skill

Exploiting Your Library's Resources

Although many people don't recognize the importance of libraries to institutions of higher education, it is undeniable that colleges and universities would not exist without them. Access to a good library is a valuable asset. If you attend (or will attend in the future) an institution of higher education, some of your tuition money goes (or will go) to support the library, so it's smart to find out what resources are available through your library.

Your instructor may invite a librarian to speak about what your library can offer, or you might take a tour of your library. Physically going to the library is a good way to see what's available. You should know which computers you can use to access the library catalogues and databases, where the books are kept (often called the book stacks), where the information desk is, and where the circulation and reserve desks are located. Your librarian is the most helpful resource if you have questions about how to find information.

If you don't go to the library in person, you should spend some time becoming familiar with the library's website, which is your gateway to the broadest range of current, reliable information. Using the website is far more efficient than searching the Internet—even using a browser designed for academic study. Through strategic use of the website, you can find information that is selected for you by subject, date, and format (book, journal article, thesis, report, etc.). Accessing information through your library almost assures that the information you find is reliable. And finally, a good library will give you access to information from places near and far.

At a minimum, you should know how to search for books and journal articles on your library's website. Here are some tips that will apply to most libraries.

Search for books when you want to find comprehensive background information on a topic.

- Use the library's online catalogue. If a book you want is in the library, you can find it yourself or put a hold on the book and pick it up when you receive an email indicating it's available.
- If the book you want is out, put it on hold. You will receive an email when the book is available.
- If the library doesn't have the book, submit an interlibrary loan request. You will receive an email when the book is available.

Search for journal articles when you want to find the most recent, specific information on a topic.

- Ask your instructor or librarian which database is the best one for you to use in your field of study.
- Read the abstract first to discover if it is worth your time to read the whole article.
- To read the whole article, link to it electronically.
- If the article you want is not available through your library, submit an interlibrary loan request. Once available, you will receive the article by email.

Sometimes students are intimidated by the library's website. However, you should consider your library as a tool that will help you achieve your academic goals. Learning library research skills will improve your efficiency in your academic work and study.

WARM-UP ASSIGNMENT
Write a Short Annotated Bibliography

Write a short annotated bibliography on a technology-related topic of your choice. To begin, develop a research question to guide your library search. As the key words in this question will determine the information you will find for your bibliography, spend some time thinking about and writing an interesting question.

For this task, write a narrow question in order to limit the amount of information you find.

A. Use one of these questions based on the information in this chapter or develop a question of your own.

- Can the use of MMORPGs help students learn vocabulary?
- Can the use of MMORPGs help students learn other aspects of language?
- Can the use of _____ technology help students learn

  _____ about a language?
- Do members of the Internet generation learn differently from other generations?
- How has technology changed the way people learn?
- What are the challenges of implementing technology in higher education classrooms?
- Why might professors resist the use of new technology in their classrooms?
- Why might students resist the use of new technology in their classrooms?

B. Go to the library (or the website) and find three sources of information that will help you answer your question. You may work with a partner to find the sources, but you should write your own summaries and evaluations. Use appropriate and mostly consistent verb tenses.

You will find that learning library search skills will take some time, especially at first. In addition, writing both a summary and an evaluation of the content will require careful reading and thinking. However, once you are familiar with your library's website search functions and feel comfortable evaluating information, you will become more efficient.

This short annotated bibliography should provide an overview of some of the key research that addresses your question.

C. You will use this assignment as the basis of a longer annotated bibliography in the Final Assignment.

To learn more about how to write an annotated bibliography and see an example, see the Models Chapter, page 289.

When you receive feedback from your instructor or your classmates on this Warm-Up Assignment, you will have information that you can use to improve your writing on the Final Assignment.

READING ③   Can Artificial Intelligence Make Teaching More Personal?

This author reports on several educational technology initiatives that use artificial intelligence (AI) to provide feedback to university students efficiently. Although Reading 1 suggested that Net Geners welcome technology use in their classrooms, not all students like the technology described in Reading 3.

VOCABULARY BUILD

A. Match the key words from Reading 3 with the definitions.

KEY WORDS		DEFINITIONS
❶ assuming (v.)	_____	a) completely or greatly
❷ attuned (adj.) to	_____	b) group things tightly together
❸ batch (n.)	_____	c) something that is said that makes you feel better or less worried
❹ cluster (v.)	_____	d) taking control or responsibility for
❺ convincing (n.)	_____	e) familiar with or aware of
❻ designated (adj.)	_____	f) state of boredom because what you are doing continues for a long time without changing
❼ profoundly (adv.)	_____	g) chosen

KEY WORDS		DEFINITIONS
8 reassurance (n.)	_____	h) group of people or things that can be dealt with together
9 tedium (n.)	_____	i) persuasion

B. Fill in the blanks with the best key words from task A. You may need to change the part of speech of the word (e.g., from verb to noun or vice versa) and the spelling to make the word fit the sentence. Use a dictionary as required.

1 The library's computers are _____ together in the lobby of the building.

2 The increasing use of educational technology is _____ affecting the delivery of course content.

3 During exams, students must leave their devices (cellphones, tablets, and computers) in the _____ area at the back of the room.

4 As technology improves, it can _____ more of the tedious marking that faculty usually complete.

5 To _____ students that they will benefit from machine grading of their assignments is a difficult persuasive task.

6 The technology clusters common errors together; as a result, faculty members become more _____ to the errors students typically make.

7 Once faculty members _____ students that the software doesn't determine their final grade, students are happier about its use.

8 The software _____ similar answers together.

9 Teaching assistants are looking forward to adopting the machine-marking software as it can eliminate much of the _____ workload of marking.

MyBookshelf > My eLab > Exercises > Chapter 6 > Vocabulary Review

Before You Read

A. Work in a group of three and discuss how you would feel about the use of the following technologies in your classroom:

☐ A computer marking your numbers-based assignments

☐ A computer marking your writing assignments

☐ A chatbot (robot) answering your email questions

☐ A robot teaching your class

☐ A computer sending you automated reminders to complete your reading and assignments

In your opinion, would these technologies enhance your learning? Would they make your learning more personal? Are they interactive?

B. Share your group's ideas with your class.

While You Read

C. The author of this text reports on two technology initiatives (included in the list in task A above) used at several universities in the United States. While you read, put a check mark beside the two technologies in the list that are described in this text.

Can Artificial Intelligence Make Teaching More Personal?

Consumer products like Alexa and Google Home can tell us how to prepare a meal and answer dinner-party trivia questions about the Treaty of Paris. So how long before tools that are powered by artificial intelligence (AI) start **assuming** more of the classroom work that professors handle today?

5 The answer is simple: they already have. At the University of Michigan at Ann Arbor, students in a statistics class last fall had their assignments evaluated by an automated text-analysis tool called Gradescope. And in 2016, some of the students in a computer science class at the Georgia Institute of Technology were surprised to learn that one of the TAs answering their questions remotely all semester was actually a chatbot
10 powered by AI.

The bigger question, however, is this: how does teaching change as these AI tools start assuming more classroom work?

That's harder to answer. A new grading tool called Gradescope—powered by AI and now being used for more than 175,000 students at 550 colleges—offers one window
15 on the possibilities.

The tool helps automate the grading process without requiring instructors to rely on multiple-choice tests. Several professors who use it say the automation has actually made it easier for them to personalize their teaching—although some of their students have needed some **convincing**.

20 Instructors also say the technology has made their grading fairer and faster—the latter an especially useful factor for courses like chemistry, in which students' mastery of new material depends on their understanding what came before. "Getting feedback from a test you took two weeks ago is not going to help," says Alegra Eroy-Reveles, an assistant professor of chemistry and biochemistry at San Francisco State University, now in her
25 third year of using the tool. "It's important to get [test results] in a timely manner."

Because Gradescope has made grading tests easier, Eroy-Reveles is giving more of them. Instead of three major exams a semester, she now gives eight smaller tests. "It will take me about three hours to grade about a hundred of them," she says. The tool can read handwritten answers and can group together all the correct formulas
30 in one **batch** and each variation of the wrong answer in separate batches. Thanks to those AI features, she's able to quickly see what her students are missing.

The timesaving tool was developed by Arjun Singh and Sergey Karayev as PhD students at the University of California at Berkeley. Working as TAs in a computer science class on artificial intelligence in 2012, they felt buried by the **tedium** of having to grade a
35 hundred tests by hand and, as Singh recalls, "writing the same thing fifty times as your students make the same mistakes fifty times."

As students of AI themselves, they figured there had to be a way to deploy machine learning to make their own
40 jobs easier. By the summer of 2014 they had written the code that could read students' names off a form and recognize patterns in handwritten answers, such as chemical formulas for acids, as long
45 as they were entered in a **designated** area on standardized test forms. Their software could also identify and **cluster** those answers into groups. "We built this because we wanted a tool for ourselves,"
50 Singh says.

With another college friend and Singh's faculty adviser, they established Gradescope as a company. They hoped that the tool's main AI feature—its ability to read patterns not programmed in ahead of time—would set it apart from the few other automated grading tools in use.

55 The tool doesn't do all the work. Instructors, using a standardized form, must still scan in all the tests and determine how much weight to assign to each answer. That's fundamental to the process, says Singh. For many professors, "the exam is the last line of defence" in a teaching environment increasingly influenced by standardized course materials provided by publishers and other courseware developers. "[Teachers]
60 want to be involved in [developing their own assessments.]"

Seth Anthony, an associate professor of chemistry at the Oregon Institute of Technology, tried Gradescope for a final exam last fall and is now using it for his general chemistry course, which has forty engineering students. He says the tool has made him more **attuned** to the patterns of students' mistakes, which he can more easily spot in weekly
65 quizzes. And because the tool requires him to establish the grading rubric upfront, he says, "I can tell that my grading is fairer as a result."

The AI features in Gradescope "are not **profoundly** deep at this point," he notes. The tool recognizes handwriting and can cluster answers, but it does not actually learn from previous patterns.

70 Still, he appreciates its benefits, even if some of his students have been a bit uneasy about receiving their grades from an automated system. For some of them, he's had to provide **reassurance** that he, as the instructor, was really determining their grades. Artificial intelligence, Anthony says, "enables me to be more personal, but I can see how students would perceive it as more impersonal."

75 "They want the personal touch."

(850 words)

Blumenstyk, G. (2018, April 8). Can artificial intelligence make teaching more personal? *The Chronicle of Higher Education*. Retrieved from: https://www.chronicle.com/article/Can-Artificial-Intelligence/243023

After You Read

D. To demonstrate your understanding of how this text contrasts with Reading 1, choose the best answers to complete the following sentences. Some sentences have more than one answer. When you have finished, discuss your answers with your class.

1. Reading 1 was about how technology use in higher education should benefit (students / professors).

2. Reading 3 described technology use that benefitted (students / professors).

3. The technology initiatives described in Reading 3 were implemented by (students / professors).

4. In Reading 3, the (students / professors) had no control over the technologies.

5. Gradescope (increases / decreases) the tedium involved in grading student work.

6. By grouping correct answers and variations of incorrect answers together, Gradescope allows professors (to avoid marking each test separately / to easily see the most frequently made errors).

7. If Gradescope allows professors to identify common student errors, the reader assumes that professors will (help students correct those errors / modify their teaching so students don't make those errors in the future.)

8. As Gradescope increases grading efficiency, professors can test students (less often / more often).

9. Seth Antony (quoted in Reading 3) believes that using Gradescope has made his grading (more personal / fairer).

10. Students are (excited / unhappy / uneasy) about the use of Gradescope.

11. Students believe that the use of these two technologies makes their educational experience (more personal / less personal).

E. Do you believe that these technologies are good for students as well as professors? Why or why not?

_____

_____

F. What do you think are professors' criteria for successful technology use in higher education classrooms? Answer this question by completing this sentence with as many options as possible. Discuss these options with your class.

Successful technology use in higher education classrooms must ...

_____

_____

_____

_____

MyBookshelf > My eLab >
Exercises > Chapter 6 >
Can Artificial Intelligence Make
Teaching More Personal?

FINAL ASSIGNMENT
Write a Longer Annotated Bibliography

Write a longer annotated bibliography. If you were not happy with your research question in the Warm-Up Assignment, now is the time to revise it. If you were happy with your research question, you can either work with the same question or broaden it to allow for a wider information search.

A. Working on your own, find another three sources that will answer your research question. Write an evaluation of each of the new sources.

B. Combine these three sources with the three from your Warm-Up Assignment to compile an annotated bibliography.

To learn more about how to write an annotated bibliography and see an example, see the Models Chapter on page 289.

Critical Connections

Once you have completed your longer annotated bibliography, you will have six sources that you can use to extend your analysis of common features in academic writing.

A. Set up a table like the one below and review your six sources to confirm if they demonstrate the characteristics of academic writing identified in Focus on Critical Thinking (page 183). For each source, put a check mark beside each characteristic that is reflected in the writing.

CHARACTERISTICS OF ACADEMIC WRITING	SOURCE 1	SOURCE 2	SOURCE 3	SOURCE 4	SOURCE 5	SOURCE 6
❶ Has a third-person perspective						
❷ Does not address the reader directly						
❸ Contains in-text citations and references						
❹ Includes long sentences						
❺ Reflects (mostly) consistent verb tense use						
❻ Contains quotes from study participants, and maintains their "authentic" voices						

B. Do you notice any differences from one source to the next? Can you explain these differences? Compare your table with two other students' tables. This should give you an insight into how common these characteristics are in academic writing and if there is much variation. In many cases, writing in a single style (like academic style) is consistent; however, you can usually observe variations. Working in your group of three, can you find any academic sources that diverge from the typical characteristics of academic writing?

CHAPTER 7

Doping in Sports

Every major sporting event brings news of athletes who have "doped" (used performance-enhancing drugs). Athletes from almost every country and every sport have been disgraced by medical tests that reveal their involvement with drugs. At the centre of the controversy are prominent sports figures like cyclists Chris Froome and Lance Armstrong, and baseball great Roger Clemens. With so many athletes testing positive for performance-enhancing drugs, is it time to legalize their use?

In this chapter,
you will

- learn vocabulary related to the use of drugs in sports;

- use connecting words and phrases common in persuasive arguments;

- synthesize information from multiple sources;

- recognize methods of persuasion;

- persuade by conceding and refuting arguments;

- compare original and summarized/paraphrased writing;

- write a short and a longer persuasive essay.

GEARING UP

DOPING CONTROL STEPS

Get notification

Report to the station

Select collection vessel

Provide sample

Minimum 90 ml of urine

Choose collection kit

Split the sample

Gravity measurement

Fill in the form

A. With your class, discuss what these elite athletes have in common. Can you add any names to this list?

- Lance Armstrong, American cyclist
- Jose Canseco and Roger Clemens, American baseball players
- Kunjarani Devi, Indian weightlifter
- Ben Johnson, Canadian sprinter
- Kostas Kenteris and Ekaterini Thanou, Greek sprinters
- Li Zhesi, Chinese swimmer

B. Do you believe performance-enhancing drugs should be legalized in sports? Survey your class to find the majority opinion. Put a check mark beside the opinion of the class:

☐ Doping in sports should be legal. ☐ Doping in sports should not be legal.

Below are the key words you will practise in this chapter. Check the words you understand, then underline the words you use. Highlight the words you need to learn.

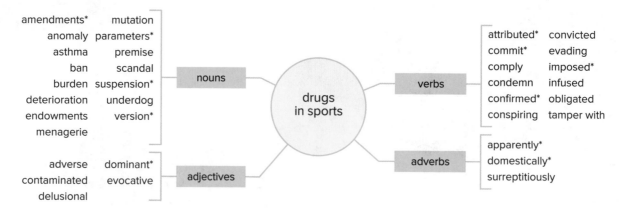

nouns

amendments*
anomaly
asthma
ban
burden
deterioration
endowments
menagerie

mutation
parameters*
premise
scandal
suspension*
underdog
version*

drugs in sports

verbs

attributed*
commit*
comply
condemn
confirmed*
conspiring

convicted
evading
imposed*
infused
obligated
tamper with

adverbs

apparently*
domestically*
surreptitiously

adjectives

adverse
contaminated
delusional

dominant*
evocative

*Appears on the Academic Word List

Chris Froome Tests Positive, and Cycling History Repeats Itself

This article was published in *The New York Times* on December 13, 2017, just after Chris Froome, a well-known competitive cyclist, tested positive for performance-enhancing drug use. Written for the general public, the language is idiomatic and engaging. In July 2018, Froome was cleared of the doping charges.

Christopher Froome in yellow jersey;
Tour de France, 2016

A. The first column of the table provides definitions for key words from Reading 1. Working with a partner, use the line numbers and definitions to identify the key words in the text and write them in the second column. Then answer the questions that follow.

DEFINITIONS AND LINE NUMBERS	KEY WORDS
LINE 3: showed that something was true by providing more proof	1. _____
LINE 4: medical condition that makes it hard to breathe	2. _____
LINE 14: event in which someone, especially someone important, behaves badly in ways that shock other people	3. _____
LINES 21, 57: when something is officially stopped for a period of time	4. _____

DEFINITIONS AND LINE NUMBERS	KEY WORDS
LINE 22: official order that prevents something from being done	5. _____
LINE 28: believed or said that a situation or event was caused by something else	6. _____
LINE 43: copy of something that has been changed slightly from the original	7. _____
LINE 51: idea that you accept is true and is the basis for developing other ideas	8. _____
LINE 60: more powerful or important than other people or things	9. _____

B. Answer the questions by filling in the blanks with the appropriate key words from the table above.

1. Which two words indicate forms of punishment for an athlete who is caught doping? _____

2. Which word indicates a type of illness? _____

3. What situation is especially embarrassing for a well-known person? _____

4. If athletes all have slightly different explanations for a doping scandal, they have their own _____ of what really happened.

5. If doctors prescribe drugs that help athletes recover faster from extreme training, the increase in doping in sports could be _____ to these drugs.

6. If you believe the _____ that athletes can't win unless they dope, you are more likely to believe that all athletes dope.

7. The well-known professional cyclist Lance Armstrong avoided a doping scandal for a long time because there were no medical tests that _____ he had used drugs.

8. Professional cyclists who doped were _____ in their sport over many years.

C. There are several idiomatic expressions that will be helpful to know. Match each idiomatic expression in column 1 with its definition in column 2. When you have finished, confirm your answers with a classmate.

IDIOMATIC EXPRESSIONS		DEFINITIONS
1 dig your heels in	_____	a) unbelievable lies
2 doozies	_____	b) face public disgrace
3 isn't going to fly	_____	c) escape from a difficult situation
4 sideways glances	_____	d) won't be accepted

IDIOMATIC EXPRESSIONS		DEFINITIONS
⑤ wiggle out of	_____	e) refuse to do something despite other people's efforts to persuade you
⑥ fall hard	_____	f) way of expressing suspicion or distrust

Before You Read

A. Before reading the article, skim paragraphs 2 and 3 and identify the following people and things:

Chris Froome: _____

salbutamol: _____

Vuelta a España: _____

Team Sky: _____

While You Read

B. As you read this short article, consider whether Juliet Macur (the author) expresses an opinion about doping in professional cycling. Do you think she is pro-doping, anti-doping, or somewhere in the middle? Be prepared to explain why you think so.

Chris Froome Tests Positive, and Cycling History Repeats Itself

Admit it: You had a feeling it would happen. I had a feeling it would happen. How could anyone not?

Chris Froome, the four-time Tour de France winner, confirmed on Wednesday that he tested positive for excessively high amounts of the asthma drug salbutamol during
5 the Vuelta a España in September, on his way to victory in that Grand Tour. The level of the drug found in his urine was twice the amount allowed by anti-doping rules.

This news comes as no surprise. Not necessarily because it was Froome, the thirty-two-year-old rider for Britain's Team Sky who has dominated cycling in recent years. But because the revelation fits right in with a Tour tradition.

infamous (adj.): well known for some bad quality or action

10 So Froome's name now goes on the growing list of cycling champions turned infamous for failed drug tests or doping admissions: Lance Armstrong, Floyd Landis, Jan Ullrich, Alberto Contador, and on and on.

entangled (adj.): trapped in a bad situation

The last time there were back-to-back Tours de France without the winner becoming entangled in a doping scandal was 1995, when Miguel Induráin of Spain won his fifth
15 and final Tour. (Yet he too, once failed a test for an asthma drug but was not punished.)

That's an entire generation of embarrassment for a sport and its biggest stars. Three of those riders—Armstrong, Landis, and Contador—have been stripped of some or all of their victories, but those falls from grace didn't happen without a fight. And it looks as if Froome is preparing to **dig [his heels] in** for one, too.

sanctimonious (adj.): behaving as if you are morally better than others in an annoying way

20 Froome, who has had asthma since childhood and has often used inhalers in public, may face a suspension of a year or more. But don't think for a second that he and his powerful, often sanctimonious team are going to … accept a ban.

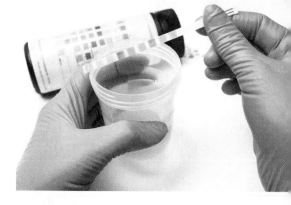

Be prepared for explanations and excuses, and they had better be good, because
25 cycling investigators have heard some **doozies**. Tyler Hamilton once blamed a doping positive on a vanishing twin in his mother's womb. Landis once attributed a suspicious surge in testosterone to too
30 many [drinks] of whiskey.

For the moment, Froome is free to continue racing, and he isn't panicking. At least not publicly.

He told *The Guardian* and *Le Monde* that his asthma had worsened during the Vuelta, so he just followed a Team Sky doctor's orders to increase the amount of salbutamol
35 he was already taking. The drug opens airways—an undeniably helpful result in a sport like cycling—and some argue that if a handful of riders can take it for asthma, then every rider should be allowed to do the same. And why wouldn't they? Salbutamol has been used to increase endurance and increase lean muscle mass—basically the reasons the World Anti-Doping Agency affixed a limit to the amount an athlete could
40 have in their system.

But even if a doctor told Froome to take more of the drug, Froome should have known better—he must know better—because that **isn't going to fly** with anti-doping experts.

rookie (n.): someone who is new, or playing in the first year of professional sports

To be even clearer: if Froome's version of events is true, he made a rookie mistake. It would also be a surprise if Froome couldn't feel the difference between the regular
45 amount of salbutamol he takes, and twice that amount. And the consequences of getting caught doing so should have been obvious to an athlete who—as he admitted—knew he was going to be tested repeatedly.

So right now we know this: something went very wrong for Froome at the Vuelta, and that something, now and perhaps forever, has put a black mark next to his name
50 in every record book.

…

pompous (adj.): self-important or arrogant

Team Sky was founded in 2009 on the pompous premise that the organization had a zero tolerance for performance-enhancing drug use and that it would fire anyone with a doping past. It was quite a bold and somewhat ridiculous idea, and the **sideways glances** only multiplied as Froome and Team Sky ascended mountain after mountain
55 with improbable ease.

We'll find out now if Team Sky's stated zero tolerance applies to its best rider. If Froome can't **wiggle out** of a suspension with an acceptable explanation, does it mean his time with Sky is over? My guess is it won't be … After all, cycling's rules are often broken or, at the very least, bent to fit the needs of a team or its star.

60 But if history has taught us anything, it is that the most dominant riders in cycling are the ones who **fall** the **hard**est.

(746 words)

Macur, J. (2017, December 13). Chris Froome tests positive, and cycling history repeats itself. *The New York Times.* Retrieved from https://www.nytimes.com/2017/12/13/sports/cycling/chris-froome-doping.html

After You Read

C. What is the author's opinion about doping in sports? Is her opinion strongly expressed?

_____

_____

D. To demonstrate your understanding of the reading, indicate whether the following statements are true or false. After, check your answers with a classmate.

STATEMENTS	TRUE	FALSE
1 The author starts the article by "speaking" directly to readers to attract their attention.		
2 At a recent cycling race, Froome tested positive for excessive amounts of the hormone erythropoietin.		
3 A professional cyclist testing positive for performance-enhancing drugs is an unusual occurrence.		
4 The author anticipates that Froome and his team will refuse to accept a ban as punishment for Froome's doping.		
5 The author suggests that cyclists seem to lie frequently to explain why they should be allowed to use performance-enhancing drugs.		
6 The author believes that Froome had no justifiable reason for taking the amount of salbutamol that he did.		
7 The author thinks that Froome should have known better than to take double the regular amount of his asthma drug, as he is not a rookie on the competitive cycling tour.		
8 Team Sky was founded on the premise that its team members were all "clean," i.e., they would never take drugs.		
9 The author indicates that anti-doping rules in cycling are strict, and they are never broken or "bent."		

MyBookshelf > My eLab >
Exercises > Chapter 7 >
Chris Froome Tests Positive

FOCUS ON
ACCURACY

Using Connecting Words and Phrases Common in Persuasive Writing

When writing a persuasive essay, it is common to use connecting words and phrases to present arguments.

A. To develop a comprehensive list of connectors, write the connectors from the box in the table next to the purpose they serve. When you have finished, check your answers with a classmate.

▶

in addition	including	in conclusion	for example
to summarize	for this reason	such as	for instance
as a result	moreover	~~one reason for this is~~	furthermore
to illustrate	a key factor is		to conclude

PURPOSE FOR CONNECTORS	CONNECTING WORDS AND PHRASES
Giving reasons	*one reason for this is,*
Adding information	
Adding examples	
Concluding	

MyBookshelf > My eLab > Exercises > Chapter 7 > Accuracy Review

B. Then, working as a class, add any additional connecting words and phrases you know that are not included in the box. You now have a useful list of connecting words and phrases to use in your writing assignments.

WARM-UP ASSIGNMENT
Write a Short Persuasive Essay

Using *only* information from Reading 1, write a short persuasive essay that argues *for* the use of performance-enhancing drugs in professional sports.

A. Your short essay should include

- an introduction with a thesis statement that is pro-doping;
- a short essay body (no more than two or three paragraphs) that includes reasons for your opinion;
- information from Reading 1 to support your points, including in-text citations (as appropriate) and a reference at the end;
- connecting words and phrases as appropriate;

- a conclusion that summarizes the essay's main points, with a concluding statement suggesting what professional sports might be like in the future when doping is allowed.

Refer to the Models Chapter (page 292) to see an example and to learn more about how to write a persuasive essay.

When you receive feedback from your instructor or your classmates on this Warm-Up Assignment, you will have information that you can use to improve your writing on the Final Assignment.

Athlete Reference Guide

The following reading is an excerpt from the *Athlete Reference Guide to the 2015 World Anti-Doping Code*. This text will increase your understanding of the responsibilities and restrictions professional athletes have when competing at national and international levels.

VOCABULARY BUILD

A. Read the sentences and for each key word in bold, choose the best synonym from the options given. When you have finished, confirm your answers with a classmate.

1 The medical tests for doping are not always reliable, so a single **adverse** analytical finding must always be confirmed by a second.

   a) negative   b) positive   c) unfavourable

2 **Amendments** are often used to update legal documents.

   a) adjustments   b) parameters   c) limits

3 If athletes do not cooperate with anti-doping rules, they **commit a violation**.

   a) do something legal   b) do something illegal   c) reveal

4 If athletes do not **comply with** anti-doping rules, they may be suspended or banned from competition.

   a) obey   b) do what they want   c) act against

5 If athletes are **conspiring** with others to hide the use of performance-enhancing drugs, they are committing a violation.

   a) convicting   b) committing a crime   c) secretly planning

6 Athletes must be careful they don't ingest any food **contaminated by** a substance on the prohibited substances list.

   a) influenced   b) made impure by   c) developed

7 If two medical tests confirm the use of prohibited substances, the athlete is **convicted of** a doping violation.

   a) officially guilty of   b) unofficially guilty of

8 Even if athletes compete only **domestically**, never internationally, they may still be subject to anti-doping regulations.

   a) in neighbouring countries   b) in their home countries   c) in northern countries

9 Athletes who use performance-enhancing drugs may be successful at **evading** detection for years.

   a) committing   b) avoiding   c) imposing

10 However, once these athletes are caught, a ban or a suspension is usually **imposed on** them.

   a) contaminated by   b) convicted of   c) forced on

11 Once a suspension is imposed, athletes are **obligated to** comply with the terms of the suspension.

    a) required to   b) considered to   c) thought to

12 New anti-doping regulations require athletes to have a "biological passport," which indicates their biological **parameters.**

    a) convictions   b) amendments   c) range of proven indicators

13 If athletes **tamper with** an anti-doping medical test, they could be banned from competition.

    a) enhance   b) manipulate   c) comply

B. Which of the key words above are related to criminal behaviour and punishment? List the words here. What does this list reveal or suggest about Reading 2?

_____

_____

_____

_____

C. In this reading, the word *prohibited* forms collocations with two nouns. Use the line numbers provided below to find these collocations.

LINE 15 _____

LINE 94 _____

Before You Read

A. Although many people know that the World Anti-Doping Agency (WADA) tests professional athletes for the use of performance-enhancing drugs, most people aren't aware of the amount of effort that the testing requires. Working in a group of three, consider the list of resources that WADA needs to test athletes accurately. Place a check mark next to each resource you think WADA needs.

WADA'S RESOURCES	
Doctors who know about performance-enhancing drugs	
People to develop the rules and policies about which substances are prohibited	
People to administer the tests all over the world	
Scientists to analyze the tests and report the results	
People to notify athletes about testing and make sure they comply	
People to develop and maintain the WADA website	
Cars and refrigerated vehicles to transport samples to laboratories all over the world	
People to plan meetings with sports organizations from around the world	

B. Does it surprise you how many people and resources WADA needs to test athletes for performance-enhancing drugs? Do you think the desire for "clean" sports is worth the expense for these resources?

_____

_____

While You Read

C. This reading is divided into five parts, and Part 5 is divided into four sections. The headings for these parts and sections are listed below, out of order. As you read, write the headings in the most appropriate places based on the content. When you have finished, compare your answers with your class.

HEADINGS FOR THE FIVE PARTS	SECTION HEADINGS FOR PART 5
Application of the Code	The whereabouts rule
Anti-Doping Violations	Does intent matter when it comes to an anti-doping rule violation?
Rules and Responsibilities	What is prohibited association?
The Code	What about dietary supplements?
The Right Stuff	

Athlete Reference Guide to the 2015 World Anti-Doping Code

The purpose of the World Anti-Doping Code is to protect the rights of the clean athlete.

Part 1: _____

The World Anti-Doping Code sets out rules that you, as an athlete, must follow. The point of this guide is to help you
5 understand the rules.

This document is merely a guide. It is no substitute for the language of the Code. To emphasize: the language of the Code is always the primary source. This guide is thus provided purely for the purpose of understanding and is in no way a
10 binding legal document.

The Code, in its first few pages, speaks of the intrinsic value of the "spirit of sport." That spirit is what drives forward the primary goal of any anti-doping program: prevention.

That is, to prevent the intentional or unintentional use of
15 prohibited substances or methods, or the commission of any other anti-doping rule violation.

Part 2: _____

What, exactly, is the World Anti-Doping Code?

The Code is the anti-doping system framework. It has
20 been accepted by the entire Olympic movement as well
as by various sports bodies and National Anti-Doping
Organizations throughout the entire world. It also has
been recognized by more than 170 governments, through
the UNESCO Convention against Doping in Sport.

25 The Code first came into effect in July 2004. A first set of
amendments took effect on 1 January 2009. A second
set took effect on 1 January 2015.

The full text of the Code can be found on the World Anti-
Doping Agency's website.

30 In support of the Code, WADA has also developed
"International Standards" for different technical and
operational areas, including the List of Prohibited
Substances and Methods, Testing and Investigations,
Therapeutic Use Exemptions, Laboratories, and the
35 Protection of Privacy and Personal Information.

...

Part 3: _____

Who is subject to the Code?

1. If you are a national- or international-level athlete, the Code applies to you.
"International-level" athletes are defined by the athletes' International Federation.
40 "National-level" athletes are defined by the athletes' National Anti-Doping
Organization.

2. Each National Anti-Doping Organization can decide whether and how the Code will
apply if you are an athlete competing **domestically** at a level that does not identify
you as "national-level." If you are competing at this level, the National Anti-Doping
45 Organization tests you, and if you return a positive test or **tamper with** the doping
control process or **commit** another anti-doping rule violation, the Code then requires
that sanctions be **imposed**.

3. If you are not participating in competition but merely engaging in recreational or
in fitness activities, National Anti-Doping Organizations also have discretion to
50 decide whether and how the Code will apply.

Part 4: _____

You must know and **comply** with all "applicable anti-doping policies and rules."

As an athlete, you have certain roles and responsibilities. These include:

- You must take responsibility for what you "ingest," meaning what you eat and
55 drink and anything that may enter your body. The essential rule is this: if it is in
your body, you are responsible for it. In legal terms, this is called "strict liability."

- You must be available for sample collection.

- You must inform medical personnel that they are **obligated** not to give you prohibited substances or methods. You must also take responsibility to make sure
60   that any medical treatment you receive does not violate the Code.

- You must cooperate with anti-doping organizations investigating anti-doping rule violations.

Coaches, trainers, managers, agents and other support personnel are often role models for athletes. They, too, have certain rights and responsibilities. These include:

65 - They must know and comply with all anti-doping policies and rules that apply to them or the athletes they support.

- They must cooperate with the athlete-testing program.

- They must use their considerable influence to promote a clean sport philosophy.

- They must cooperate with Anti-Doping Organizations investigating anti-doping
70   rule violations.

- They must not use or possess any prohibited substance or method without a valid justification.

Part 5: _____

As an athlete, the Code specifically says that you are responsible for knowing what
75 [constitutes] an anti-doping rule violation.

Such violations can involve more than just a positive test—which, in the language of the Code, is called an "**Adverse** Analytical Finding."

For example, it is also an anti-doping rule violation to use and possess prohibited substances and methods.

80 There are also other types of anti-doping rule violations. The Code spells these out:

- Tampering or attempted tampering with any part of doping control. For example, intentionally interfering with a doping control officer, intimidating a potential witness, or altering a sample by adding a foreign substance.

- Possession of prohibited substance or method. It's not OK to buy or have on you
85   a banned substance for the purposes of giving it to a friend or relative, except under certain very limited justified medical circumstances—say, buying insulin for a diabetic child.

trafficking (n.): the buying and selling of illegal drugs

- Trafficking or attempted trafficking in a prohibited substance or method. [You are not permitted to] administer or attempt to administer a prohibited substance or
90   method to an athlete.

- Complicity. This covers a wide range of acts: assisting, encouraging, aiding, abetting, **conspiring**, covering up or "any other type of complicity" involving an anti-doping rule violation or attempted violation by "another person."

- Prohibited Association.

95 - Whereabouts Failure.

- **Evading**, refusing, or failing to submit a sample collection. You should be aware that an anti-doping rule violation can be proven by any reliable means. This includes laboratory results and other evidence—the term used is "non-analytical" proof. This evidence can include but is not limited to the "Athlete Biological Passport" (a
100   study over time of a number of your biological **parameters**), admissions, witness testimony, and various types of documentary evidence.

Section 1: _____

As noted before, you are responsible—"strictly liable"—for anything and everything in your system. To establish an anti-doping rule violation for use or presence of a
105 prohibited substance, it is not necessary to demonstrate intent, fault, negligence, or knowing use on your part.

It is not a defence to an anti-doping rule violation that, for instance, someone in your entourage or camp gave you a substance; or that a banned substance was not listed on a product label; or that a prohibited substance or method would not have improved
110 your performance.

If you use or try to use a prohibited substance or method, that is doping. The "success" or "failure" of the use or attempted use does not matter. It is considered doping.

Section 2: _____

You should not take a supplement if there is any doubt as to what it might contain.

115 In many countries, the regulation of dietary supplements can be very lax. It is not unusual for supplements marketed in health-food stores or over the Internet to contain prohibited substances that are not disclosed on the product label. Over the past few years, a significant number of positive tests have been attributed to mislabelled or **contaminated** supplements.

120 To use but one example, there have been a large number of cases in recent years, including at the Olympic Games, of athletes from different sports testing positive for the banned stimulant methylhexaneamine (MHA). This stimulant might also be known as, among other things, 1,3-dimethylamylamine or DMAA; it might also be called geranium root extract or geranium oil (even if it does not come from
125 geranium oil or plants). These names might—or might not—be on a product label. But methylhexaneamine rarely is, even though it is on the Prohibited List.

wary (adj.): cautious because something could be dangerous or illegal

You should be extremely **wary** of products that, among other things, claim to build muscle, aid in recovery, provide energy, or help with weight loss. Because you will be held strictly liable for the consequences of a positive test caused by a mislabelled
130 supplement, the best advice is this: you should not take a supplement if there is any doubt as to what it might contain.

Section 3: _____

The primary purpose of the whereabouts requirements is to facilitate out-of-competition testing.

135 Providing whereabouts information gives an Anti-Doping Organization the ability to locate you and, as well, to rely on unannounced controls to maximize the potential for doping athletes to be caught. Unannounced testing is the cornerstone of an effective anti-doping program.

Relatively few athletes are in a "Registered Testing Pool" and need to provide accurate
140 and current whereabouts information.

If you have been notified that you are in a registered testing pool, that means you have to provide whereabouts information quarterly. That filing includes regularly scheduled activities and a one-hour window each day where you must be available for testing. The activities and testing window must be kept updated.

145   • If you fail to file your quarterly form on time, you commit a filing failure.

    • If you are not where you say you are going to be during the daily one-hour window, you commit a missed test violation. You have the right to contest any potential filing failure or missed test violation before the relevant Anti-Doping Organization. Any combination of three filing failures or missed tests within a
150   twelve-month period—if not successfully contested by you—results in an anti-doping rule violation.

    • If you take part in a team sport, and are in a registered testing pool, you are subject to the same whereabouts rules as athletes who compete in an individual sport.

    • A team-sport or individual athlete may delegate some or all whereabouts filings to
155   a coach, manager, or other third party; however, each athlete ultimately remains responsible for submitting accurate and complete whereabouts information.

    • Team whereabouts can also be submitted to an Anti-Doping Organization for activities that involves a team.

    • Anti-Doping Organizations may require certain athletes who are not in a registered
160   testing pool to provide less detailed whereabouts information. If you are one of these athletes, failure to comply with whereabouts requirements is not considered an anti-doping rule violation but may carry other consequences set by your Anti-Doping Organization.

Section 4: _____

165   • There have been several high-profile examples where athletes have continued to work with coaches who have been banned or with other individuals who have been criminally convicted for providing performance-enhancing drugs.

    • A new feature of the Code taking effect at the start of 2015 makes it an anti-doping rule violation for you to associate with this sort of "athlete support person" once
170   you have been specifically warned not to engage in that association.

    The details:

    • You must not work with coaches, trainers, doctors, or others who are ineligible because of an anti-doping rule violation or who have been criminally convicted or professionally disciplined in relation to doping.

175   • Some examples of this type of prohibited association include obtaining training, strategy, nutrition or medical advice, therapy, treatment, or prescriptions. Moreover, the athlete support person may not serve as an agent or representative. Prohibited association need not involve any form of compensation.

    • This provision does not apply in circumstances where the association is not in a
180   professional or sport-related capacity. Examples: a parent-child or husband-wife relationship.

(1859 words)

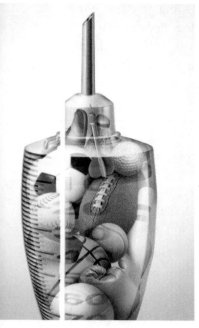

World Anti-Doping Agency. (2015). *Athlete reference guide to the 2015 world anti-doping code* (pp. 3–9). Retrieved from https://www.wada-ama.org/en/resources/education-and-prevention/athlete-reference-guide-to-2015-code-online-version

After You Read

D. To demonstrate your understanding, answer the following questions.

1 In Part 1, the authors write about "the spirit of sport," but this is not defined in the reading. Define the expression in your own words. Do you believe in the spirit of sport?

_____

_____

_____

_____

2 What is the purpose of Part 2?

_____

_____

_____

_____

3 As stated in Part 3, the anti-doping rules apply to what levels of athletes?

_____

_____

_____

_____

4 Part 4 states the requirements for athletes and coaches (and all other people who work with athletes). Check the appropriate columns to indicate which requirements apply to athletes, coaches, or both.

REQUIREMENTS	ATHLETES' REQUIREMENTS	COACHES' REQUIREMENTS
1 You are responsible for what you ingest.		
2 You must be available for sample collection.		
3 You must not have medical treatment that contradicts the Code.		
4 You must cooperate with anti-doping investigations.		
5 You must promote the spirit of sport.		
6 You must not possess any prohibited substance.		

5 What is the formal term for a positive doping test?

_____

6. In point form, list the anti-doping violations.

- _____
- _____
- _____
- _____
- _____
- _____
- _____
- _____

7. What does *strict liability* mean?

_____

_____

_____

8. Why should athletes be careful if they take dietary supplements?

_____

_____

_____

9. In your own words, briefly describe the whereabouts rule.

_____

_____

_____

_____

10. In a single sentence, explain the term *prohibited association*.

_____

_____

_____

11. What is the tone of this reading? What language is used to convey this tone? How would you feel if you were an athlete who was thinking about competing at a national or international level?

_____

_____

_____

_____

MyBookshelf > My eLab >
Exercises > Chapter 7 >
Athlete Reference Guide

FOCUS ON WRITING

Synthesizing Information from Multiple Sources in Writing

One type of written task instructors may ask you to complete requires you to synthesize information from two or more sources. This involves applying knowledge learned from one source to information learned from another source (or other sources). Here is an example of a task that requires synthesizing information from two sources.

> Referring to WADA's *Athlete Reference Guide to the 2015 World Anti-Doping Code*, explain why Chris Froome should be banned from racing after his adverse analytical finding.

In order to answer this question, you need to have good knowledge of content from both Readings 1 and 2. The solution to writing a good answer is to organize the information within your body paragraphs as demonstrated below.

A. In the following paragraph, underline information from Reading 1 and highlight information from Reading 2. Circle information that is the writer's opinion. When you have finished, compare your answers with those of a classmate.

Recently, Macur (2017) reported that cyclist Chris Froome, a four-time Tour de France winner, tested positive for levels of salbutamol that exceeded the limits set by the World Anti-Doping Agency (WADA) during the Vuelta a España Tour. Froome is an experienced cyclist who uses salbutamol regularly to treat asthma. However, Froome exceeded the allowable limits for the drug when testers found in his urine "twice the amount allowed by anti-doping rules." As a veteran of the cycling tour, Froome should be familiar with WADA's *Athlete Reference Guide to the 2015 World Anti-Doping Code*, which states that athletes have "strict liability" for the food and drugs they ingest. The *Guide* clearly states (in Part 4) that athletes must take responsibility for any substances that are found in their bodies. From the perspective of the *Guide*, it is clear that Froome must be held accountable for exceeding the allowable limits of drug use and should be banned from racing for a period of time.

B. Work with a partner to answer the following questions about the above paragraph.

1 What is the purpose of the first sentence?

_____

_____

2 In the first half of the paragraph, what information does the writer summarize?

_____

_____

3 In the second half of the paragraph, what information does the writer summarize?

_____

_____

4 Does the author write in general terms or provide specific details from the readings?

_____

_____

5 Which other verb does the writer use as a synonym for *reported*?

_____

_____

6 What is the purpose of the concluding sentence?

_____

_____

C. The following paragraph expresses an opposing viewpoint but follows a similar structure. Again, underline information from Reading 1, highlight information from Reading 2, and circle the writer's opinion.

For readers familiar with the recent history of competitive cycling, it is hardly surprising that Chris Froome was caught doping during the last Vuelta a España Tour (Macur, 2017). Froome's adverse analytical finding revealed that his urine contained twice the allowable amount of salbutamol, a drug used to treat asthma. It is widely known that Froome suffers from asthma, and he takes an allowable dose of the drug to help him breathe. Froome reported that during the Vuelta Tour, his asthma intensified and his team doctor recommended that he double his usual dose. According to WADA's *Athlete Reference Guide to the 2015 World Anti-Doping Code,* the team's doctor has a responsibility to "comply with all anti-doping policies" (Part 4). The doctor should have been aware that doubling Froome's regular dose would push Froome over the allowable amount, triggering the adverse analytical finding. Under these circumstances, the team doctor should be held accountable for Froome's positive drug test and the doctor should be removed from the team.

Note the following elements that the two paragraphs have in common.

- The topic sentences have different grammatical structures than the original text, so they do not seem repetitive.
- The writer uses synonyms to avoid repetition.
- The information from one source is summarized first; the information from the second source follows.
- Concrete examples support the main point of the paragraph.
- The concluding sentences express the writer's opinion, shifting the reader's attention from specific examples to general statements.

D. With your partner, search the Internet for a story of an athlete caught using performance-enhancing drugs. Then, write a paragraph in which you synthesize information from your first source with information from Reading 2 to explain why that athlete should (or should not) be banned from competition.

E. When you have finished, show your work to another pair of students and ask them to underline information from your Internet source, highlight information from Reading 2, and circle the sentence(s) that reveal(s) your opinion. Your classmates might also make useful suggestions about your use of synonyms and specific examples. When you are satisfied with your paragraph, write it on the board or post it to a class website or wiki.

MyBookshelf > My eLab > Exercises > Chapter 7 > Focus on Writing

FOCUS ON CRITICAL THINKING

Recognizing Methods of Persuasion: Ethos, Pathos, Logos

Aristotle, the famous Greek philosopher who lived from 384 to 322 BCE, wrote about methods of persuasion (or rhetorical appeals) that are still relevant today. Aristotle's methods provide a framework for recognizing and developing persuasive arguments.

Aristotle wrote that all persuasive arguments rely on one or more of the following elements:

a) The speaker's or writer's credibility, called *ethos*

b) The audience's emotional response to a story, called *pathos*

c) The logic of the speaker based on reasoning, facts, and figures, called *logos*

A. Here are three persuasive statements that demonstrate these three methods. Label each method with one of Aristotle's terms. When you have finished, compare your answers with a classmate. You will use this information to analyze Reading 3.

    1 Although Lance Armstrong's spectacular cycling race results have been invalidated because of his long-term use of performance-enhancing drugs, we should remember his inspirational recovery from cancer and all the good his LiveStrong Foundation does for other cancer survivors. _____

    2 Nobody knows more about the inequities of doping than Beckie Scott, a Canadian cross-country skier who placed third in the 2002 Olympics in the five-kilometre race but eventually received the gold medal after the women who finished first and second were disqualified for adverse analytical findings. _____

    3 Many people believe that professional athletes are role models for young competitors, so it is particularly important for professionals to not use performance-enhancing drugs. However, there is no empirical proof that young athletes, who might cut their hair in the same style as their role models, will take performance-enhancing drugs just because that's what their role model does. _____

Malcolm Gladwell is a well-known Canadian who writes about popular culture. At the time he wrote this essay, Lance Armstrong, the now infamous cyclist who confessed to doping, was in the middle of a public scandal that revealed the extent of his sophisticated and long-term use of performance-enhancing drugs. You may be surprised by Gladwell's perspective on this issue.

VOCABULARY BUILD

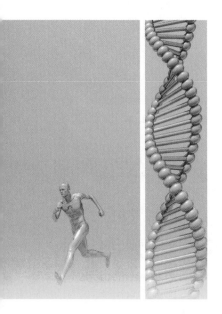

A. Read the sentences and classify each word in bold according to its part of speech in the table below. When you have finished, verify your answers with a classmate.

① **Apparently**, he had committed several violations before.

② His win was an **anomaly**. It was completely unexpected.

③ The violation was a **burden** on the athlete.

④ Don't **condemn** athletes who are trapped by difficult circumstances.

⑤ Athletes who dope are not **delusional**; they know they are committing violations.

⑥ When athletes train hard, there is a **deterioration** in their hematocrit numbers.

⑦ Cyclists' various genetic **endowments** ensure there is no "level playing field."

⑧ The colour of his face is **evocative** of the colour of the earth near his home.

⑨ He extracted his blood ahead of time, then **infused** it before the race.

⑩ People's genetic differences create a fantastic **menagerie** of human variation.

⑪ He had a rare genetic **mutation** that made him a superior athlete.

⑫ A doping athlete may **surreptitiously** move drugs from one location to another.

⑬ Athletes who believe they are **underdogs** may be tempted to dope.

NOUN	VERB	ADJECTIVE	ADVERB

B. In the table above, highlight the words for which you need definitions. Working with your partner, write the definitions on a separate page. Keep the paper to help you review the vocabulary later.

C. Two expressions about fairness in sports will help you express your ideas in the Final Assignment. The first expression is *a level playing field*, which refers to a situation where all athletes have an equal opportunity to win a competition. Find a synonym for that expression in line 1 of Reading 3.

_____

Before You Read

In this non-academic persuasive essay, Malcolm Gladwell refers to two books: *The Sports Gene* (2013) by David Epstein, and *The Secret Race* (2012) by Tyler Hamilton.

In 2013, David Epstein was a senior writer for the popular magazine *Sports Illustrated*. Tyler Hamilton is the cyclist mentioned in Reading 1 who tested positive for performance-enhancing drugs and revealed that all his teammates, including Lance Armstrong, were doping.

A. Discuss with your class why Gladwell refers to these two books and authors in his essay. What benefit does this add?

While You Read

B. Gladwell supports his arguments with six examples of athletes in various sports. As you read, write the names of the athletes and their sports next to the arguments they support in the table. When you have finished, confirm your answers with the class.

ARGUMENTS	EXAMPLES OF ATHLETES AND SPORTS
A. Nature creates an uneven set of genetic endowments and natural advantages	1. *Eero Mäntyranta – cross-country skiing*
B. Sports organizations allow athletes to alter their natural endowments with surgery. Why not allow athletes to use drugs?	
C. Sports organizations encourage athletes to modify their bodies (sometimes dangerously) through diet and training. Why not allow athletes to use science to improve their performance?	

Man and Superman

a sporting chance (exp.): a fair chance

*In athletic competitions, what qualifies as **a sporting chance**?*

Toward the end of *The Sports Gene* (Penguin/Current), David Epstein makes his way to a remote corner of Finland to visit a man named Eero Mäntyranta. Mäntyranta lives in a small house next to a lake, among the pine and spruce trees north of the
5 Arctic Circle. He is in his seventies. There is a statue of him in the nearby village. "Everything about him has a certain width to it," Epstein writes. "The bulbous nose in the middle of a softly rounded face. His thick fingers, broad jaw, and a barrel chest covered by a red knit sweater with a stern-faced reindeer across the middle. He is a remarkable-looking man." What's most remarkable is the colour of his face. It is a
10 "shade of cardinal, mottled in places with purple," and **evocative** of "the hue of the red paint that comes from this region's iron-rich soil."

Mäntyranta carries a rare genetic **mutation**. His DNA has an **anomaly** that causes his bone marrow to overproduce red blood cells. That accounts for the colour of his skin, and also for his extraordinary career as a competitive cross-country skier. In cross-
15 country skiing, athletes propel themselves over distances of ten and twenty miles—a physical challenge that places intense demands on the ability of their red blood cells to deliver oxygen to their muscles. Mäntyranta, by virtue of his unique physiology, had

something like 65 percent more red blood cells than the normal adult male. In the 1960, 1964, and 1968 Winter Olympic Games, he won a total of seven medals—three
20 golds, two silvers, and two bronzes—and in the same period he also won two world-championship victories in the thirty-kilometre race. In the 1964 Olympics, he beat his closest competitor in the fifteen-kilometre race by forty seconds, a margin of victory, Epstein says, "never equalled in that event at the Olympics before or since."

In *The Sports Gene*, there are countless tales like this, examples of all the ways that
25 the greatest athletes are different from the rest of us. They respond more effectively to training. The shape of their bodies is optimized for certain kinds of athletic activities. They carry genes that put them far ahead of ordinary athletes.

Epstein tells the story of Donald Thomas, who on the seventh high jump of his life cleared 7 feet 3.25 inches—practically a world-class height. The next year, after a grand
30 total of eight months of training, Thomas won the world championships. How did he do it? He was blessed, among other things, with unusually long legs and a strikingly long Achilles tendon—10.25 inches in length—which acted as a kind of spring, catapulting him high into the air when he planted his foot for a jump. (Kangaroos have long tendons as well, Epstein tells us, which is what gives them their special hop.)

35 Why do so many of the world's best distance runners come from Kenya and Ethiopia? The answer, Epstein explains, begins with weight. A runner needs not just to be skinny but—more specifically—to have skinny calves and ankles, because every extra pound carried on your extremities costs more than a pound carried on your torso. That's why shaving even a few ounces off a pair of running shoes can have a significant
40 effect. Runners from the Kalenjin tribe, in Kenya—where the majority of the country's best runners come from—turn out to be skinny in exactly this way. Epstein cites a study comparing Kalenjins with Danes; the Kalenjins were shorter and had longer legs, and their lower legs were nearly a *pound* lighter. That translates to 8 percent less energy consumed per kilometre. (For evidence of the peculiar Kalenjin lower leg, look

45 up pictures of the great Kenyan miler Asbel Kiprop, a tall and elegant man who runs on what appear to be two ebony-coloured pencils.) According to Epstein, there's an evolutionary explanation for all this: hot and dry environments favour very thin, long-limbed
50 frames, which are easy to cool, just as cold climates favour thick, squat bodies, which are better at conserving heat.

Distance runners also get a big advantage from living at high altitudes, where the body is typically forced to
55 compensate for the lack of oxygen by producing extra red blood cells. Not *too* high up, mind you. In the Andes, for example, the air is too rarefied for the kind of workouts necessary to be a world-class runner. The optimal range is six to nine thousand feet. The best
60 runners in Ethiopia and Kenya come from the ridges of the Rift Valley, which, Epstein writes, are "plumb in the sweet spot." When Kenyans compete against Europeans or North Americans, the Kenyans come to the track with an enormous head start.

65 What we are watching when we watch elite sports, then, is a contest among wildly disparate groups of people, who approach the starting line with an uneven set of genetic **endowments** and natural advantages. There will be Donald Thomases who barely have to train, and there will be Eero Mäntyrantas, who carry around in their blood, by dumb genetic luck, the ability to finish forty seconds ahead of their

70 competitors. Elite sports supply, as Epstein puts it, a "splendid stage for the fantastic **menagerie** that is human biological diversity." The menagerie is what makes sports fascinating. But it has also burdened high-level competition with a contradiction. We want sports to be fair and we take elaborate measures to make sure that no one competitor has an advantage over any other. But how can a fantastic menagerie ever

75 be a contest among equals?

…

visual acuity (n.): clear sight

Epstein tells us that baseball players have, as a group, remarkable eyesight. The ophthalmologist Louis Rosenbaum tested close to four hundred major- and minor-league baseball players over four years and found

80 an average **visual acuity** of about 20/13; that is, the typical professional baseball player can see at 20 feet what the rest of us can see at 13 feet. When Rosenbaum looked at the Los Angeles Dodgers, he found that half had 20/10 vision and a small number fell below 20/9,

85 "flirting with the theoretical limit of the human eye," as Epstein points out. The ability to consistently hit a baseball thrown at speeds approaching a hundred miles an hour, with a [challenging] array of spins and curves, requires the kind of eyesight commonly found in only

90 a tiny fraction of the general population.

Eyesight can be improved—in some cases dramatically—through laser surgery or implantable lenses. Should a promising young baseball player cursed with normal vision be allowed to get that kind of corrective surgery? In this instance, Major League Baseball says yes. Major League Baseball also permits pitchers to replace the ulnar

95 collateral ligament in the elbow of their throwing arm with a tendon taken from a cadaver or elsewhere in the athlete's body. Tendon-replacement surgery is similar to laser surgery: it turns the athlete into an improved version of his natural self.

But when it comes to drugs, Major League Baseball—like most sports—draws the line. An athlete cannot use a drug to become an improved version of his natural self, even

100 if the drug is used in doses that are not harmful and is something that—like testosterone—is no more than a copy of a naturally occurring hormone, available by prescription to anyone, virtually anywhere in the world.

…

pariah (adj.): someone who is hated and avoided by everyone; outcast

The other great doping **pariah** is Lance Armstrong. He **apparently** removed large quantities of his own blood and then **infused** himself before competition, in order

105 to boost the number of oxygen-carrying red blood cells in his system. Armstrong wanted to be like Eero Mäntyranta. He wanted to match, through his own efforts, what some very lucky people already do naturally and legally. Before we **condemn** him, though, shouldn't we have to come up with a good reason that one man is allowed to have lots of red blood cells and another man is not?

110 "I've always said you could have hooked us up to the best lie detectors on the planet and asked us if we were cheating, and we'd have passed," Lance Armstrong's former teammate Tyler Hamilton writes in his autobiography, *The Secret Race* (co-written with Daniel Coyle; Bantam). "Not because we were delusional—we knew we were breaking the rules—but because we didn't think of it as cheating. It felt fair to break the rules."

115 *The Secret Race* deserves to be read alongside *The Sports Gene*, because it describes the flip side of the question that Epstein explores. What if you aren't Eero Mäntyranta?

acutely (adv.): intensely

Hamilton was a skier who came late to cycling, and he paints himself as an **underdog**. When he first met Armstrong—at the Tour DuPont, in Delaware—he looked around at the other professional riders and became **acutely** conscious that he didn't look 120 the part … The riders' "leg veins looked like highway maps. Their arms were toothpicks … They were like racehorses." Hamilton's trunk was oversized. His leg veins did not pop. He had a skier's thighs. His arms were too muscled, and he pedalled with an ungainly "potato-masher stroke."

When Hamilton joined Armstrong on the US Postal Service racing team, he was 125 forced to relearn the sport, to leave behind, as he puts it, the romantic world "where I used to climb on my bike and simply hope I had a good day." The makeover began with his weight. When Michele Ferrari, the key Postal Service adviser, first saw Hamilton, he told him he was too fat, and in cycling terms he was. Riding a bicycle quickly is a function of the power you apply to the pedals divided by the weight you 130 are carrying, and it's easier to reduce the weight than to increase the power. Hamilton says he would come home from a workout, after burning thousands of calories, drink a large bottle of seltzer water, take two or three sleeping pills—and hope to sleep through dinner and, ideally, breakfast the following morning. At dinner with friends, Hamilton would take a large bite, fake a sneeze, spit the food into a napkin, and then 135 run off to the bathroom to dispose of it. He knew that he was getting into shape, he says, when his skin got thin and papery, when it hurt to sit down on a wooden chair because his buttocks had disappeared, and when his jersey sleeve was so loose around his biceps that it flapped in the wind. At the most basic level, cycling was about physical transformation: it was about taking the body that nature had given 140 you and forcibly changing it.

…

paradox (n.): idea that seems strange because it incorporates two contradictory things

Hematocrit … was [what] they cared about most. It refers to the percentage of the body's blood that is made up of oxygen-carrying red blood cells. The higher the hematocrit, the more endurance you have. (Mäntyranta had a very high hematocrit.) The **paradox** of endurance sports is that an athlete can never work as hard as he wants, 145 because if he pushes himself too far his hematocrit will fall. Hamilton had a natural hematocrit of 42 percent—which is on the low end of normal. By the third week of the Tour de France, he would be at 36 percent, which meant a 6 percent decrease in his power—in the force he could apply to his pedals. In a sport where power differentials of a tenth of a percent can be decisive, this "qualifies as a deal breaker."

150 For the members of the Postal Service squad, the solution was to use the hormone EPO (erythropoietin) and blood transfusions to boost their hematocrits as high as they could without raising suspicion. (Before 2000, there was no test for EPO itself, so riders were not allowed to exceed a hematocrit of 50 percent.) Then they would add maintenance doses over time, to counteract the **deterioration** in their hematocrit 155 caused by races and workouts. The procedures were precise and sophisticated.

Testosterone capsules were added to the mix to aid recovery. They were referred to as "red eggs." EPO, a naturally occurring hormone that increases the production of red blood cells, was [called] Edgar. During the Tour de France, and other races, bags of each rider's blood were collected in secret locations at predetermined intervals,
160 then **surreptitiously** [transported] from stage to stage in refrigerated containers for strategic transfusions. The window of vulnerability after taking a drug—the interval during which doping could be detected—was called "glowtime." Most riders who doped (and in the Armstrong era, it now appears, nearly all the top riders did) would take two thousand units of Edgar subcutaneously every couple of days, which meant
165 they "glowed" for a dangerously long time. Armstrong and his crew practised microdosing, taking five hundred units of Edgar nightly and injecting the drug directly into the vein, where it was dispersed much more quickly.

…

Hamilton was eventually caught and was suspended from professional cycling. He became one of the first in his circle to implicate Lance Armstrong, testifying before
170 federal investigators and appearing on [the popular TV show] *60 Minutes*. He says that he regrets his years of using performance-enhancing drugs. The lies and duplicity became an unbearable **burden**. His marriage fell apart. He sank into a depression. His book is supposed to serve as his apology. At that task, it fails. Try as he might—and sometimes he doesn't seem to be trying very hard—Hamilton cannot explain
175 why a sport that has no problem with the voluntary induction of **anorexia** as a performance-enhancing measure is so upset about athletes infusing themselves with their own blood.

anorexia (n.): a psychological illness that makes people stop eating

"Dope is not really a magical boost as much as it is a way to control against declines," Hamilton writes. Doping meant that cyclists finally could train as hard as they wanted.
180 It was the means by which pudgy underdogs could compete with natural wonders. "People think doping is for lazy people who want to avoid hard work," Hamilton writes. For many riders, the opposite was true:

> EPO granted the ability to suffer more; to push yourself farther and harder than you'd ever imagined, in both training and racing. It rewarded
> 185 precisely what I was good at: having a great work ethic, pushing myself to the limit and past it. I felt almost giddy: this was a new landscape. I began to see races differently. They weren't rolls of the genetic dice, or who happened to be on form that day. They didn't depend on who you were. They depended on *what you did*—how hard you worked, how
> 190 attentive and professional you were in your preparation.

This is a long way from the exploits of genial old men living among the pristine pines of northern Finland. It is a vision of sports in which the object of competition is to use science, intelligence, and sheer will to conquer natural difference. Hamilton and Armstrong may simply be athletes who regard this kind of achievement as
195 worthier than the gold medals of a man with the dumb luck to be born with a random genetic mutation.

(2525 words)

Gladwell, M. (2013, September 2). Man and superman. *The New Yorker*. Retrieved from https://www.newyorker.com/magazine/2013/09/09/man-and-superman

After You Read

C. To demonstrate your understanding, answer the following questions.

1 What is Gladwell's thesis? In other words, what is Gladwell trying to persuade his readers to believe about the use of performance-enhancing drugs in sports?

_____

_____

2 Which of Aristotle's methods of persuasion did Gladwell use to make his arguments?

_____

_____

_____

_____

D. Discuss the following questions with your class.

1 Did Gladwell persuade you?

2 What arguments did you find persuasive?

3 What is your opinion about whether performance-enhancing drugs should be allowed in sports?

MyBookshelf > My eLab >
Exercises > Chapter 7 >
Man and Superman

Academic
Survival Skill

Persuading by Conceding and Refuting Arguments

In Reading 3, Gladwell clearly expresses his pro-doping opinion about the use of performance-enhancing drugs in professional sports. However, there are many arguments against their use. Several of these are listed in the table below.

A. Read the anti-doping arguments listed in the first column. As a class, add as many additional arguments as you can think of to the last rows.

When you are writing a persuasive essay, one useful technique is to concede the reasonableness of the opposite perspective before refuting it with your own point. This concede and refute pattern is demonstrated in the second column of the table.

B. Read the sentences in the second column and underline the transition words and phrases that signal the move from conceding a point to refuting it.

ANTI-DOPING ARGUMENTS	CONCEDING AND REFUTING ANTI-DOPING ARGUMENTS
1 The equity argument • All athletes should compete on a level playing field without the unfair advantage that performance-enhancing drugs provide.	Proponents of the equity argument believe that athletes should compete on a level playing field without the unfair advantages of performance-enhancing drugs. However, this argument does not acknowledge that Nature has never provided a level playing field, which is no more than an idealized fantasy.
2 The spirit of sport argument • The natural purity of sports should not be damaged by the use of performance-enhancing drugs, which are unnatural and artificial.	Advocates of the spirit of sport argument believe that there is a natural purity to athletic competition that is destroyed by the use of performance-enhancing drugs. Unfortunately, the belief that sports were "pure" in the past is untrue. Since the very first Olympic Games, athletes have searched for ways to enhance their performance through scientific means (Kremenik et al., 2006).
3 The health argument • Anti-doping regulations protect athletes' health.	While it is reasonable to be concerned about the health of child athletes, it is paternalistic to desire to protect the health of adults. For example, we do not prevent adults from smoking, which is not in the best interests of the smoker.
4 The role model argument • To protect the health of young athletes, the behaviour of professional athletes (role models) should be regulated.	Although the role model argument points to an emotional concern for the health of young athletes, it has not been proven that the use of performance-enhancing drugs by professional athletes encourages young athletes to dope (Petersen, 2010).
5 The money argument • The massive amounts of resources used to police athletes could be used for more critical needs.	Despite the fact that WADA catches and punishes the few athletes that dope, it requires large amounts of resources to police all athletes, develop technology to detect doping, and constantly update policies and lists of banned substances. Surely, these resources could be better spent on research and education.
6 The lazy athlete argument • Performance-enhancing drugs provide a way for lazy athletes to beat athletes who do not dope.	Some people may believe that doping allows athletes to win without having to train hard. In fact, using performance-enhancing drugs allows athletes to train harder, beyond the limits of their natural capabilities. There is no such thing as a lazy professional athlete.
7 The legalization argument • If performance-enhancing drugs were legalized, all athletes would have to take them to have a chance at winning.	Opponents of doping argue that if it were legalized, athletes would effectively have to dope to have a chance at winning. This would force athletes to take drugs that could be dangerous to their health. Conversely, advocates of doping believe that if doping were legalized, athletes could take drugs under the supervision of a doctor, which would encourage safe use of the drugs.
8	
9	

References

Kremenik, M., Onodera, S., Nagao, M., Yuzuki, O., & Yonetani, S. (2006). A historical timeline of doping in the Olympics (Part 1 1896–1968). *Kawasaki Journal of Medical Welfare, 12*(1), 19–28.

Petersen, T. (2010). Good athlete – bad athlete? On the "role model argument" for banning performance-enhancing drugs. *Sports, Ethics and Philosophy, 4*(3), 323–340.

C. Answer the questions referring to the table above.

1 Which examples in the second column move from conceding to refuting in a single sentence? _____

② What pattern do these sentences use to accomplish this?

_____

③ Which examples in the second column move from conceding to refuting in two sentences? _____

④ In examples 1, 2, and 7, which words mean "people who support" an idea?

_____

⑤ In example 7, what word means "people who don't support" an idea?

_____

D. To practise, work with a partner and write sentences that concede and then refute a pro-doping argument (as presented in Reading 3). When you have finished, write your best sentences on the board to receive feedback from your instructor and your class.

PRO-DOPING ARGUMENTS	CONCEDING AND REFUTING PRO-DOPING ARGUMENTS
❶ The Nature is unfair argument • Nature creates an uneven set of genetic endowments and natural advantages.	
❷ The surgical enhancement argument • Some sports organizations (such as Major League Baseball in the US) allow athletes to alter their natural endowments with surgery. Why not allow athletes to use drugs to enhance their performance?	
❸ The dangerous training argument • Sports organizations encourage athletes to modify their bodies (sometimes dangerously) through diet and training. Why not allow athletes to use science to improve their performance?	

FOCUS ON READING

Comparing Original and Summarized/ Paraphrased Writing

As a developing academic writer, you are likely interested in how other writers summarize and paraphrase. In Reading 3, Gladwell summarizes and paraphrases sections of *The Sports Gene* (Epstein, 2013) and *The Secret Race* (Hamilton & Coyle, 2012). To learn more about summarizing and paraphrasing, compare the original texts with Gladwell's.

A. Answer the questions referring to the examples on page 238.

1 In both examples, Gladwell quotes from the original texts. Underline the quotes in Gladwell's writing and the same words in the original texts. Why does Gladwell quote these sections rather than paraphrase in his own words?

_____

_____

_____

_____

_____

2 If you read Example 1 closely, you will see that Gladwell doesn't always keep the content of the paraphrase in the same order as it was presented in the original writing. Why not?

_____

_____

_____

_____

_____

3 Read the examples closely to look for shifts in perspective from first person (in the original texts) to third person (in Gladwell's paraphrases). What is gained or lost in this shift?

_____

_____

_____

_____

_____

4 What did you learn by comparing the original writing with Gladwell's paraphrases?

_____

_____

_____

_____

_____

EXAMPLE 1

EPSTEIN'S ORIGINAL

Liris [Mäntyranta's daughter] told me [Epstein] ... that her father's unique gene mutation had caused his skin to redden as he got older, but I didn't quite expect this shade of cardinal, mottled in places with purple (p. 267) ... In the 15K race, Mäntyranta finished forty seconds ahead of the next skier—a margin of victory never equalled in that event at the Olympics before or since—while the next five finishers were within twenty seconds of one another. In the 30K race he won by over a minute (p. 269) ... [The 1960] Olympic title was just a preamble. Two golds and a silver followed in Innsbruck in 1964. Then a silver and two bronzes in Grenoble, France in '68, and a [host] of world championship medals along the way. In all, he placed in five hundred races (p. 273) ... At times, Eero's extraordinary red blood cell count—measured at up to 65 percent higher than that of an average man—sullied his sterling career. Despite the fact that his blood levels had been documented since he was a kid, [there was] speculation ... that his unusual blood profile was the result of doping. It was not until twenty years after his retirement from skiing that scientists pinpointed the truth (p. 274).

GLADWELL'S PARAPHRASE

Mäntyranta carries a rare genetic mutation. His DNA has an anomaly that causes his bone marrow to overproduce red blood cells. That accounts for the colour of his skin, and also for his extraordinary career as a competitive cross-country skier. In cross-country skiing, athletes propel themselves over distances of ten and twenty miles—a physical challenge that places intense demands on the ability of their red blood cells to deliver oxygen to their muscles. Mäntyranta, by virtue of his unique physiology, had something like 65 percent more red blood cells than the normal adult male. In the 1960, 1964, and 1968 Winter Olympic Games, he won a total of seven medals—three golds, two silvers, and two bronzes—and in the same period he also won two world-championship victories in the thirty-kilometre race. In the 1964 Olympics, he beat his closest competitor in the fifteen-kilometre race by forty seconds, a margin of victory, Epstein says, "never equalled in that event at the Olympics before or since."

EXAMPLE 2

HAMILTON & COYLE'S ORIGINAL

You can tell a rider's fitness by ... the veins in his legs ... Their leg veins looked like highway maps. Their arms were toothpicks. On their bikes, they could slither through the tightest pack of riders at full speed, one hand on the handlebars. Looking at them was inspiring; they were like racehorses.

Looking at myself—that was a different feeling. If they were thoroughbreds, I was a work pony ... My legs showed zero veins. I had narrow shoulders, ski-racer thighs, and thick arms that fit into my jersey sleeves like sausages into casing. Plus, I pedalled with a potato-masher stroke ... The plain truth was, I had no real business in the Tour DuPont. I didn't have the power, experience, or bike-handling skills to compete with the European pros, much less beat them over twelve days (p. 21).

GLADWELL'S PARAPHRASE

Hamilton was a skier who came late to cycling, and he paints himself as an underdog. When he first met Armstrong—at the Tour DuPont, in Delaware—he looked around at the other professional riders and became acutely conscious that he didn't look the part ... The riders' "leg veins looked like highway maps. Their arms were toothpicks ... They were like racehorses." Hamilton's trunk was oversized. His leg veins did not pop. He had a skier's thighs. His arms were too muscled, and he pedalled with an ungainly "potato-masher stroke."

FINAL ASSIGNMENT
Write a Longer Persuasive Essay

Write a persuasive essay in which you agree or disagree with this statement.

The World Anti-Doping Association (WADA) should be disbanded and the resources it uses should be spent on medical research.

A. In your essay,

- use at least one example of each of Aristotle's methods of persuasion (ethos, pathos, and logos) to support your argument;
- synthesize information from the three readings in this chapter (as well as from other readings);
- use connecting words to signal how you are organizing your arguments;
- use the concede and refute pattern as appropriate.

Refer to the Models Chapter (page 292) to see an example of a persuasive essay and to learn more about how to write one.

Critical Connections

In this chapter, you learned about Aristotle's three methods of persuasion: ethos, pathos, and logos. Other readings in this book also demonstrate these persuasive elements.

A. Working with a partner, select several of the readings listed below and identify which methods of persuasion the authors used. When you have finished, share your findings with your class.

Chapter 1: The "Jobless Recovery," page 35
logos (data about unemployment) and pathos (appeal to the reader's emotions about helping young people succeed)

Chapter 2: Towards an Explanation of the Growth in Young Entrepreneur Activities: A Cross-Country Survey of Work Values of College Students, page 65

Chapter 3: So Fresh and So Clean, page 78

Chapter 4: Dr. Sustainability: Environmental Scientist of the Year, page 106

Chapter 4: How Do Green Buildings Pay?, page 127

Chapter 5: The Social Life of Autonomous Cars, page 169

Chapter 6: Using Technology as a Learning Tool, Not Just the Cool New Thing, page 178

Chapter 6: In-Game Culture Affects Learners' Use of Vocabulary Learning Strategies in Massively Multiplayer Online Role-Playing Games, page 190

Chapter 8: Naming the Substances We Detect, page 254

Emerging Contaminants

Water scientists are discovering new (emerging) contaminants in rivers and lakes that may harm the natural environment. The sources of these contaminants are medicines for animals and people, and human personal care products (PCPs) such as deodorants and soaps. These contaminants, which are flushed down toilets and washed down drains, travel through our wastewater treatment plants and beyond into rivers and lakes where they cause physical changes to the fish population. What long-term effect will these contaminants have on the health of fish, other animals, and humans?

In this chapter, you will

- learn vocabulary related to emerging contaminants;

- explore the many uses of *that*;

- analyze critical expression;

- practise expressing critical thoughts;

- discover the organization of a problem-solution text;

- combine different organizational patterns to suit your writing purpose;

- describe and evaluate a solution for a problem-solution text;

- write a problem-solution essay.

GEARING UP

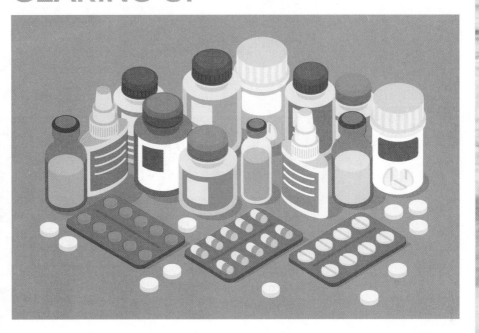

A. Working in a small group, generate two lists: one of frequently used personal care products (PCPs), which wash off into the water when people shower or bathe; and a second of common medicines, which are flushed into wastewater.

PERSONAL CARE PRODUCTS (PCPS)	COMMON MEDICINES
deodorants	*painkillers*

B. If scientists discovered that these products and medicines caused damage to the health of fish and other animals, do you think people would be willing to stop using them? Why?

_____

_____

Below are the key words you will practise in this chapter. Check the words you understand, then underline the words you use. Highlight the words you need to learn.

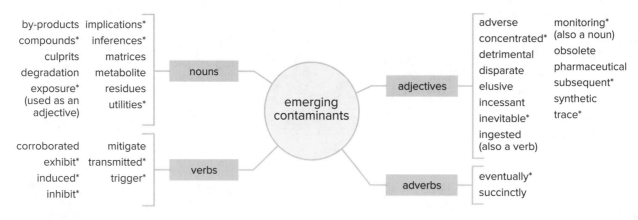

nouns

by-products   implications*
compounds*   inferences*
culprits   matrices
degradation   metabolite
exposure*   residues
(used as an   utilities*
adjective)

verbs

corroborated   mitigate
exhibit*   transmitted*
induced*   trigger*
inhibit*

emerging
contaminants

adjectives

adverse   monitoring*
concentrated*   (also a noun)
detrimental   obsolete
disparate   pharmaceutical
elusive   subsequent*
incessant   synthetic
inevitable*   trace*
ingested
(also a verb)

adverbs

eventually*
succinctly

*Appears on the Academic Word List

READING ❶

Pharmaceuticals May Be Poisoning America's Drinking Water

This reading is an excerpt from a magazine that was republished in *Pollution*, one in a series of textbooks called *Opposing Viewpoints*. The author presents one view of emerging contaminants in the water supply.

A. Read the following sentences adapted from Reading 1. Use the context to help you choose the best definition for each of the words in bold. When you have finished, confirm your answers as a class.

WORDS IN CONTEXT		DEFINITIONS
❶ A growing number of **compounds** are showing up in America's drinking water.		a) process that changes a complex compound to a simpler form
❷ Reverse osmosis water filtration uses large amounts of electricity and produces a highly **concentrated** wastewater stream.		b) carefully checking a situation to see how it changes over time
❸ If we are able to identify certain compounds that seem to be the **culprits** in potential human health risks, technology could be developed to remove those compounds rather than take out all impurities.		c) improve a situation or make its effects less harmful
❹ You may be successful at removing the original contaminant, but through **degradation**, you may be worse off than when you started.		d) substances containing atoms of two or more elements

WORDS IN CONTEXT		DEFINITIONS
5 Some fish in close proximity to wastewater discharge points **exhibit** multiple sexual abnormalities.	_____	e) public services that provide water, gas, or electricity
6 We just don't know what the **exposure** risk is to many of these compounds.	_____	f) relating to drugs and medicines
7 First we need to figure out whether we need to **mitigate**, and if we do, then we'll address those larger issues of how to do it.	_____	g) display
8 "These contaminants are active at very low concentrations in the water," says Jeff Armstrong, senior scientist in the ocean-**monitoring** group for the Orange County, California Sanitation District.	_____	h) reasons for a problem or difficulty
9 Before water **utilities** can choose an effective technology, though, the harmful CECs have to be identified.	_____	i) start or set in motion
10 Hidden among the well-known problems faced by water professionals is another emerging issue: rising amounts of **pharmaceutical** compounds in surface water and drinking water.	_____	j) additional substances that are produced by a natural or industrial process
11 These contaminants **trigger** abnormal reproductive responses in fish and possibly in humans.	_____	k) contact (e.g., with danger)
12 Ozone creates **by-products** that can cause cancer.	_____	l) stronger because most of the water has been removed from it

B. The readings in this chapter contain a number of technical words and phrases related to wastewater treatment. Working with a partner, review the words and phrases and their definitions in Table A. Then categorize the terms under the correct headings in Table B.

Table A

TECHNICAL WORDS/PHRASES	DEFINITIONS
1 chlorine	chemical often used in swimming pools to disinfect, clean, and purify water
2 effluent	clean water that leaves a wastewater treatment facility; wastewater effluent is cleaner than the water that enters the plant
3 endocrine-disrupting compounds	chemical compounds that change or modify (disrupt) hormone levels in the body
4 endocrine disruptors	synonym for endocrine-disrupting compounds
5 estrogenic compounds	medical compounds that contain estrogen, the hormone that regulates female characteristics
6 granular activated carbon filters	filters made of specially treated carbon that are used to remove impurities from wastewater
7 hormones	chemicals produced naturally by the body to regulate growth and development; people with growth problems may take synthetic (artificial) hormones
8 influent	dirty water entering a wastewater treatment facility through underground pipes (sewers)
9 outfall	place where wastewater effluent is released (discharged) into a body of water; fish that swim near the wastewater outfall may be affected by compounds in the water

TECHNICAL WORDS/PHRASES	DEFINITIONS
⑩ ozonation	process used to purify wastewater by dissolving ozone gas in the water, changing organic material to carbon dioxide and deactivating bacteria
⑪ pathogen	germ, bacterium, or virus that causes disease
⑫ reverse osmosis filtration	high-energy method used to clean wastewater by forcing dirty water through a membrane to remove impurities
⑬ trace organic compounds	very small amounts of naturally occurring substances
⑭ wastewater treatment facilities	buildings and equipment used to clean dirty water, sometimes referred to as WWTFs
⑮ wastewater treatment plants	buildings and equipment used to clean dirty water (synonym for WWTFs)

Table B

WORDS/PHRASES THAT DESCRIBE POSSIBLE CONTAMINANTS	WORDS/PHRASES THAT FORM COLLOCATIONS WITH WASTEWATER	OTHER WORDS/PHRASES THAT REFER TO WATER TREATMENT
endocrine disruptors	*wastewater outfall*	*chlorine*

C. Based on your understanding of the words you learned in these activities, explain to a classmate the problem of emerging contaminants and possible solutions.

Before You Read

A. The article begins with an abstract. Read the abstract, then write short answers to the following questions. When you have finished, check your answers with a classmate.

① What type of compounds does the author write about and where are they found?

_____

② What term does the author use to describe these compounds?

_____

③ What is the problem with current wastewater treatment facilities?

_____

④ What happens to fish that live near the wastewater treatment plants' discharge areas?

_____

Wastewater treatment plant

⑤ Why is fish health important?

_____

⑥ What does the author hope for in the future?

_____

_____

While You Read

B. In this reading, the author uses five headings to organize the content. The headings are listed out of order here. As you read, write the headings in the appropriate sections in the text.

> The Challenge of Identifying CECs
>
> Increasing Sexual Abnormalities
>
> Determining the Effects
>
> The Use of Take-Back Programs
>
> The Sources and Treatment of CECs

When you have finished, work with a classmate to compare where you placed each heading.

Pharmaceuticals May Be Poisoning America's Drinking Water

*A growing number of **pharmaceutical compounds** are showing up in America's drinking water, claims Patricia Frank in the following essay. More Americans than ever are being treated with prescription drugs that often end up in wastewater facilities that are not designed to filter out these compounds of emerging concern (CECs), she maintains. As*
5 *a result, Frank asserts, fish found close to watershed and wastewater discharge areas show reproductive abnormalities, which is raising concerns about the impact of CECs on human health. Growing public concern may pressure wastewater treatment facilities to find ways to safely remove CECs from America's drinking water, she contends.*

Hidden among the well-known problems faced by water professionals—aging
10 infrastructure, dwindling supply—is another emerging issue: rising amounts of pharmaceutical compounds in surface water and drinking water. And, considering the increasing numbers of people being treated with drugs at earlier ages and an aging population taking multiple medications for a variety of health conditions, more of
15 those compounds likely will find their way into the nation's wastewater facilities.

Early signs of the problem were discovered by the US Geological Survey (USGS) research in 1999. Of the sixty pharmaceuticals the
20 agency was testing for, it found thirty of them in 139 streams in thirty states. In addition, 80 percent of the streams had one or more contaminants, 54 percent had five or more, and 13 percent showed twenty or more.

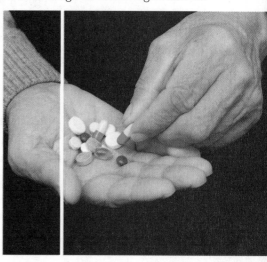

25 "We can measure over 150 compounds in water alone," says Dana Kolpin, a research hydrologist and member of the USGS study team. "Now, the big question is what kind of environmental consequences [do they pose] to terrestrial and aquatic ecosystems and, maybe in the long term, even human health. We just don't know what the **exposure** risk is to many of these compounds."

30 _____

Scientists from the ... USGS, other government agencies, and universities are attempting to determine the potential effects of chronic exposure to pharmaceutical mixtures—otherwise known as compounds of emerging concern (CECs)—such as endocrine disruption and the development of antibiotic resistance in the aquatic 35 environment, soil, plants, animals, and humans.

Though the amounts being measured often are in parts per million or parts per billion, many of the compounds are designed to have effects at low levels. "These CECs are active at very low concentrations in the water and in the sediments," says Jeff Armstrong, senior scientist in the ocean-**monitoring** group for the Orange County, 40 California Sanitation District. "It's not so much the death of the animals [that is a concern], it is reproductive effects or effects on other areas of the endocrine system, the ability to fight off infection, or other aspects of reproduction."

Endocrine disruptors are chemicals that mimic or block hormones or **trigger** abnormal reproductive responses in fish and possibly in humans. Nevertheless, our ability to 45 measure the compounds is ahead of our knowledge of their long-term effects.

_____

However, some fish in close proximity to wastewater discharge points **exhibit** multiple sexual abnormalities, such as male fish with deformed testes or low to no sperm counts, for example. Some fish are classified as "intersex" with sex characteristics of 50 both genders. Kolpin says a large proportion of the male fish have either female egg protein or female characteristics.

Following a high number of fish deaths in the Potomac River basin and the Shenandoah watershed between 2003 and 2005, the USGS and scientists from Virginia and West Virginia analyzed samples of thirty smallmouth bass from six sites. A microscopic 55 examination of the fish testes discovered 42 percent of the male bass had developed eggs. A second USGS study found an even higher number of intersex fish—79 percent. "[In the Potomac, we found] a big portion of the male fish having either female egg yolk protein or female characteristics," Kolpin says. Douglas Chambers, the study's lead scientist, says that all water samples contained detectable levels of at least one 60 known endocrine-disrupting compound.

Pacific Ocean flatfish found in sediment near Orange County, California's Huntington Beach effluent discharge point, exhibited similar effects. "We're finding that male fish are producing [endocrine-disrupting compounds] in concentrations that normal males should not," Armstrong says. "That means they're being exposed to some kind 65 of estrogenic compound. We're finding the fish near our outfall and [the estrogenic compound] seems to be in higher concentrations [there, which indicates] that something's coming out in the treated wastewater that might be causing this."

"It's really not certain what's going on, but [there is no doubt] that there is evidence of endocrine-type biomarkers in fish downstream from wastewater outfall," says
70 Shane Snyder, research and development project manager for the Southern Nevada Water Authority in Las Vegas. "The degree of magnitude of the effect seems like it's going to be related to the treatment type, the degree of mixing and the mobility of the fish."

---

75 The contaminants may originate from hospitals and medical facilities, vet clinics, pharmaceutical manufacturers, and people using prescription and over-the-counter medications and personal care products. "[Medical facilities] can be a big source of … pharmaceuticals, X-ray and MRI contrast agents, and chemotherapy drugs," Kolpin says. "Maybe they need to have separate wastewater treatment so they're not just
80 put in with residential waste."

Designed to remove conventional pollutants, such as suspended solids and easily biodegradable organic materials, most conventional wastewater treatment plants do not remove CECs. The concentration of the compounds that remains in wastewater treatment plant effluent depends on the type of treatment, the specific compounds,
85 as well as the concentration in the influent entering the plant.

Techniques for removing compounds from drinking water included 1) advanced oxidation [with either ozone or chlorine], 2) membrane filtration [with or without] granular activated carbon, and 3) nano-filtration combined with reverse osmosis, which eliminates all the drugs. Each technology serves a function, but each can
90 produce an unwelcome side effect.

renders (v.): makes

[Oxidation with] conventional ozone **renders** certain CECs inactive, but its use comes with a price, Snyder warns. "Ozone creates **by-products** [that can cause] cancer … [It's] great [that] you're putting in ozone, but what about all the cancer-causing by-products they form?"

95 [Oxidation with] chlorine, the most commonly used wastewater disinfectant …, is the least effective in removing the CECs. Kolpin's concern is the creation of chlorination by-products. The [Environmental Protection Agency] already has set drinking water standards of 100 parts per billion for one group of
100 by-products, called trihalomethanes, because of their potential to cause cancer. "You may be removing the parent compound [of CECs but] by creating these chlorinated **degradation** products, [you] may be worse off than when you started," he says. "Certainly chlorination has the advantages of removing
105 pathogens, but we are not certain that it's the best route to remove CECs. It needs to be researched."

[As a form of filtration,] reverse osmosis (RO) offers the most promise as the technology can remove CECs to the point where they are no longer detectable. However, it uses large amounts of electricity and produces a highly **concentrated** wastewater stream.
110 "[RO] creates a stream of concentrated waste; what do you do with the concentrated waste stream that you've generated?" Snyder says.

Techniques that combine ozone and [filtration with] granular activated carbon (GAC) are effective for removing industrial and agricultural pollutants, and also improve the water's taste and odour. The filters get dirty and must be washed periodically; otherwise, the water can become infected with *Cryptosporidium* and *Giardia*.

Before water **utilities** can choose an effective technology, though, the harmful CECs have to be identified. "First we need to figure out whether we need to **mitigate**, and if we do, then we'll address those larger issues of how to do it," Armstrong says.

Still, common wastewater treatments can be useful in removing CECs. "The tertiary treatment, like reverse osmosis (RO) or micro- or nano-filtration, removes pretty much 100 percent of [CECs]," Armstrong says. "There's a lot in the literature that [says] ozonation renders these [compounds] biologically inactive. The problem is doing that on a large scale. [We process] 965 million litres of wastewater a day. There's no way we can remove all CECs from that much wastewater, so we have to look to other ways to figure out what kind of mitigation strategy's going to work for us."

CECs will not be regulated in the near future, at least. "Due to insufficient data …, it appears that pharmaceuticals will not be regulated any time soon," says Snyder …

Meanwhile, the Las Vegas [Valley] Water District has added ozone to its expanded wastewater treatment facility. Ozone was chosen for its disinfection power … "Ozone is extremely effective for destroying estrogenicity, and that's where our concern lies for the fish," Snyder says.

Granular activated carbon

Because 50 to 90 percent of **ingested** drugs are excreted, state and local governments are attempting to involve the public through drug take-back programs to stem the flow at one of its source points. "We'll deal with that in the treatment plants as best we can, but keeping the extraneous pharmaceuticals out of the environment is where the majority of the action seems to be at the municipal level today," Armstrong says.

…

The public also seems ready to address the issue. In May 2006, the San Francisco Bay Area Pollution Prevention Group collected 3634 pounds of pharmaceutical waste from 1500 residents, and South Portland, Maine, recently sponsored a one-day event and collected 55,000 pills. The state's legislators currently are exploring instituting turn-in, mail-back, and other disposal programs.

Making it convenient for the public to participate in drug take-back programs appears to be helping. San Mateo County, California, featured repainted and donated postal service mailboxes, which made their program as easy to access as mailing a letter. Their pilot program in four locations collected nearly 590 pounds of unwanted drugs in just four months, at a cost of $924, plus the costs of the police to collect the drugs.

Despite the best efforts to control the drugs that enter the wastewater stream, water
155 utilities still can expect challenges to meet growing needs and the delivery of safe
drinking water to their customers, including removing CECs. "I'm hoping if we are
able to identify certain compounds that seem to be the **culprits** in potential human
health risks, that technology could be developed to mitigate those, rather than take
out everything," Snyder says. "People have the perception that utilities like ours pull
160 from some giant coffer of money and we can do whatever we want to get down to
the last nanogram [of contaminant], but the public will pay."

(1756 words)

Frank, P. (2011). Pharmaceuticals may be poisoning America's drinking water. In L. I. Gerdes (Ed.),
Pollution (pp. 78–85). Farmington Hills, MI: Greenhaven Press.

After You Read

C. To demonstrate your comprehension, write short answers to the following
questions.

1 What are the three problems that water professionals are facing, as stated
in the first two sentences of the reading?

_____

_____

2 After finding so many pharmaceutical compounds in rivers (in the US),
what are scientists most worried about?

_____

_____

3 What are the possible impacts of endocrine disruption and the development
of antibiotic resistance?

_____

_____

4 What seems to be happening to male fish that live in water close to
wastewater discharge points?

_____

_____

5 What are some sources of pharmaceutical contaminants?

_____

_____

6 What are conventional wastewater treatment plants (WWTPs) designed
to do?

_____

_____

7 The three technologies that can be used to remove CECs all have problems. List the problems associated with each technology.

• Oxidation by adding ozone: _____

_____

• Oxidation by adding chlorine: _____

_____

• Reverse osmosis (RO) filtration: _____

_____

• Ozone combined with reverse osmosis: _____

_____

_____

8 There are further problems related to CECs in the water. Provide more details about each of these problems.

• Amount of water to clean: _____

_____

• Insufficient data: _____

_____

_____

9 How could the use of pharmaceutical "take-back programs" help reduce the problem of CECs in the water?

_____

_____

10 The author of this article frequently quotes expert Dr. Shane Snyder, research and development project manager for the Southern Nevada Water Authority in Las Vegas. Review the quotes (starting on lines 68, 91, 110, 130, 135, and 156) and summarize Snyder's opinion about how best to remove CECs from the water. You will read more quotes from Snyder in Reading 2.

_____

_____

_____

_____

D. Discuss with the class how worried people should be about CECs in the water supply.

MyBookshelf > My eLab >
Exercises > Chapter 8 >
Pharmaceuticals May Be Poisoning
America's Drinking Water

The Many Uses of *That*

In Reading 1, the word *that* serves a variety of functions. Examining these functions can help you understand the diversity of ways you use *that* in your own writing. Below, you will find one example of each of the functions of *that* in Reading 1.

1. *That* as a **demonstrative pronoun**: refers to an idea, person, or thing that has already been mentioned.

   Example:

   > 50 to 90 percent of ingested drugs are excreted ... "We'll deal with *that* in the treatment plants as best we can ...," Armstrong says.

2. *That* as a **determiner**: used before a noun to indicate which item you are referring to.

   Example:

   > The technology used to detect CECs in the water has improved significantly over the last decade. *That* technology has become increasingly sensitive to increasingly trace amounts of compounds.

3. *That* as an **intensifier**: emphasizes an adjective, adverb, verb, or determiner. (In this example, *much* is a determiner.)

   Example:

   > There's no way we can remove all contaminants of emerging concern (CECs) from *that* much wastewater, so we have to look to other ways to figure out what ... is going to work for us.

4. *That* as a **relative pronoun**: begins a relative clause that describes or adds details about a noun or noun phrase.

   Example:

   > More Americans than ever are being treated with prescription drugs *that* often end up in wastewater facilities *that* are not designed to filter out these compounds of emerging concern (CECs), she maintains.

5. *That* as a **subordinate conjunction**: introduces a clause that functions as a noun in the sentence (subject, object, or other complement).

   Example A: noun clause as object of a verb (following a verb)

   > We are finding *that* male fish are producing endocrine-disrupting compounds.

   Example B: noun clause as object of a verb, used to introduce reported (or indirect) speech

   > Douglas Chambers, the study's lead scientist, says *that* all water samples contained detectable levels of at least one known endocrine-disrupting compound.

Example C: noun clause as adjective complement (following an adjective)

Certainly chlorination has the advantages of removing pathogens, but <u>we are not certain</u> ***that*** it's the best route to remove CECs.

Example D: noun clause as noun complement (following a noun)

<u>People have the perception</u> ***that*** utilities like ours pull from some giant coffer of money and we can do whatever we want to get down to the last nanogram [of contaminant], but the public will pay.

A. To practise using *that*, complete the sentences below according to the instructions in parentheses.

① The use of improved technology to detect pharmaceutical compounds in the water allows for greater discovery of the compounds; ...
(use *that* as a demonstrative pronoun)

_____

_____

② Reverse osmosis may remove most CECs from water, but ...
(use *that* as a determiner)

_____

_____

③ Pharmaceutical compounds are composed of medicines ...
(use *that* as a relative pronoun)

_____

_____

④ Scientists have discovered ... (use *that* as a subordinate conjunction to introduce a noun clause acting as object of the verb)

_____

_____

⑤ There is no doubt ... (use *that* as a subordinate conjunction to introduce a clause as noun complement)

_____

_____

⑥ Dr. Shane Snyder reported ... (use *that* as a subordinate conjunction to introduce reported speech)

_____

_____

READING ② Naming the Substances We Detect

Reading 2, a persuasive essay, was published in a magazine written for water engineers and scientists. These authors present a different view of CECs in water.

VOCABULARY BUILD

A. The key words in Reading 2 are listed in column 1. Working with a partner, find the key words using the line numbers indicated in column 2. Then use context clues or a dictionary to write short definitions of the key words in column 3. Verify your definitions with another pair of students. Finally, to help you remember the words, apply them to your own experience by answering the prompts in column 4. Share your answers with the class.

KEY WORDS	LINE NUMBERS	DEFINITIONS	APPLIED TO YOUR EXPERIENCES
❶ **disparate** (adj.)	83		Name two disparate subjects that you study.
❷ **elusive** (adj.)	54		Name something that is elusive.
❸ **implications** (n.)	6		What are the implications of a high grade?
❹ **inevitable** (adj.)	27		Name something that is inevitable in your life.
❺ **inferences** (n.)	30		Based on information from Reading 1, what inferences can you make?
❻ **obsolete** (adj.)	51		Name two things that were useful in the past but are now obsolete.
❼ **succinctly** (adv.)	84		Name two complex ideas that you would like to write about succinctly.

B. Search for these key words (listed in column 1 with their definitions) from Reading 2 using the line numbers indicated. Write the words that form collocations with the key words in column 3.

KEY WORDS	LINE NUMBERS	COLLOCATIONS
❶ **synthetic** (adj.) Definition: artificial, not natural, or man-made	12, 18, 75	synthetic synthetic synthetic
❷ **trace** (adj.) Definition: present in very small amounts	2, 4, 11	trace trace trace

Before You Read

A. Working with a partner, highlight the topic sentence of each paragraph. Reread the topic sentences in order and spend some time thinking about the content. Then close the book and tell your partner what this reading is about.

While You Read

B. Reading 2 is a persuasive essay. Underline the thesis sentence in the first paragraph and confirm your choice with another student. Then, as you read, underline sentences, parts of sentences, or specific words that display persuasive elements. When you have finished, discuss with your class whether the authors have succeeded in persuading you to accept their thesis statement.

Naming the Substances We Detect

There is a movement in the water and wastewater industry to find a name to use when discussing the large number of substances that are found in water at trace concentrations. Several terms have been proposed and used in technical and media communications, including the terms *microconstituents*, *trace organics*, and *endocrine-disrupting*
5 *compounds*. However, these names are not well understood by either the public or the media, resulting in confusion regarding the implications for human health. A major challenge surrounding the topic is communicating the significance of trace concentrations and how these compounds should be addressed from a regulatory standpoint. The water and wastewater industry needs to change its
10 vocabulary and develop a clear method of communicating about these trace substances in a way that **fosters** public trust and understanding.

fosters (v.): creates

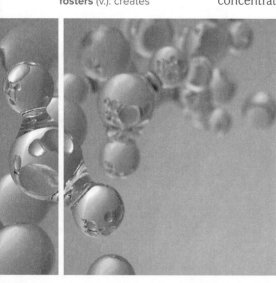

Many synthetic organic chemicals have found their way into the environment. They include pharmaceuticals, detergents, insecticides, pesticides, cosmetics, fragrances, plasticizers, and many more—there
15 is scarcely any part of our modern lives where we do not come into contact with them. Society chooses to use them for many good reasons, including the fact that they can extend our lifespan and improve our quality of life. Synthetic organics have been the subject of many attention-grabbing press accounts due to the fact that they
20 tend to bioaccumulate (show up in increasing quantities the higher up an animal is in the food chain) and because they may be linked to sexual abnormalities in fish.

People are understandably concerned when they read that these substances are detected in drinking water. Media has taken the descriptive scientific name of
25 endocrine-disrupting compounds out of context while cartoons have humanized the sex-change effects observed in fish, leading some to believe similar reproductive problems are inevitable in humans. This fails to reflect the fact that humans do not spend 100 percent of their lifetimes immersed in water, as do fish. Of course, it is important to understand the influences on aquatic life, but it confuses the real findings
30 to draw inappropriate inferences for human health. The other critical thing that is often overlooked in media reports is the fact the concentrations being detected are exceedingly small. As Southern Nevada Water Authority (SNWA) researcher Dr. Shane Snyder recently noted, "The highest concentration of any pharmaceutical compound in US drinking water is approximately five million times lower than the therapeutic
35 dose." Imagine drinking a glass of water that had one five-millionth of an ibuprofen tablet dissolved in it. Is it reasonable to think that this could have a measurable effect on your body? You would need to drink five million glasses of water in order to consume the equivalent of a single tablet (and that might not even be enough to take care of your headache).

40 Unfortunately, we are not given the tools in our education or media communication to differentiate between our considerable exposure to these substances during our everyday activities and our minimal exposure to them in water, nor to understand what effects, if any, they might really have. When the media runs an alarming headline calling these everyday substances contaminants, compounds of emerging concern

45 or, worse, unknowable unknowns, those of us who are not scientifically trained to understand those terms grow fearful. Our gut reaction is to demand the complete removal of these trace substances.

Highly advanced wastewater treatment processes like reverse osmosis can reduce concentrations to below current detection limits, effectively
50 meeting the common definition of removal. However, current detection limits may soon be obsolete, as detection technology grows more and more advanced, allowing detection of smaller and smaller concentrations. "Zero" and "completely removed" will always remain elusive, but we can expect the concentration of the compounds to be
55 "reduced" so they do not pose a threat to human health.

Although water treated by reverse osmosis meets the current definition of pure (non-detectable concentrations), this advanced wastewater treatment requires a large capital investment and a large amount of electricity to operate. The ecological impacts of this cannot be ignored in light of the current global realization of the
60 negative effects of **rampant** energy consumption. Treatment technologies need to be thoughtfully considered and selected to provide the right level of treatment for the intended use. Regulation of these substances should only follow, not precede, a very thoughtful, thorough, and scientific examination of the risks and environmental and public health impacts of such choices.

65 The critical question is not whether we can find things in water or what one word we should call them, but, rather, do they exist in concentrations that cause harm? Continued research is needed to assist decision-making about future management of these substances. It is inappropriate to equate detection of such materials with unacceptable risk to humans or the aquatic environment.

rampant (adj.): extensive

Reverse osmosis system for drinking water

70 The water and wastewater industry is actively engaged in the discussion about the threat of harm, potential regulation, and the best way to effectively communicate with the public in a way that builds trust and reduces fear. The industry has just begun to realize there is public and media confusion regarding substance 75 detection, the impact of the small concentrations of synthetic organic compounds, and their implications for human health. This confusion **underscores** the need for the water industry professionals and scientists to communicate clearly with each other and with the public.

80 In summary, within the water industry, there has been an extraordinary focus on naming the substances we are detecting. The industry is looking for just the right word or phrase to group together a broad and disparate group of substances that are by-products of everyday modern life so that we can talk about them neatly, succinctly, 85 and, above all, scientifically. Unfortunately, such a grouping and generalized characterization of these substances tends to frustrate rather than advance public understanding, as it implies there is a scientifically valid commonality of risk from the materials at trace concentrations. This well-intentioned simplification suggests that a host of potentially harmful substances are being detected in our nation's waters. 90 What we need is an honest presentation of scientific findings about detection and risk in familiar terms, without confusing the issue with a **catch-all umbrella phrase**, especially one with **ominous** overtones that leads us to believe there is something new and evil lurking in our waters.

Scientists and water professionals have a responsibility to help people understand 95 risks and to pay attention to the impact their words have on a community that has poor understanding of water science.

(1067 words)

Callaway, E., Macpherson, L., & Simpson, J. (2010). Talking substance about detection ... or naming the substances we detect? *Influents, 5,* 30–31. Retrieved from https://www.weao.org/influents

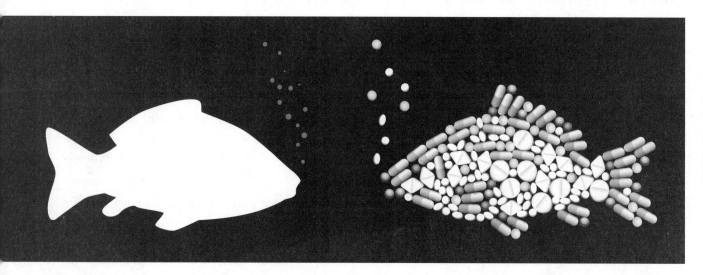

After You Read

C. Answer the following questions.

1 Paraphrase the thesis statement that you identified in While You Read.

_____

_____

_____

_____

2 Which two risks from synthetic organics (emerging contaminants) are presented in the second paragraph?

_____

_____

_____

3 Why are humans not likely to respond to endocrine-disrupting compounds in the same way as fish? (Give two reasons.)

_____

_____

_____

_____

4 Why is the public so worried about emerging contaminants?

_____

_____

5 What problems are associated with using reverse osmosis to eliminate contaminants?

_____

_____

_____

_____

_____

6 According to the authors, what is the critical question?

_____

_____

7 What statement is inappropriate to make at this time?

_____

_____

⑧ In both the introduction and the conclusion of this essay, the authors state that the water industry is searching for a single term that will describe all the compounds now found in water. Why is this simplification a problem?

_____

_____

_____

D. In line 32, the authors include a quote from Dr. Shane Snyder, who was also quoted in Reading 1. Reread Snyder's quotes in Readings 1 and 2. What opinion does Snyder seem to hold about CECs in the water in each of the readings? Discuss as a class what Snyder's true opinion about CECs is.

E. Have another discussion with your classmates about how worried people should be about CECs in the water supply. Have your opinions changed?

MyBookshelf > My eLab >
Exercises > Chapter 8 >
Naming the Substances We Detect

FOCUS ON WRITING

Analyzing Critical Expression

The ability to express critical thoughts politely is an important skill in academic writing. In Reading 2, the authors are critical of the media and public scientific education.

A. Use the line numbers in the first column to identify words and phrases in Reading 2 that express criticism. Write these in the second column. In the third column, identify the target of the authors' criticism. The first one has been done for you.

READING 2	WORDS/PHRASES THAT EXPRESS CRITICISM	TARGET OF AUTHORS' CRITICISM
LINES 5–6	_However, these names are not well understood by either the public or the media, resulting in confusion …_	_Uninformed public and media_
LINES 18–19		
LINES 24–26		
LINES 30–31		
LINES 40–41		
LINE 68		

READING 2	WORDS/PHRASES THAT EXPRESS CRITICISM	TARGET OF AUTHORS' CRITICISM
LINES 85–88		
LINES 88–89		
LINES 94–96		

MyBookshelf > My eLab >
Exercises > Chapter 8 >
Focus on Writing

Expressing Critical Thoughts

FOCUS ON CRITICAL THINKING

When you write for an academic purpose, you want
to show how your ideas are contextualized, or based
on other people's thoughts and writing. While you may agree with some
of those writers (or some of their points), you will likely disagree with others.
Expressing your disagreement in an acceptable manner is a useful skill.

A. To practise expressing disagreement or criticism, read the media headlines
in the first column. Then, in the second column, use words and phrases
from the table in Focus on Writing to write sentences that are critical
of each headline. The first one has been done for you.

MEDIA HEADLINES	CRITICAL SENTENCES
❶ Drug Waste Clogs Rivers around the World, Scientists Say (*The Guardian*, April 11, 2018)	*This attention-grabbing headline implies that rivers have stopped flowing due to pharmaceutical compounds in the water supply. Headlines like this lead people to believe that our water supply is unsafe.*
❷ Your Tap Water Likely Contains at Least Eight Drugs (*The Institute for Natural Healing*, May 1, 2017)	
❸ Sorry, Did You Just Say There Are Hormones in My Tap Water? (*Water for Health*, May 14, 2018)	
❹ There Are Drugs in Your Drinking (and Bottled) Water (*Tonic*, April 17, 2017)	
❺ Cocktails of Chemicals and Drugs in Our Water Supply Remain Unfiltered (*Wake Up World*, March 5, 2017)	
❻ Are You Drinking Prescription Drugs in Your Tap Water? (*Focus for Health*, March 2, 2018)	

Discovering the Organization of a Problem-Solution Text

Readings 1 and 2 are examples of problem-solution texts, which typically have four parts. This organizational pattern is common in academic and technical texts.

A. The first three components of a typical problem-solution text are given in the first column of the table. The first paragraph of Reading 2 (page 254) contains these three parts; since it is the introduction, each part is presented as a summary statement. Read the paragraph and identify the line numbers that match each component; write them in the second column. After, discuss your answers as a class.

COMPONENTS OF A PROBLEM-SOLUTION TEXT	EXAMPLES FROM READING 2
❶ Description of the current situation	LINES _____
❷ Statement of the problem (Note the use of a transition word as the authors move from describing the situation to stating the problem.)	LINES _____
❸ Description of a possible solution	LINES _____

B. Working with a partner, now consider a larger section of Reading 2 and identify all four components. As this section is part of the body of the text, each component is developed more fully than the summary statements you identified in task A. Read lines 12 to 55 and identify the line numbers that match each component; write them in the second column.

COMPONENTS OF A PROBLEM-SOLUTION TEXT	EXAMPLES FROM READING 2
❶ Description of the current situation	LINES _____
❷ Statement of the problem	LINES _____
❸ Description of a possible solution	LINES _____
❹ Evaluation of the solution (Note the use of a transition word as the authors move from describing a possible solution to evaluating the solution.)	LINES _____

C. Reread lines 86 to 115 of Reading 1 (pages 247–248) and take a close look at the repeated move from solution to evaluation of the solution. Identify the line numbers that match each component; write them in the second column.

COMPONENTS OF A PROBLEM-SOLUTION TEXT	EXAMPLES FROM READING 1
❶ Description of possible solutions (several)	LINES _____86–90_____
❷ Description of a possible solution (ozonation)	LINES _____
❸ Evaluation of the solution	LINES _____
❹ Description of a possible solution (chlorine)	LINES _____
❺ Evaluation of the solution	LINES _____

COMPONENTS OF A PROBLEM-SOLUTION TEXT	EXAMPLES FROM READING 1
❻ Description of a possible solution (reverse osmosis)	LINES _____
❼ Evaluation of the solution	LINES _____
❽ Description of a possible solution (ozonation and granular activated carbon filters)	LINES _____
❾ Evaluation of the solution	LINES _____

In this excerpt from Reading 1, the move from solution to evaluation is not generally marked by a transition word or phrase, except in the case of the reverse osmosis solution. However, the text might have been improved if some form of transition had been used.

The four parts of problem-solution texts do not always appear in order from description of the situation to evaluation of the solution. While the description of the situation and problem typically come first as a form of introduction, the remaining parts can vary in order, as you see in Readings 1 and 2.

WARM-UP ASSIGNMENT
Describe and Evaluate a Solution for a Problem-Solution Text

You will write the last two parts of a problem-solution text: the description of a solution and your evaluation of it.

A. Start by selecting one of the solutions to the problem of emerging contaminants that were mentioned in Readings 1 and 2:
- Oxidation by adding ozone
- Oxidation by adding chlorine
- Filtration with granular activated carbon
- Reverse osmosis (RO) filtration

B. Find and document reliable sources of information on your chosen solution. Paraphrase and summarize these sources, providing accurate references in the citation style required in your discipline.

When you receive feedback from your instructor or your classmates on this Warm-Up Assignment, you will have information that you can use to improve your writing on the Final Assignment.

C. Write at least two paragraphs describing the solution. Then, use a transition to signal the move to your evaluation, and write another complete paragraph. As your evaluation is likely to be critical of the solution, use words and phrases learned in Focus on Writing (page 258) and Focus on Critical Thinking (page 259) to express criticism in an appropriate academic manner. This Warm-Up Assignment text will be integrated into the Final Assignment.

Refer to the Models Chapter (page 296) to see an example of a problem-solution text and to learn more about how to write one.

Reading 3 is an excerpt from a book chapter that summarizes the research on the effects of emerging contaminants, or microconstituents, in the water. The author uses the term *aqueous* (relating to water) *matrices* (plural of *matrix*) to imply the complexity and interconnectedness of global water and wastewater systems.

VOCABULARY BUILD

A. The sentences below contain key words from Reading 3. Working with a partner, choose the correct meaning of the key word in bold to complete each of the sentences. If you are not sure of the meaning, locate the word in the reading and consider the context. When you have finished, compare answers as a class.

① If someone experiences an **adverse** (line 167) effect, they experience a …

a) positive influence   b) negative impact   c) neutral outcome

② If research results are **corroborated** (line 24), it means they have been …

a) confirmed by another research study

b) contradicted by another research study

c) destroyed by another research study

③ If a pharmaceutical compound has a **detrimental** (line 4) effect, it has …

a) a neutral effect   b) a positive impact   c) an adverse outcome

④ If a CEC will enter the water **eventually** (line 26), it means this will …

a) definitely happen at some point in the future

b) possibly happen at some point in the future

c) not happen at some point in the future

⑤ If fish have **incessant** (line 31) exposure to CECs in the water, it means they have …

a) very little exposure   b) occasional exposure   c) continuous exposure

⑥ If an adverse effect is poison-**induced** (line 118), that means the poison …

a) prevented it   b) caused it   c) supported it

⑦ If birds **ingested** (line 136) medicine, they …

a) excreted it   b) ate it   c) tolerated it

⑧ When CECs **inhibit** (line 98) a fish's natural response to removing poison from its body, they …

a) improve the natural response

b) prevent the natural response

c) control the natural response

⑨ When pharmaceutical compounds enter water **matrices** (line 19), they enter …

a) simple systems

b) complex but simplified systems

c) complex, interconnected systems

⑩ When medicines break down into **metabolites** (line 27), they break down into ...

  a) by-products

  b) unknown compounds

  c) compounds that reform in water

⑪ If scientists find drug **residues** (line 110) in the water, they find ...

  a) large quantities of the drug

  b) small, unused deposits of the drug

  c) active amounts of the drug

⑫ If a person has a **subsequent** (line 120) exposure to a compound, it means that she/he has been exposed ...

  a) more than once

  b) for the first time

⑬ If bacteria are **transmitted** (line 134) through the water, it means that the bacteria are ...

  a) reduced by the water

  b) stopped by the water

  c) spread by the water

MyBookshelf > My eLab > Exercises > Chapter 8 > Vocabulary Review

Before You Read

As this text is a summary of research relating to the complex issue of CECs in water, it is composed of many short sections; each section summarizes one aspect of the issue.

A. List the nineteen headings found in the article in the appropriate column to produce an outline of the content. Check your answers with the class.

HEADING NUMBERS	MAIN HEADINGS	SUBHEADINGS
❶	*Introduction*	
❷		
❸		
❹		
❺		
❻		
❼		
❽		
❾		

HEADING NUMBERS	MAIN HEADINGS	SUBHEADINGS
⑩		
⑪		
⑫		
⑬		
⑭		
⑮		
⑯		
⑰		
⑱		
⑲		

B. Review the headings and subheadings in the table, and highlight the ones that you believe will present new information, or information that you haven't read about in Readings 1 and 2.

While You Read

C. You are now familiar with the structure of a problem-solution text.

Complete the following table, listing the four parts of a problem-solution text in the first column. In Reading 3, these four components can be found from lines 20 (after the abstract) to 185 (excluding the conclusion).

D. As you read, list the lines of the reading (between lines 20 and 186) that correspond to each section in the second column. Because this reading is an excerpt from a longer chapter, not all parts are equally well developed here. Pay careful attention to identify all the sections of a typical problem-solution text, particularly at the end of the reading.

FOUR PARTS OF A PROBLEM-SOLUTION TEXT	READING 3 LINE NUMBERS
Description of the current situation	LINES _____
	LINES _____
	LINES _____
	LINES _____

E. When you have finished, confirm your answers with your class.

Pollution of Aqueous Matrices with Pharmaceuticals

*The world is witnessing an increasing contamination of the environment by pharmaceuticals due to their escalating consumption and **recalcitrant** nature. Water bodies like rivers, lakes, and even surface water have been found to be contaminated with drugs. Exposure to these contaminants is already showing **detrimental** effects in fish, frogs, birds, etc.,*
5 *with the development of antibiotic-resistant pathogens being another **repercussion**. Chronic exposure to pharmaceuticals, even in trace quantities, may also affect human health adversely in the long term. Although a decade ago it was difficult to provide substantial data for such pollution, the recent development*
10 *of highly sensitive and specific analytical tools has led to the detection of pharmaceuticals in many drinking water sources also. In this chapter, we discuss various aspects of this issue, beginning with the causes of pollution, the enormity of*
15 *consequences, types of aquatic sources reported to be contaminated, drugs usually found, and finally the variety of techniques that can be used to detect and characterize pharmaceuticals in aqueous **matrices**.*

20 Introduction

Pharmaceuticals play a very important role in health care as they are manufactured and used for specific biological activities in humans and animals. However, in the last two decades, pharmaceuticals have also been recognized as environmental contaminants in various matrices, as **corroborated** by many studies (Richardson &
25 Bowron, 1985). It is obvious that a xenobiotic produced or consumed in large amounts would **eventually** make its way into the environment and may persist as a contaminant either in an intact form, as a degradation product, or a **metabolite** of the parent. It is not unreasonable to anticipate that many of the detected pharmaceutical contaminants may have been present in the environment for decades, but have come into notice
30 only recently due to tremendous progress in the analytical techniques for trace analysis (Buchberger, 2011). It is also very reasonable to assert that with **incessant** increase in production and consumption of pharmaceuticals with each passing year, the environmental pollution with pharmaceuticals is rising progressively.

The Reasons for Pollution of Aquatic Sources
35 with Pharmaceuticals

As indicated above, the problem of pollution of aquatic sources with pharmaceuticals is most noteworthy [because it] is of a continuous nature. The major reasons for this are enumerated below.

Consumption on the Rise

40 Consumption of pharmaceuticals is increasing rapidly because of the emergence of new diseases and rise in consumer population due to enhancement of lifespan (older people consume more drugs). Improvements in living standards and hence better affordability of drugs, complemented with new drug discoveries and the progress of pharmaceutical companies, are also contributing toward increased consumption
45 (Behnke, 2012).

Continuous Infusion in the Environment

Continuous infusion of a pollutant into the aquatic environment is sufficient for effecting incessant, multi-generational life cycle exposures to sensitive aquatic
50 species. Chemical stability is not an issue as long as the pollutant is continually introduced (such as via sewage treatment plant effluent). Current criteria for establishing the importance of pollutants, based on chemical stability as measure of tenacity, may be overlooking entire ranks
55 of potential pollutants, for example, pharmaceuticals and the bioactive ingredients in personal care products (Daughton, 2000).

Diverse Nature of Pharmaceuticals

Pharmaceuticals and personal care products (PPCPs) are a very large and diverse
60 suite of pollutants. Many of them may be present together at the same time in an aquatic body, making it difficult to monitor them.

Inefficient Sewage Treatment [Plants]

Modern sewage treatment [plants] are not constructed to specifically eliminate pharmaceuticals from drinking water supplies. Due to their specific chemistry, each
65 pharmaceutical requires an exclusively designed degradation technique for its complete destruction. Waste management plants use generalized degradation techniques; therefore, many pharmaceuticals are not completely destroyed (Vera-Candioti et al., 2008). Also, the presence of antibiotics in wastewater treatment plant (WWTP) influents could disrupt the degradation processes that are driven by bacterial
70 degradation, for example activated sludge, thus hindering the degradation of other drugs as well.

Conversion from Inactive to Active Form

Many metabolites ... get transformed in the environment to give higher concentrations of the active metabolite, which may exceed the safe exposure levels and thus cause
75 harm to the aquatic wildlife ...

Why Is It Such a Big Problem?

Pharmaceuticals are potent in nature as compared to other pollutants. Hence, their coming into water supplies is a serious matter of concern. They can have an impact in the following ways.

80 Impact on Wildlife

A study was carried out wherein the four most abundantly used pharmaceuticals (namely acetaminophen, carbamazepine, diltiazem, and cimetidine) and six sulphonamide-related
85 antibiotics were investigated for their acute toxicity employing three representative model species: (1) a marine bacterium (Vibrio fischeri), (2) a fresh water invertebrate (Daphnia magna), and (3) Japanese medaka fish (Oryzias latipes).
90 Researchers anticipated immobility of test fish, high mortality rate, etc. Utilizing a series of

Japanese Medaka fish

conservative assumptions, the predicted environmental concentrations (PECs) of the pharmaceuticals tested were calculated, and their hazard quotients were derived. [The fish tested high] for acetaminophen and sulphamethoxazole, suggesting potential
95 ecological risks and the need for further investigation (Kim et al., 2007; Brausch et al., 2012; Liu et al., 2012) …

Multi-Drug Resistance as a Line of Defence for Aquatic Organisms

Certain pharmaceutical compounds have the ability to **inhibit** the active transport system required for preventing intracellular exposure of many aquatic organisms
100 (analogous to multi-drug transporters). Once inhibited, the lack of this system could lead to the intracellular accumulation of many toxicants. Multi-drug transport capacity seems to be better developed in aquatic life as it is routinely exposed to toxicants; organisms in more isolated areas are vulnerable to toxic [compounds] when facing first-time exposure (Daughton, 2000; Boxall et al., 2012).

105 ### Synergistic Effects of Pharmacologically Similar Drugs

innocuous (adj.): harmless

Isolated pharmaceutical compounds in the aquatic environment may be **innocuous** per se, but when a large number of similar drugs are present, their cumulative concentration could exceed safe exposure levels, especially when the drugs act by the same mode of action. In 2006, researchers from the University of Insubria in Italy conducted a study
110 by exposing human embryonic cells … to a low-level mixture of thirteen drug **residues**. Even at low doses, the drug residues actually stopped the cells from reproducing (Pomati et al., 2006).

Bioaccumulation

Pharmaceuticals are usually lipophilic and often have a low biodegradability. Still there
115 is a higher probability of increase in the concentration of a chemical in a biological organism over time, compared to chemical's concentration in the environment (Halling-Sørensen et al., 1998).

Toxicant-Induced Loss of Tolerance

Initial exposure to low doses of drugs sensitizes
120 [the immune system], and **subsequent** exposure levels, below those previously tolerated, trigger [adverse] symptoms (Miller, 1997).

Allergic Responses

125 Sometimes, very low doses of an antibacterial-like penicillin can trigger effects in allergic individuals (Wicher & Reisman, 1980).

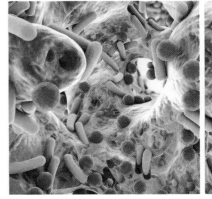

Antibiotic-resistant bacteria

Resistance to Antibiotics

The development of antimicrobial resistance in the environment is another eventuality.
130 In a recent study, it was shown that the proportions of multi-resistant bacterial strains sampled downstream from a manufacturing site of penicillin were higher than in the upstream isolates. As these bacteria were multi-resistant, it also indicated toward the cross-resistance prevalent due to penicillin contamination. These resistant bacteria may be directly **transmitted** to humans via drinking water if groundwater is also
135 contaminated (Li et al., 2009). Another instance is the pandemic of avian flu during which wildfowls **ingested** oseltamivir (Tamiflu) at a quantity less than its minimum

inhibitory concentration, together with the virus in their daily water intake. As both the drug and the pathogen were present together in the gastrointestinal tract of wildfowls, selection of resistant bacteria occurred. These resistant bacteria were perhaps also
140 transmitted to humans, who were living in close proximity to aquatic life. This is corroborated by the fact that 18 percent of Japanese children are resistant to oseltamivir due to its widespread use and contamination of surface waters in Japan (Fick et al., 2007; Singer et al., 2007).

Effect on Non-Target Species Is Less Understood

145 The modes of action of most pharmaceuticals in humans are poorly understood and even less implicit is the [number] of effects on non-target species. Thus, what is visible to us at present may only be the tip of the iceberg (Daughton, 2000; Brausch et al., 2012).

Overall Impact on Human Health

150 Very few reports address the potential effect to human health due to the presence of trace levels of pharmaceuticals in the environment. Christensen (1998) and Webb et al. (2003) evaluated the potential human health impact for several drug substances found in surface and drinking water and reported no significant impact to human health. A similar study was carried out in the USA for human risk assessment posed
155 by twenty-six active pharmaceutical ingredients (APIs) and their metabolites, covering fourteen classes of drugs. The predicted no effect concentrations (PNECs) for these drugs were assessed in drinking water as a consequence of fish ingestion. The PNECs were compared to measured environmental concentrations (MECs) from the published literature and to maximum predicted environmental concentrations generated using
160 the pharmaceutical assessment and transport evaluation model. For all the twenty-six compounds, the study indicated no appreciable human health risks from the presence of trace concentrations of the drugs in surface water and drinking water (Schwab et al., 2005). Yet, there are uncertainties in these assessments as the drugs and their metabolites, although appearing insignificant independently, do positively contribute
165 to the overall toxic load of the environment. It has been insinuated that increasing levels of estrogen in the environment, via its use for purposes such as menopause symptom relief and birth control pills, could be causing **adverse** effects on humans, such as reduced male sperm counts and sperm motility and younger ages of puberty in girls (Buhner, 2002). Thus, the views regarding potential harmful effects to humans
170 are varied as of now.

. . .

[Removal, Regulation, Prevention, and Consumer Awareness]

The developments on the analytical front have helped significantly in understanding the extent of the problem of pollution of water sources with pharmaceuticals. Analytical technologies have been successfully employed to monitor the levels of pharmaceuticals
175 present in influents and effluents of WWTPs, and to the levels pharmaceuticals are removed with a particular technique used in influent treatment, including tertiary treatment processes. Unfortunately, the list of chemical contaminants in water sources, which may or may not always be of significant human health concern, is ever expanding. Therefore, whether analytical monitoring and upgrading of treatment
180 facilities are the right approaches, is a matter of concern. Instead, it has been proposed that greater emphasis shall be paid to the prevention of ingress of pharmaceuticals

in water matrices and bringing in stronger regulations. In addition, … consumer awareness [should be increased] so as to avert unregulated disposal of drugs in the environment by individuals. These major concerns are strongly highlighted recently
185 by World Health Organization (2011; 2012).

Conclusion

The contamination of the environment, particularly aquatic sources, by pharmaceuticals is increasing at an alarming rate. A number of factors are playing a role in this, with inefficient waste disposal systems being one of the major ones. Although various
190 regulations and guidelines have been passed in many countries to minimize the impact of pharmaceuticals on the environment, in many places, there is a lack of compliance with the regulations. Pollution with pharmaceuticals has already started taking a toll on the aquatic flora and fauna, and there is not much time left before the adverse effects of this will start showing up in humans. As pharmaceuticals gain
195 entry into the different components of the environment, from a variety of sources and due to the cyclic path they follow in the various environmental matrices, it becomes a difficult task to effectively monitor all of them. Nevertheless, it is essential to obtain some experimental data regarding the levels of pharmaceuticals in the environment, including water sources, in specific areas, so as to be able to warn the
200 local regulatory authorities and public about the seriousness of this issue. Fortunately, newer and improved techniques are available as of now, which can be employed for precise estimation of the types and quantities in which pharmaceuticals exist as pollutants. It is hoped that the situation can be controlled by greater emphasis on take-back programs, improving regulations, public guidance, and consumer education.

(2007 words)

References

Behnke, J. (2012). Pharmaceuticals in the water: The albatross around Texas's neck. *Texas Tech Administrative Law Journal, 13*, 325–391.

Boxall A. B., Rudd, M. A., Brooks, B. W., Caldwell, D. J., Choi, K., Hickmann, S., ... Van der Kraak, G. (2012). Pharmaceuticals and personal care products in the environment: What are the big questions? *Environmental Health Perspectives, 120*(9), 1221–1229. doi:10.1289/ehp.1104477

Brausch, J. M., Connors, K. A., Brooks, B. W., & Rand, G. M. (2012). Human pharmaceuticals in the aquatic environment: A review of recent toxicological studies and considerations for toxicity testing. *Review of Environmental Contaminant Toxicology, 218*, 1–99. doi: 10.1007/978-1-4614-3137-4_1

Buchberger, W. W. (2011). Current approaches to trace analysis of pharmaceuticals and personal care products in the environment. *Journal of Chromatography A, 1218*(4), 603–618. doi: 10.1016/j.chroma.2010.10.040

Buhner, S. H. (2002). The environmental impacts of technological medicine. In S. H. Buhner (Ed.), *The lost language of plants: The ecological importance of plant medicines to life on Earth* (pp. 92–101). Vermont, USA: Chelsea Green Publishing.

Christensen, F. M. (1998). Pharmaceuticals in the environment—a human risk? *Regulatory Toxicology and Pharmacology, 28*(3), 212–221. doi:10.1006/rtph.1998.1253

Daughton, C. G. (2000). *Pharmaceuticals in the environment: Overarching issues and concerns*. Paper presented at the American Chemical Society National Meeting, San Francisco, CA.

Fick, J., Lindberg, R. H., Tysklind, M., Haemig, P. D., Waldenström, J., Wallensten, A., & Olsen, B. (2007). Antiviral oseltamivir is not removed or degraded in normal sewage water treatment: Implications for development of resistance by influenza A virus. *PLOS ONE, 2*(10), 986–991. doi:10.1371/journal.pone.0000986

Halling-Sørensen, B., Nors Nielsen, S., Lanzky, P. F., Ingerslev, F., Holten Lützhøft, H. C., & Jørgensen, S. E. (1998). Occurrence, fate and effects of pharmaceutical substances in the environment—a review. *Chemosphere, 36*(2), 357–393.

Kim, Y., Choi, K., Jung, J., Park, S., Kim, P. G., & Park, J. (2007). Aquatic toxicity of acetaminophen, carbamazepine, cimetidine, diltiazem and six major sulfonamides, and their potential ecological risks in Korea. *Environment International, 33*(3), 370–375. doi:10.1016/j.envint.2006.11.017

Li, D., Yang, M., Hu, J., Zhang, J., Liu, R., Gu, X., & Wang, Z. (2009). Antibiotic-resistance profile in environmental bacteria isolated from penicillin production wastewater treatment plant and the receiving river. *Environmental Microbiology, 11*(6), 1506–1517. doi:10.1111/j.1462-2920.2009.01878.x

Liu, X., Lee, J., Ji, K., Takeda, S., & Choi, K. (2012). Potentials and mechanisms of genotoxicity of six pharmaceuticals frequently detected in freshwater environment. *Toxicology Letters, 211*(1), 70–76.

Miller, C. S. (1997). Toxicant-induced loss of tolerance—an emerging theory of disease? *Environmental Health Perspectives 105*(Supplement 2), 445–453.

Pomati, F., Castiglioni, S., Zuccato, E., Fanelli, R., Vigetti, D., Rossetti, C., & Calamari, D. (2006). Effects of a complex mixture of therapeutic drugs at environmental levels on human embryonic cells. *Environmental Science and Technology, 40*(7), 2442–2447.

Richardson, M. L., & Bowron, J. M. (1985). The fate of pharmaceutical chemicals in the aquatic environment. *Journal of Pharmacy and Pharmacology, 37*(1), 1–12.

Schwab, B. W., Hayes, E. P., Fiori, J. M., Mastrocco, F. J., Roden, N. M., Cragin, D., ... Anderson, P. D. (2005). Human pharmaceuticals in US surface waters: A human health risk assessment. *Regulatory Toxicology and Pharmacology, 42*(3), 296–312.

Singer, A. C., Nunn, M. A., Gould, E. A., & Johnson, A. C. (2007). Potential risks associated with the proposed widespread use of Tamiflu. *Environmental Health Perspectives, 115*(1), 102–106.

Vera-Candioti, L., Gil García, M. D., Martínez Galera, M., & Goicoechea, H. C. (2008). Chemometric assisted solid-phase microextraction for the determination of anti-inflammatory and antiepileptic drugs in river water by liquid chromatography-diode array detection. *Journal of Chromatography A, 1211*(1–2), 22–32. doi:10.1016/j.chroma.2008.09.093

Webb, S., Ternes, T., Gibert, M., & Olejniczak, K. (2003). Indirect human exposure to pharmaceuticals via drinking water. *Toxicology Letters, 142*(3), 157–167.

Wicher, K., & Reisman, R. E. (1980). Anaphylactic reaction to penicillin (or penicillin-like substance) in a soft drink. *Journal of Allergy and Clinical Immunology, 66*(2), 155–157. doi.org/10.1016/0091-6749(80)90063-9

World Health Organization. (2011). *Guidelines for drinking-water quality* (4th ed.). Geneva, Switzerland. Retrieved from http://apps.who.int/iris/bitstream/handle/10665/44584/9789241548151_eng.pdf;jsessionid=3341A18E7AF4A715043CA83FD0A9F5E2?sequence=1

World Health Organization. (2012). *Pharmaceuticals in drinking-water.* Geneva, Switzerland. Retrieved from http://apps.who.int/iris/bitstream/handle/10665/44630/9789241502085_eng.pdf?sequence=1&isAllowed=y

---

Jindal, K., Narayanam, M., & Singh, S. (2014). Pollution in aqueous matrices in pharmaceuticals. In P. P. Singh, & V. Sharma (Eds.). *Water and health* (pp. 355–359, 365–366, 368–369). New Delhi: Springer.

After You Read

F. To demonstrate your comprehension, complete the following sentences.

① A journal article reports the results of a specific research project; this chapter _____

_____

② It is possible that CECs were in our water supply long before scientists began to research this issue because _____

_____

③ CECs accumulate in our lakes and rivers because _____

_____

_____

④ CECs have been shown to cause damage to _____

_____

⑤ Bioaccumulation of CECs can lead to _____

_____

⑥ With regards to human health, _____

_____

⑦ Possible solutions to CECs in wastewater include _____

_____

⑧ In the conclusion, the authors indicate that they believe that _____

_____

G. Check the facts. Indicate if the statements below are true or false. Then confirm your answers with your class.

STATEMENTS		TRUE	FALSE
❶	When a CEC enters the water system, it can degrade to various metabolites and persist in the environment for a long time.		
❷	Even if compounds degrade and become inactive in the water system, there will always be active compounds in the water because there is continuous infusion of medicines into the water supply.		
❸	Contaminants can be removed from the water supply through generalized removal processes.		
❹	Several research studies have demonstrated that common medicines have an effect on the health of fish.		
❺	Research seems to show that fish that are exposed to CECs have some tolerance to the compounds; fish that have never been exposed before may be vulnerable at first exposure.		
❻	Research conducted at a university in Italy demonstrated that human embryonic cells did not react to exposure to trace amounts of various drug compounds.		
❼	Li et al. (2009) discovered that penicillin-resistant bacteria existed in higher numbers downstream from a penicillin manufacturing plant.		
❽	Although studies have not yet proven a direct link between CECs and negative impacts on human health, the authors point out that it is difficult to study the effects of the accumulation of CECs on human health.		

MyBookshelf > My eLab >
Exercises > Chapter 8 >
Pollution of Aqueous Matrices

Combining Different Organizational Patterns to Suit Your Writing Purpose

As your English skills improve, you will notice that the texts you read and write are increasingly complex; they are no longer organized according to a single pattern. Instead, you may recognize different patterns within longer texts. In this chapter's readings, you may have recognized the following patterns:

• Definition in Reading 1, page 245

• Compare and contrast in Reading 2, page 254 (This is not a conventional compare and contrast pattern as the authors do not compare and contrast directly; however, the placement of the three wastewater treatment technologies one after the other invites a comparison from the reader.)

• Process text in the description of the solution in the Warm-Up Assignment, page 261 (as you describe how the solution works)

• Persuasive text in the conclusions of all three readings

The authors of these texts follow different organizational patterns to suit their purposes—as you should also do when you write. Knowledge of the conventional patterns of organization is an important foundation that can help you as you read and write increasingly complex texts.

FINAL ASSIGNMENT

Write a Problem-Solution Essay

Write a problem-solution text that includes all four components: situation, problem, solution, and evaluation.

A. Paraphrase and summarize the readings in this chapter, providing appropriate citations and references, to complete the first two components (situation and problem).

B. Integrate the solution and evaluation from your Warm-Up Assignment (page 261) into the text. Write another solution and evaluation section in order to compare and contrast the two solutions. Finally, write a conclusion for your problem-solution text.

C. In your text, you should include
- a definition (in your situation component);
- process descriptions (as part of your solution component);
- a compare and contrast text (also in your solution component);
- expressions of critical thought (in your evaluation component);
- a persuasive text (in your conclusion).

Refer to the Models Chapter (page 296) to see an example of a problem-solution text and to learn more about how to write one.

Critical Connections

Work in a group of three and find three current news articles (online or in print) about problems in society. Skim the articles to become familiar with the content. Group members should select the article that they find the most interesting.

A. Working individually, list in point form the four components of a problem-solution text that relate to your article.
- Describe the situation.
- State the problem.
- Describe a solution.
- Evaluate the solution.

B. Next, write down which points you agree with and which you disagree with. Express your critical thoughts about the ones you disagree with, using the expressions you learned in Focus on Critical Thinking (page 259).

C. In your group of three, share your answers to these tasks. Then share your best outcomes with the class. Post your ideas to a shared website.

MODELS CHAPTER

This chapter provides models of the assignments that you may be required to write as you progress through this textbook. All of the models are about standardized testing, allowing you to see how the same information can be arranged to meet the demands of different writing assignments.

Before each model assignment,

you will find

- instructions that highlight the key characteristics of the writing assignment;

- the outline that the writer used to prepare for the writing assignment.

MODEL 1   How to Write an Extended Definition

Definitions, and extended definitions, are common in academic writing. To write a definition, start with a sentence that includes the term you want to define. Then, use one of the following strategies to define the term or use several strategies to extend the definition.

- Provide an equation (if the term can be represented mathematically).
- Write a description.
- Make reference to the root word of the term.
- Describe the evolution of the term.
- Explain what the term is, and is not.
- Describe the process represented by the term.

MODEL 2   How to Describe a Data Set

Show data in table, graph, or chart form. When describing data in academic writing, follow these guidelines.

- Start with a sentence that points the reader to the data; for example, Table 1 shows/demonstrates/indicates/illustrates/provides/reveals/summarizes/presents ...
- Continue with sentences that describe the data, drawing attention to the most important trends. Do not simply repeat what the data show; include information in order to "add value" to the data.
- Finish by telling the reader the significance of the data.

Example of an Extended Definition Including a Data Set

What is PISA and what do the results show?

WRITER'S PLAN	
DEFINITION	• PISA: Programme for International Student Assessment • conducted by the Organization for Economic Co-operation and Development (OECD) • tests fifteen-year-olds in OECD and partner countries: seventy-two countries in 2015 • reading, math, and science tests
DATA SET	• figures show average student scores for top twenty-six countries in science, math, and reading for 2015 • science scores were used to select top twenty-six countries; math and reading scores superimposed on science scores; therefore, math/reading scores show more variability • Singapore had the highest scores in all three subjects • in general, reading scores remain below math/science scores, suggesting that math/science tests assess similar skills while reading tests assess distinct skills • size of country and politics do not seem to matter • speculation that poverty has a depressing effect on scores

PISA Results for 2015

The Programme for International Student Assessment (PISA) is a standardized test program that assesses the math, science, and reading skills of fifteen-year-old students in many countries. The program is run by the Organization for Economic Co-operation and Development (OECD), and countries that participate in PISA are affiliated with that organization. The purpose of the multi-country comparison is to enhance the quality of education and educational policies in member countries.

The initial offering of PISA was completed in 2000, and the tests are now offered every three years. Each year that the tests are administered, one of the three fields of knowledge (math, science, or reading) is emphasized, although the tests cover all three subjects. In 2015, the emphasis was on science skills. Over 540,000 students from seventy-two countries completed the tests (OECD, 2016). The PISA results have inspired many research studies that attempt to explain the variation in scores.

Figure 1 shows the average student scores for the top twenty-six countries in science, math, and reading for 2015. The reading scores were used to select the top twenty-six countries while math and reading scores were superimposed on the science scores; consequently, the math and reading scores show more variability than the science scores. Reading scores remain mostly below the math and science scores, suggesting that the math and science sections of the test assess similar skills while the reading section tests distinct skills.

In 2015, students in Singapore scored the highest in all three subjects. Singapore reached this milestone by creating a high-quality educational system. It appears that the size of the country has no bearing on test score, and that politics and religion have little impact. However, there is speculation that poverty has a depressing effect on scores (Strauss, 2010).

Figure 1: Average science, math, and reading scores for the top 26 countries participating in PISA, 2015

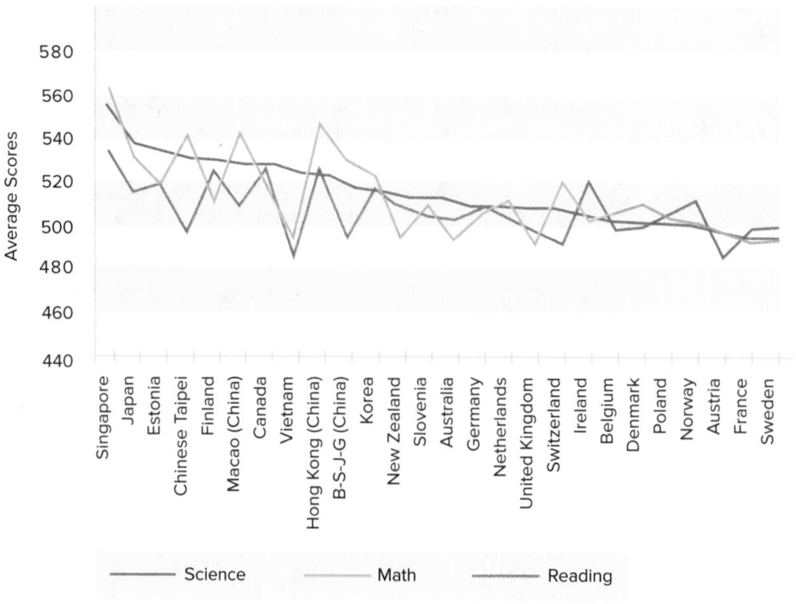

Source: Graph generated from OECD 2015 data

References

OECD. (2016). *PISA 2015 results (Volume 1): Excellence and equity in education.* Paris, France: OECD Publishing. doi.org/10.1787/9789264266490-en

Strauss, V. (2010, December 9). How poverty affected U.S. PISA scores. *Washington Post.* Retrieved from http://voices.washingtonpost.com/answer-sheet/research/how-poverty-affected-us-pisa-s.html

MODEL 3 How to Write a Process Essay

Process essays are written to explain *how* something is done. Therefore, a process essay often explains the steps in a process. The following guidelines will help you write an effective process essay.

• Like all essays, a process essay generally has three sections: an introduction, a body, and a conclusion.

• The introduction announces the topic of the essay. Although there are many good ways to start an essay, the introduction usually begins with a general statement about why the topic is important. The introduction might also start with a definition.

• The introduction finishes with a *thesis statement*. A thesis statement is a sentence that includes the topic of the essay and the opinion that the essay will present. It may or may not include the main steps of the process that you are writing about.

• The body of the essay will contain a number of paragraphs. For a short process essay, usually each paragraph describes one step in the process.

• Each body paragraph should start with a topic sentence that clearly indicates the topic of the paragraph. If your thesis listed the main steps of the process, you can repeat the key words (or synonyms of the key words) from the thesis.

• Each body paragraph should finish with a sentence that clarifies the point of the paragraph.

• The conclusion summarizes the main steps in the process. It often finishes with a sentence that restates (but does not repeat) the thesis.

Example Process Essay

How is a standardized test developed?

WRITER'S PLAN	
INTRODUCTION	• definition of a standardized test: description + distinct from a classroom test

BODY	• six steps in development
	  – state the purpose of the test
	  – write test specifications
	  – write test items
	  – evaluate the test items
	  – determine scoring procedures
	  – validate the test and develop new versions

CONCLUSION	• standardized test development a continuous process

Developing a Standardized Test

Almost all language students, even very young students, are familiar with tests. The majority of language tests students take are developed by their teachers and are known as *classroom tests*. However, there is another type of test that students are taking with increasing frequency: *standardized tests*. Zwaagstra (2011) states that standardized tests are distinct from classroom tests because they are developed by expert test developers, written by students at a set time in their learning, and scored by trained raters in a single location. In theory, when two students from very different schools write a standardized test, they should receive the same score if they have similar knowledge and skills. Standardized tests allow students, teachers, parents, and administrators to compare student proficiency. Brown and Abeywickrama (2010) divide the process of creating a standardized test into six steps.

The first step in developing a standardized language test is to state the purpose of the test. Carr (2011) explains test purpose as determining the decisions that can be made based on the test results. For example, will the test measure language proficiency for the workplace or for academic study (or something else)? Will students with high scores be hired for a job, admitted into a university, or placed in a high-level program? Test developers express the purpose of the test when they decide what it will be used to measure.

As the development and administration of a standardized test require the cooperation of many people, the second step of development is writing test specifications. Test "specs," as they may be referred to, define all elements of the test, such as the skills to be assessed, method of assessment, number of test items, delivery method, length, scoring, and method to return scores. In short, the specifications establish key information that must be shared for the test development process to be a success.

Once the test specs have been written and shared, developers begin to write items. At this stage, test questions are developed according to the specifications. Questions can range from multiple-choice, fill-in-the-blank, or matching items to more open-ended tasks that require students to read and listen to texts and speak or write in response. Essentially, the test itself is written during this step.

Although the test is written, it is not yet ready for use; evaluating the items is the fourth step in the development of a standardized test. Hughes (2003) points out that language test items must be tested on native speakers as well as on non-native speakers to identify any problems. For example, if native speakers have trouble answering a question, then it should not be used to test non-native speakers. Test items that produce unexpected responses should also be eliminated at this stage. The evaluation stage is key to ensure the questions are as good as they can be.

Determining scoring procedures is the next step in the development process. For closed questions, this can be relatively simple; a correct answer and the number of marks allocated to the item are determined. For items that require interaction or extensive response, scoring can involve the development of a rubric. Any open-ended questions require rater training to ensure that all raters score consistently. It is also important that the number of marks per question reflects the amount of time students have spent studying for that question. At the end of this stage, all scoring issues must be solved.

Finally, developers must prove the validity of the test. While the meaning of validity has changed over time, Carr (2011) states that for a test to be valid, developers must prove in a variety of ways that it is useful. To do this, developers show that questions represent tasks students would perform in real-life contexts; that the test scores reflect a student's likelihood of success; that scoring procedures are reliable; that the test is free of cultural bias; that test language is authentic; and that test feedback has a positive impact on learning and teaching. If a test meets all of these criteria, then developers can say that it is valid.

Clearly, the development of a standardized test is a lengthy process requiring the collaboration of many people. It is also true that standardized tests are rarely ever finished. The continual need to develop new versions that are equivalent in difficulty to the original test ensures ongoing efforts. Standardized test development is a challenging process that never ends.

References

Brown, D., & Abeywickrama, P. (2010). *Language assessment: Principles and classroom practices* (2nd ed.). White Plains, NY: Pearson Longman.

Carr, N. (2011). *Designing and analyzing language tests.* Oxford, UK: Oxford University Press.

Hughes, A. (2003). *Testing for language teachers* (2nd ed.). Cambridge, UK: Cambridge University Press.

Zwaagstra, M. (2011, October). Standardized testing is a good thing. *Frontier Centre for Public Policy: Policy Series* 119. Retrieved from http://www.fcpp.org/files/1/PS119StandardizedTesting.pdf

MODEL 4   How to Write a Compare and Contrast Essay

Compare and contrast essays are written to show the similarities and differences between two items. When you compare items, you show the similarities; when you contrast items, you show the differences. The following guidelines will help you write effective compare and contrast essays.

- Decide what points of comparison or contrast you wish to explain to your reader.
- Decide which pattern of organization fits your information best. There are two standard ways to organize a compare and contrast essay: block style organization and point-by-point style organization. Generally, block style organization is best

for less technical information while point-by-point style organization is best for more technical information. As advanced language learners, your content is likely to be technical or more complex, so a point-by-point style of organization is demonstrated here.

- Like other kinds of essays, a compare and contrast essay generally has three sections: an introduction, a body, and a conclusion.

- The introduction announces the topic of the essay. Although there are many good ways to start an essay, the introduction usually begins with a general statement about why the topic is important. The introduction might also start with a definition.

- The introduction finishes with a *thesis statement*. A thesis statement is a sentence that includes the topic of the essay and the opinion that the essay will present. It may or may not include the main points of comparison or contrast.

- The body of the essay will contain a number of paragraphs. For a short compare and contrast essay, usually each paragraph explains one point of comparison or contrast.

- Each body paragraph should start with a topic sentence that clearly indicates the topic of the paragraph. You can do this by repeating key words (or synonyms of the key words) from the thesis.

- Each body paragraph should finish with a sentence that clarifies the point of the paragraph.

- The conclusion summarizes the points of comparison and/or contrast. It often finishes with a sentence that restates (but does not repeat) the thesis.

Example Point-by-Point Style Compare and Contrast Essay

Explain the differences and similarities between classroom and standardized language tests.

WRITER'S PLAN		
INTRODUCTION	• classroom tests versus standardized tests • different based on purpose, development, and impact	
BODY	**CHARACTERISTICS FOR COMPARISON AND CONTRAST**	
	CLASSROOM TESTS	**STANDARDIZED TESTS**
— PURPOSE	• criterion-referenced	• criterion- or norm-referenced
— DEVELOPMENT	• simple, quick • usually involve only one teacher	• complex, time-consuming • six-step process that is never finished
— IMPACT	• generally low-stakes • extensive feedback, often formative • less stressful • test preparation individualistic	• usually high-stakes • minimal feedback • more stressful • test preparation often systemic
CONCLUSION	• classroom and standardized language tests different in purpose, development, and impact • a need for both types of tests	

Classroom versus Standardized Language Tests

Almost all language students, even very young students, are familiar with tests. The majority of language tests students take are developed by their teachers and are known as *classroom tests*. In most cases, these tests are developed by a single instructor and vary from teacher to teacher. However, there is another type of test that students are taking with increasing frequency: standardized tests. Zwaagstra (2011) states that standardized tests are distinct from classroom tests because they are developed by expert test developers, written by students at a set time in their learning, and scored by trained raters in a single location. Classroom and standardized tests may have similar purposes, but they differ in their development methods and their impact.

Classroom and standardized tests may share a common purpose; they may both be criterion-referenced tests. A criterion-referenced test is designed to measure the extent to which students achieve the criteria established in the test objectives. The test scores show how successful students were in achieving the objectives. While learners can compare their scores, the purpose of the test is to compare each learner's performance to the test objectives (Brown & Abeywickrama, 2010).

A norm-referenced test has a different purpose. Norm-referenced tests are designed to compare learners and rank them from highest to lowest. The purpose of this kind of test is not to measure whether students achieved the test objectives but to determine which student among a large group of students is "the best." Scores are percentile rankings that demonstrate how a student ranks in relation to others. It doesn't matter if the top score is 50 or 100 percent in the test; the students with the top scores are the top performers in the group, and they receive the top ranking. Examples of norm-referenced standardized tests include the Law School Admissions Test (LSAT), Graduate Management Admissions Test (GMAT), and Medical College Admissions Test (MCAT). The purpose of a criterion-referenced test is thus fundamentally different from that of a norm-referenced test.

While most standardized and classroom tests are criterion-referenced, they are developed through very different processes. Brown and Abeywickrama (2010) have determined six steps in the development of a standardized language test. These steps are stating the purpose of the test, writing test specifications, writing test items, evaluating test items, determining the scoring procedures, and validating the test. The stages are appropriate for communicating large amounts of information about the test to the multitude of people involved in developing them. However, while classroom test development may also involve multiple stages, it is often abbreviated for practical reasons. For example, most classroom tests are developed by a single teacher. As a result, the teacher does not need to write test specifications to be shared among many developers. Teachers may not have time to test items with native speakers as recommended by Hughes (2003). And they may not spend time validating the test through a variety of measures to prove that it is useful. Therefore, the test development processes for these two types of tests contrast significantly.

Finally, classroom and standardized tests are distinct in their impact. In the language-testing field, "impact" is often replaced with the term *washback*, which is defined as the influence of testing on teaching and learning (Alderson & Wall, 1993). Washback encompasses effects that are both personal and wide-ranging. Consequently, these two types of tests can be contrasted based on what's at stake, the extent of feedback, and the level of test preparation required; each of these considerations falls under the umbrella of washback.

While it may be important for a student to do well on classroom tests, the results are generally low-stakes. Students are often assessed multiple times during a course, so each test score is less likely to have a significant impact on the students' final grades. If students perform poorly on one test, they might be motivated to study harder for the next test, and they are still likely to pass the course. Consequently, students may be less anxious about taking a classroom test. In contrast, the score from a standardized test may determine whether students are admitted to a desirable university or obtain higher-paid employment. As a result, these tests are considered high-stakes. Students are often stressed by the one-time-only nature of standardized tests, whose scores influence their futures. Clearly, classroom tests are low-stakes compared to high-stakes standardized tests.

Classroom and standardized tests are distinguishable by the extent of the feedback provided with the scores. Classroom instructors, who are often dedicated to their students' success, may spend hours grading and responding to errors in the hope that students benefit from their efforts. Class time may be spent reviewing test content when the tests are returned to the students. Instructors provide extensive feedback and content review to improve student knowledge and skill; feedback therefore serves a formative purpose. However, this is not the concern of the raters who score standardized tests. They are required to produce consistent scores but not comment on student proficiency. Students may receive a single score with little or no indication of their strengths or weaknesses. The purpose of these scores is simply to quantify students' proficiency and not to provide information about how to do better next time. In this way, classroom tests often provide formative assessment while standardized tests do not.

Test preparation for these two types of testing will also vary. For classroom tests, students are likely to study on their own, or perhaps with another student or a group of students. They use their textbooks and class notes to review content that will be tested. In contrast, students studying for a standardized test usually have several options. They can take a test preparation course, either online or in a classroom. They can purchase a test preparation book or practise sample tests online. They might even go online to read blogs by students who have already completed the same test. Of course, they may decide to study on their own; however, in most cases, a wide range of study options is available. Therefore, classroom and standardized tests also differ in the study options open to students who take them.

In summary, classroom and standardized tests may be compared and contrasted to gain a greater understanding of their purposes, feedback, and impact (or washback). While most classroom tests and many standardized tests are criterion-referenced, teachers often provide formative assessment on classroom tests, which are low-stakes compared to standardized tests. High-stakes standardized tests rarely result in substantive feedback. While these two types of tests are distinct, they both serve a useful purpose within the educational community.

References

Alderson, J., & Wall, D. (1993). Does washback exist? *Applied Linguistics, 14*, 115–129.

Brown, D., & Abeywickrama, P. (2010). *Language assessment: Principles and classroom practices* (2nd ed.). White Plains, NY: Pearson Longman.

Hughes, A. (2003). *Testing for language teachers* (2nd ed.). Cambridge, UK: Cambridge University Press.

Zwaagstra, M. (2011, October). Standardized testing is a good thing. *Frontier Centre for Public Policy: Policy Series* 119. Retrieved from http://www.fcpp.org/files/1/PS119StandardizedTesting.pdf

MODEL 5 — How to Write a Report

A report explains an existing complex situation and makes recommendations about how to improve it. The following guidelines will help you write an effective report.

- Divide the report into sections. Each section begins with a section title or heading. Many reports are divided into introduction, methods, challenges, and recommendations sections. However, your section titles will depend on the information that you need to explain. In the example report, the sections are *introduction, driving forces, description of an existing test, recommendations,* and *conclusion.*

- Select logical section titles.

- In the introduction, define important terms and explain why the situation is complex.

- In methods, explain how you gathered information about the situation.

- In the challenges section, explain the problems or challenges that result from the complexity of the situation.

- In the recommendations section, make recommendations about how to improve the situation. Predict the benefits that will result from the adoption of the recommendations.

- You may include direct or indirect quotations in any of these sections.

Example Report

Would an English language proficiency test help solve communication problems at the Global Information Systems Technology company?

WRITER'S PLAN	
INTRODUCTION	• Global Information Systems Technology (GIST): sells information technology systems worldwide • working language English • wants to implement an English training program and an oral proficiency test • test a requirement before assignment to key English accounts • quotation from director of Human Resources • definition of a standardized test
DRIVING FORCES	• not all employees communicating well in English • problems with daily communication (example) • problems with large account management (example) • problems with marketing and sales (example) • quotation from director of marketing and sales
DESCRIPTION OF AN EXISTING TEST THAT COULD ADDRESS THE DRIVING FORCES	• Public Service Commission of Canada (PSCC) • describe Second Language Evaluation Test of Oral Proficiency • quotation from director of Second Language Assessment Program at the PSCC • quotation from test taker
RECOMMENDATIONS	• GIST implement a program of English training and an oral proficiency test similar to the PSCC

WRITER'S PLAN	
CONCLUSION	• The implementation of an English language assessment will improve the English proficiency of GIST employees. This will improve internal communications and the financial performance of the company.

The Need for an English Oral Proficiency Test for the Global Information Systems Technology (GIST) Company

Report submitted by Second Language Assessment Inc.

Introduction

Global Information Systems Technology (GIST) is a company that sells information technology systems to governments around the world. The company specializes in communication facilitation among government employees as well as government-to-public information flow. It employs 12,000 people in twenty different countries and operates in high-stress and confidential environments.

Many GIST employees are multilingual; however, the working language in the company is English, and the majority of business transactions are conducted in that language. GIST offers a training program for employees wishing to improve their English skills. It now wants to adopt an English oral proficiency test to measure the fluency of its employees after program completion and before salespeople are assigned to important English accounts. Janet Turner, director of Human Resources for GIST, indicates how important it is to adopt a reliable oral proficiency test. "Our employees are highly trained in information systems technology and they are hired for their expertise, but increasingly we need them to be skilled in English as well—to communicate accurately in English to support our clients. A standardized oral English proficiency test will help us achieve improved English fluency in our employees."

A standardized test, produced by test-development experts and scored by trained raters, will support GIST in its goal to reliably measure the English oral proficiency of its employees.

Driving Forces

Not all GIST employees are communicating well in English. Three recent critical incidents are driving the move to adopt an oral English proficiency test.

1. A month ago, lack of communication between two teams working on similar projects in different countries resulted in a duplication of effort that cost GIST one million dollars. Failure to speak fluent English resulted in weak communication between teams.

2. Last quarter, GIST lawyers wrote a contract that contained an error due to inaccurate communication between the lawyers and the account negotiation team. GIST was forced to pay $1.5 million to cover the cost of the error.

3. Recently, GIST's marketing team was unable to close a deal in an English-speaking country because the government purchasing team did not believe GIST's technical support people could communicate accurately in English. Had the deal been completed, GIST would have gained a $125 million account.

The frustrated director of Marketing and Sales, Eric Stauffer, claims that poor oral English proficiency is costing the company. "If we can't speak English, we can't make money, or at least, not as much money," he said. "It's hurting us financially."

Description of an Existing Test: PSCC Test of Oral Proficiency

The Public Service Commission of Canada (PSCC) designed a test of second-language oral proficiency in 2008 in response to the latest research in language assessment. A team of applied linguists, second-language test developers, and psychometric professionals developed the test according to a needs analysis based on the language demands of the tasks employees must perform. "The development of this test was a thorough process," reports Marie Brisson, head of PSCC Second Language Assessment Branch. "We piloted the test extensively before implementation, and it can measure oral skill level proficiency with great accuracy." She indicated the test is used to test oral proficiency in both English and French.

The four-stage test is conducted one-on-one; an individual candidate interacts with a language assessor. The first stage requires candidates to answer questions about familiar situations at work or volunteer activities. The second stage involves listening to pre-recorded voice-mail messages and work conversations. Candidates must answer questions about what they have heard. The third stage requires employees to talk for several minutes on a topic determined by the assessor and answer several questions about the presentation. In the final stage, the candidate listens to a pre-recorded conversation about work, summarizes the content, and answers questions. The level of difficulty increases from stage to stage, and the assessor may stop the test at any stage if he believes the candidate's proficiency has been fully demonstrated.

"This test allowed me to show what I was capable of," Carolyn Stitt said. She was one of the first employees to pilot the test to measure her proficiency in French. "The test content reflects the kinds of things I have to do in my job, so the test really makes sense. Preparing for it helps you speak better in your second language."

Recommendations

1. It is recommended that GIST develop an English language oral proficiency test to improve the English-speaking skills of its employees.

2. Before the test is developed, GIST should complete a language analysis of the tasks required of its employees. Test tasks should then reflect the requirements of the workplace.

3. The overall test structure should follow the model of the PSCC Test of Oral Proficiency.

4. The test should be piloted and revised as required before full implementation.

5. GIST should hire English assessor experts to ensure test scores are accurate and reliable.

Conclusion

The implementation of an English language assessment will improve the English proficiency of GIST employees. This will improve both internal communications and the financial performance of the company.

How to Write a Paraphrase

The goal of a paraphrase is to restate the ideas of another author without copying the author's words. Paraphrasing is an effective way to avoid plagiarism. Use the following guidelines to write a paraphrase.

- All paraphrases start with a reference to the original author. Common ways to start paraphrases are the following:

In her 2018 article, (author's name) states that …

In his book of 2018, (author's name) suggests that …

According to (author's name) in her article of 2018, …

(Author's name) website maintains that …

- A paraphrase is approximately the same length as the original writing.

- To restate the main ideas of an author without repeating the same words, you can use writing techniques such as finding synonyms for key words, changing the structure of the sentence, changing word forms, and changing the voice from active to passive (or passive to active). See pages 152–154 for examples of these writing techniques.

- You may need to use more than one of these writing techniques to complete a successful paraphrase.

Example Paraphrase

Paraphrase the following text:

> The Programme for International Student Assessment (PISA) is an ongoing programme that offers insights for education policy and practice, and that helps monitor trends in students' acquisition of knowledge and skills across countries and in different demographic subgroups within each country. PISA results reveal what is possible in education by showing what students in the highest-performing and most rapidly improving education systems can do. The findings allow policymakers around the world to gauge the knowledge and skills of students in their own countries in comparison with those in other countries, set policy targets against measurable goals achieved by other education systems, and learn from policies and practices applied elsewhere. While PISA cannot identify cause-and-effect relationships between policies/practices and student outcomes, it can show educators, policymakers, and the interested public how education systems are similar and different—and what that means for students. (144 words)
>
> ### Reference
>
> OECD. (2016). *PISA 2015 results (Volume 1): Excellence and equity in education* (p. 25). Paris, France: OECD Publishing. doi.org/10.1787/9789264266490-en

Example paraphrase:

The 2016 Organization for Economic Co-operation and Development (OECD) report entitled *PISA 2015 results (Volume 1): Excellence and equity in education* states that the Programme for International Student Assessment (PISA) provides continuous data on student progress in education for a wide range of countries. Policymakers and educators can use this information to monitor trends in student progress within their own countries and reference their students' accomplishments to similar cohorts and subgroups in other countries. Similarly, this data can be used to establish educational goals and identify countries that excel in creating educational contexts that promote successful student learning. PISA results should be treated with caution as the data do not demonstrate a causal relationship between educational systems and student achievement; however, the results are a strong indictor that differences among educational systems matter, and those differences can have significant impacts for students. (143 words)

Reference

OECD. (2016). *PISA 2015 results (Volume 1): Excellence and equity in education* (p. 25). Paris, France: OECD Publishing. doi.org/10.1787/9789264266490-en

---

MODEL 7   How to Write a Summary

The goal of a summary is to restate the ideas of another author without copying the author's words. Summarizing, like paraphrasing, is an effective way to avoid plagiarism. Follow these guidelines to write a summary.

- All summaries, like paraphrases, start with a reference to the original author. Common ways to start summaries are the following:

  In her 2018 article, (author's name) states that ...

  In his book of 2018, (author's name) suggests that ...

  According to (author's name) in her article of 2018, ...

  (Author's name) website maintains that ...

- A summary, unlike a paraphrase, is approximately one-quarter to one-third the length of the original writing.

- To summarize an original text, you should

  - read the original text carefully;

  - underline the main points of the original text, leaving out supporting details, repetitions, and examples;

  - paraphrase the underlined sentences.

- To paraphrase the underlined sentences, you can use writing techniques such as finding synonyms for key words, changing the structure of the sentence, changing word forms, and changing the voice from active to passive (or passive to active). See pages 152–154 for examples of these writing techniques.

- You may need to use more than one of these writing techniques to complete a successful summary.

Example Summary

Summarize the following text:

> "What is important for citizens to know and be able to do?" In response to that question and to the need for internationally comparable evidence on student performance, the Organization for Economic Co-operation and Development (OECD) launched the triennial survey of fifteen-year-old students around the world known as the Programme for International Student Assessment, or PISA.

PISA assesses the extent to which fifteen-year-old students, near the end of their compulsory education, have acquired key knowledge and skills that are essential for full participation in modern societies. The assessment focuses on the core school subjects of science, reading, and mathematics. Students' proficiency in an innovative domain is also assessed (in 2015, this domain is collaborative problem-solving). The assessment does not just ascertain whether students can reproduce knowledge; it also examines how well students can extrapolate from what they have learned and can apply that knowledge in unfamiliar settings, both in and outside of school. This approach reflects the fact that modern economies reward individuals not for what they know, but for what they can do with what they know. (179 words)

Reference

OECD. (2016). *PISA 2015 results (Volume 1): Excellence and equity in education* (p. 25). Paris, France: OECD Publishing. doi.org/10.1787/9789264266490-en

Example summary:
The 2016 report entitled *PISA 2015 results (Volume 1): Excellence and equity in education* states that the Organization for Economic Co-operation and Development (OECD) initiated the Program for International Student Assessment (PISA) to address the need for global comparative data on student educational performance. Every three years, PISA assesses fifteen-year-old students' knowledge in the domains of science, reading, and mathematics. (60 words)

Reference

OECD. (2016). *PISA 2015 results (Volume 1): Excellence and equity in education* (p. 25). Paris, France: OECD Publishing. doi.org/10.1787/9789264266490-en

MODEL 8 · How to Write a Cause and Effect Essay

Cause and effect essays are written to demonstrate that something is the cause of something else (the effect). The following guidelines will help you write an effective cause and effect essay.

• Like all essays, a cause and effect essay generally has three sections: an introduction, a body, and a conclusion. Unlike in a report, these section titles are usually not used as headings in the essay.

• The introduction announces the topic of the essay. Although there are many good ways to start an essay, the introduction usually begins with a general statement about the cause of a situation or an event and the significance of the effects.

• The introduction finishes with a thesis statement. A thesis statement is a sentence that presents the cause and effect relationship you will write about as well as an opinion about the relationship. It may or may not list the specific effects that you will write about.

• The body of the essay will contain a number of paragraphs. For a short cause and effect essay, usually each paragraph explains one effect.

- Each body paragraph should start with a topic sentence that clearly indicates the topic of the paragraph. If your thesis listed specific effects, you can repeat key words (or synonyms of the key words) from the thesis.
- Each body paragraph should finish with a sentence that clarifies the point of the paragraph.
- The conclusion summarizes the main effects and why the essay opinion is correct. It often finishes with a sentence that restates (but does not repeat) the thesis.

Example Cause and Effect Essay

What effects do standardized tests have on students hoping to study in English-medium universities?

WRITER'S PLAN	
INTRODUCTION	• standardized English language tests have significant impacts on English language learning students hoping to study in a country where English is the language of instruction at the post-secondary level • definition of washback
TEST RESULTS VALUE STUDENTS DIFFERENTLY	• standardized tests have serious consequences • student worth dependent on scores
LOCAL KNOWLEDGE DEVALUED	• tests only measure what test developers value
UNETHICAL TEST PREPARATION	• test preparation unethical; attempts to improve scores without improving proficiency • costs are high
CONCLUSION	• standardized English language tests have unfortunate negative washback effects on students by suggesting that their value is dependent on their test results, by devaluing local knowledge, and by encouraging them to participate in unethical test preparation courses

The Effects of Standardized Testing on University-Level English Language Learners

Standardized English language tests have significant effects on English language learning students hoping to study in a country where English is the language of instruction at the post-secondary level. The effects of standardized testing on university-level English language learners have been variously referred to as test influence, backwash, washback, or impact. In 2005, Taylor defined the terms *washback* and *impact*, indicating that many teachers and researchers use the term *washback* to refer to the consequences tests have on students, and the term *impact* to refer to the consequences tests have on educational systems. She notes that washback/impact can be either negative or positive. This essay will address the effects of standardized English language tests on students, so the term *washback* will be used to describe these outcomes. Although the washback from these tests varies from student to student, it appears the washback may be predominantly negative.

In his 2003 book entitled *Values in English Language Teaching*, Johnston dedicates a chapter to the critical discussion of the washback of standardized tests on English-language learners. He claims that tests have serious consequences for students. He maintains that students who succeed on standardized tests are valued by society; students who fail these tests are less valued. Similarly, students' sense of self-worth may be diminished if they do not meet the test requirements. Johnston points out that learners who do not succeed on tests might do well in other contexts. For example, a learner might fail a test but nevertheless find a good job. However, while students may realize that test failure doesn't represent their true worth, low test scores may mean a significant change in their future plans.

In any context, a test can measure only small samples of student proficiency due to time constraints. Standardized tests measure only the knowledge that test developers believe is important (Johnston, 2003). Knowledge that lies outside the test domain may be just as significant for students, but it is not assessed in a standardized test. For example, students may value local cultural knowledge or idiomatic vocabulary, but these items are not likely to be included in a standardized test. As a result, standardized tests assess a narrow range of knowledge and devalue other knowledge.

Johnston writes that test preparation courses for standardized tests are unethical because they attempt to improve scores without improving student proficiency. For example, in most cases, test preparation courses are intensive, but it is unlikely that language proficiency will improve significantly over a weekend. Students are attracted to these courses in hopes of achieving high scores, and they are willing to invest significant amounts of money in them. Johnston believes these preparation courses take money from students without offering evidence of improved English proficiency, which he believes is immoral.

In conclusion, Johnston writes about the moral implications of standardized testing. His work exposes how society devalues students who are less successful on standardized tests, and how this threatens students' self-valuation. He points to the narrow band of knowledge that is prioritized by standardized tests and the immorality of test preparation courses. For all of these reasons, the washback effects of standardized tests on English language learners are predominately negative.

References

Johnston, B. (2003). The morality of testing and assessment. In *Values in English language teaching* (pp. 61–78). Mahwah, NJ: Lawrence Erlbaum Associates.

Taylor, L. (2005). Washback and impact. *ELT Journal 59*(2), 154–155. doi.org/10.1093/eltj/cci030

MODEL 9 **How to Write an Annotated Bibliography**

The purpose of an annotated bibliography is to summarize and evaluate information about a specific topic. It should save the reader time by providing enough information to enable the reader to decide which texts are worth reading. The following guidelines will help you write an effective annotated bibliography.

• Identify which texts (journal articles, books, or other) you will summarize and evaluate.

• For each text, write a reference.

• Under each reference, summarize the information in the original text. Although an academic summary is generally one-quarter to one-third the length of the original text, the summary sections of an annotated bibliography are very short, usually only a few sentences.

- After each summary, evaluate the information. The evaluation section should indicate why the information is important, innovative, accurate, or noteworthy. It might be part of the summary paragraph (if this is the case, be sure to use a transition word or phrase to indicate the shift from summary to evaluation), or it might appear in a separate paragraph.
- You may find it easier to write the evaluations after you have finished summarizing all the texts. That way, you will be better able to evaluate the importance of each text in relation to the other texts.
- The total annotation for each text can range in length; however, a general guideline is that it should consist of approximately 150 words.

Example Annotated Bibliography

Topic: Washback in standardized testing around the world

Barnes, M. (2017). Washback: Exploring what constitutes "good" teaching practices. *Journal of English for Academic Purposes, 30*, 1–12.

In her 2017 article, Barnes uses classroom observations and teacher interviews to determine the teaching practices of four instructors who teach both English for Academic Purposes (EAP) and TOEFL test preparation courses. This study reveals that in their EAP classes, teachers employ methods that best reflect their beliefs in the importance of a student-centred, process approach to learning whereas in the TOEFL preparation classes, the same teachers use more teacher-centred methods that emphasize product (i.e., high test score) over process. Barnes speculates that the nature of the TOEFL test drives instructors to modify their teaching methods in ways that contradict their beliefs about good language teaching practices.

Barnes's research addresses the negative washback effects of standardized testing on teaching methods. Her mixed-methods research (using both observations and interviews) is well positioned to capture complexity in the testing context. More research is needed to determine whether the more teacher-centred methodology common to TOEFL preparation classes affects student TOEFL scores. (168 words)

Chou, M. (2015). Impacts of the test of English listening comprehension on students' English learning expectations in Taiwan. *Language, Culture and Curriculum, 28*(2), 191–208.

Chou (2015) reports on the impacts a test of English listening comprehension had on students in Taiwan. Using a student questionnaire, Chou surveyed 590 eighteen-year-old Taiwanese students to learn about the washback effects of the listening comprehension test that was added to the traditional English language tests of reading, vocabulary, and grammar for college admission. Chou found that while the test had some negative washback effects (e.g., science students, and those who identified as "average" or "weak" in English listening comprehension, stated that they suffered increased stress and reduced study time for the traditional English skills tests), overall the new test created positive washback effects through improved English listening comprehension and increased motivation to improve listening comprehension skills.

Although a standardized English listening comprehension test may create some negative washback for some students, this study reveals that the positive washback effects are stronger. Despite using only surveys for data collection, the research reflects a complex educational context in which both negative and positive washback effects are apparent. (168 words)

Kim, E. (2017). The TOEFL iBT writing: Korean students' perceptions of the TOEFL iBT writing test. *Assessing Writing, 33*, 1–11.

According to Kim (2017), the TOEFL iBT writing tasks should be critically re-examined from a student perspective. Kim's evaluation of data collected from two TOEFL test taker websites reveals Korean test takers' test preparation strategies and challenges. Her data indicates that test takers are frustrated by lack of time and the inability to demonstrate their writing ability through discipline-specific writing tasks. Similarly, test takers resent the lack of feedback despite test creators' assertions that E-rater Scoring Engine (which is used to score the written tasks) generates written feedback. In addition, students feel that memorization of "templates" is the best strategy to prepare for writing test tasks rather than seeking to improve their English writing proficiency.

Kim's study gathers data from an innovative source to report the negative washback of the TOEFL iBT writing tasks on test takers. However, as this is the only source of data, and it is likely that test takers are most likely to post negative, rather than positive, comments online, the results may be skewed. A mixed-method research design might reveal more nuanced washback effects. (173 words)

Ma, F. (2014). College English test: To be abolished or to be polished. *Journal of Language Teaching and Research, 5*(5), 1176–1184.

In this 2014 article, Ma documents both the negative and positive washback of the College English Test (CET), the national English language standardized test in mainland China. The Ministry of Education develops and maintains the test, which assesses writing, reading, listening, and translation (a speaking test is available to students who score well on the CET). Positive washback effects include motivating students to study English, encouraging institutions to improve teaching quality, and creating test-development expertise. Negative washback effects include driving a test-oriented educational culture that focuses more on test scores than language proficiency. Ma recommends the reform of the CET by privatizing the test and revising it according to communicative testing principles.

Ma reports on the positive and negative washback effects of the CET through a careful analysis of existing literature. While the author does not attempt empirical research in this case, the discussion provides an insightful overview of the English language-testing context in China, and the recommendations are thoughtful. (160 words)

Muñoz, A., & Álvarez, M. (2010). Washback of an oral assessment system in an EFL classroom. *Language Testing, 27*(1), 33–49.

Muñoz and Álvarez, in their 2010 article, report on the impact a classroom-based oral language assessment system had on teaching and learning. In their research, they used experimental and control groups, and a mixed-method design that gathered data from teacher and student surveys, classroom observations, and external evaluations of the students' oral performance. Their study revealed that ongoing teacher guidance and support created positive washback through a focus on student progress and learning processes. Informing students about how learning objectives related to assessments and incorporating student self-assessment into the learning process resulted in positive washback by making explicit the connections between educational goals and assessments.

This study is one of the few that reports on an assessment system that has positive washback on teachers, teaching, and students. It is notable that the study explores an assessment system rather than a standardized test. Impressively, the researchers gathered data from a wide variety of sources to capture the complexity of the assessment context. (162 words)

Taylor, L. (2005). Washback and impact. *ELT Journal 59*(2), 154–155.

In this short 2005 article, Taylor defines the terms *washback* and *impact*, indicating that many teachers and researchers use the term *washback* to refer to the consequences tests have on students, and the term *impact* to refer to the consequences tests have on educational systems. She notes that washback/impact can be either negative or positive and are both complex in nature. Moving forward, researchers should design studies that empirically measure the extent of washback and impact.

This article is one in a series of short articles designed to provide definitions of key concepts in applied linguistics. It is significant as it establishes clear definitions for *washback* and *impact* and points to the direction future research should take. (117 words)

MODEL 10 | How to Write a Persuasive Essay

Persuasive essays are written to persuade, or convince, people that a particular opinion about a topic is correct. The following guidelines will help you write an effective persuasive essay.

• Like all essays, a persuasive essay generally has three sections: an introduction, a body, and a conclusion. You may not use these section titles as headings in the essay.

• The introduction announces the topic of the essay. Although there are many good ways to start an essay, the introduction usually begins with a general statement about why the topic is important. The introduction might also begin with a definition.

- The introduction finishes with a *thesis statement*. A thesis statement is a sentence that includes the topic of the essay and the opinion that the essay will present. It may or may not include the main reasons why the opinion of the essay is correct.

- The body of the essay will contain a number of paragraphs. For a short persuasive essay, usually each paragraph explains one reason why the essay opinion is correct.

- In the body of the essay, you may include paraphrases and summaries of other writers' ideas to support your points.

- Each body paragraph should start with a topic sentence that clearly indicates the topic of the paragraph. You can do this by repeating key words (or synonyms of the key words) from the thesis.

- Each body paragraph should finish with a sentence that clarifies the point of the paragraph.

- The conclusion summarizes the main reasons why the essay opinion is correct. It often finishes with a sentence that restates (but does not repeat) the thesis.

Example Persuasive Essay

Standardized language tests are harmful. Agree or disagree and explain why.

WRITER'S PLAN		
INTRODUCTION	• definition of standardized test (Zwaagstra, 2011) • controversial • do more harm than good	
BODY	**STANDARDIZED TESTS ARE HARMFUL**	**STANDARDIZED TESTS ARE USEFUL**
— TIME	• teachers must teach to the test • take up time that could be better spent on learning (BCTF, 2009)	• if tests and teaching and real-world tasks are aligned, then the tests are useful (Zwaagstra, 2011)
— COST	• too expensive • PISA cost to test 1500 students: US$700,000 (Schneider, 2009) • total cost (470,000 students participating in 2009): $219 million	• similar to the drug enforcement argument: too expensive, so we shouldn't do it • consequences of not using them
— POWER AND CONTROL	• create power imbalances between testers and test takers • tests undemocratic (Shohamy, 2001)	• test administrators now follow Shohamy's recommendations • standardized testing now more democratic
— MORALITY	• morality of testing • tests establish criteria that measure worth of students • destroy teacher-student relationship (Johnston, 2003)	• objective measure of language competency still needed

CONCLUSION	• administration must make standardized tests effective so that
	  — time spent on test preparation is useful and not wasted
	  — administrative costs do not exceed the usefulness of test scores
	  — tests are not simply tools used to control power and a social agenda
	• tests are viewed as one way to measure proficiency but do not reflect the total worth of an individual	

Are Standardized Tests Harmful?

Zwaagstra (2011) states that standardized tests are distinct from classroom tests because they are developed by expert test developers, written by students at a set time in their learning, and scored by trained raters in a single location. There is a great deal of controversy about standardized tests and whether they are harmful or useful. However, while the administration of standardized tests may be flawed, their use is essential.

One of the greatest objections to standardized tests is the time required to prepare students for them. The British Columbia Teachers' Federation expresses this view in its objections to provincial standardized tests (BCTF, 2009). It argues that time spent preparing students to write the tests is time that could be better spent on teaching and providing students with feedback that will help them learn. Their webpage states that the standardized tests assess only a small part of their provincial curriculum, and that preparing students to take the tests emphasizes those elements of the curriculum that are tested, at the expense of others.

This argument commands respect as it demonstrates the teachers' desires to do the best for their students, yet the solution is not to reduce the use of standardized tests. Instead, the tests should be redesigned, with the assistance of federation members, to assess curricular elements that teachers feel are important to their students' progress. As Zwaagstra (2011) points out, once the standardized tests align with the provincial curriculum, the time required to prepare students for the test will no longer detract from regular teaching. Teaching to the test and teaching the curriculum will be one and the same. As a result, this argument should not be used to reduce the use of standardized tests.

It is common to hear the argument that the costs of standardized testing outweigh their benefits. In an article published in *Education Next*, Schneider (2009) estimates that the cost of administering the Programme for International Student Assessment (PISA) tests to 1500 students (the minimum number required for inclusion in the program) is US$700,000. While PISA does not release the total costs of its standardized testing program, if Schneider's cost estimate is correct, it would have cost US$219 million to test the 470,000 students in the seventy-four countries that participated in PISA 2009 (Statistics Canada, 2010). It could reasonably be argued that this money might be better spent in some other way.

However, this line of reasoning is similar to the argument that countries should allow the use of drugs for non-medicinal purposes because it costs too much to enforce laws against such use. Yet, countries continue to pay the costs of enforcing these laws because the alternative is undesirable. Similarly undesirable, the consequences of eliminating standardized tests would mean that applicants could be hired or admitted to positions for which they are unqualified; schools would stop trying to improve the quality of their education. Consequently, the cost of administering standardized tests can not be used to justify their elimination.

In her article, "Democratic assessment as an alternative," Shohamy (2001) reasons that standardized tests support power imbalances that exist between test administrators and students. She suggests that those who create and administer standardized tests hold power over students, who have less power. She views these tests as undemocratic, stating that they value a narrow range of knowledge and ignore knowledge that falls outside that range. This effect devalues the knowledge of students and makes them subservient to powerful test administrators.

Shohamy's belief that standardized tests are undemocratic is often cited by other researchers, suggesting that her points have meaning for many people. And in fact, her arguments have encouraged test administrators to adopt a critical language-testing approach that involves students in test creation, ensures designers develop fair tests, and requires test administrators to work continuously to improve test quality. Shohamy's writing has been influential in improving the quality of standardized tests to the point where they are now more democratic than before.

Johnston (2003) expresses a concern when he writes about the morality of standardized testing. He believes that standardized tests are used to compare students and that successful students are assumed to have desirable characteristics while less successful students are devalued. He points to teacher-student relationships, which he says are often supportive in the classroom yet become mistrustful and suspicious in a testing situation. He suggests that the decision to use standardized tests is a moral one. Although the morality of testing is important to consider, Johnston's concerns do not eliminate the need for objective measures of language competency. When principals hire teachers, employers hire translators, or schools admit students, they must know whether those applicants can meet the proficiency requirements of the position. It would not be reasonable (or moral) to hire a French teacher without knowing that person's proficiency in French.

Arguments against standardized testing have merit, but this does not mean that these tests are harmful. Standardized test administrators must work to minimize the potentially harmful effects of the tests and maximize their usefulness. In this way, time spent on test preparation is not wasted, administrative costs do not exceed the usefulness of test scores, and tests become more than tools used by powerful majority groups to enforce a social agenda. In addition, standardized test results should be recognized for what they are: measures of proficiency rather than a measure of an individual's worth. Current test administrators confront these challenges to standardized testing and produce useful results that allow educational institutions and employers to make good decisions about whom to admit and hire.

References

British Columbia Teachers' Federation. (2009, December 9). BCTF concerns about the Foundation Skills Assessment. Retrieved from http://www.bctf.ca/IssuesInEducation.aspx?id=5728

Johnston, B. (2003). The morality of testing and assessment. In *Values in English language teaching* (pp. 61–78). Mahwah, NJ: Lawrence Erlbaum Associates.

Schneider, M. (2009, Fall). The international PISA test: A risky investment for states. *Education Next, 9*(4). Retrieved from http://educationnext.org/the-international-pisa-test/

Shohamy, E. (2001). Democratic assessment as an alternative. *Language Testing, 18*(4), 373–391. doi.org/10.1177/026553220101800404

Statistics Canada. (2010). *Measuring up: Canadian results of the OECD PISA study. The performance of Canada's youth in reading, mathematics and science. 2009, First results for Canadians aged 15.* (81-590-XPE no.4). Ottawa, ON: Statistics Canada.

Zwaagstra, M. (2011, October). Standardized testing is a good thing. *Frontier Centre for Public Policy: Policy Series* 119. Retrieved from http://www.fcpp.org/files/1/PS119StandardizedTesting.pdf

How to Write a Problem-Solution Essay

A problem-solution essay describes a problem and provides a possible solution.

- Problem-solution essays have six sections: introduction, description of a situation, statement of the problem, description of a solution, evaluation of the solution, and conclusion. Section headings are usually not included in the essay.

- The introduction announces the topic of the essay. Although there are many good ways to start an essay, the introduction usually begins with a general statement about why the topic is important.

- The introduction finishes with a *thesis statement*. A thesis statement is a sentence that includes the topic of the essay and the opinion that the essay will present. The expressed opinion indicates whether a solution is possible or whether one solution is better than another.

- The body of the essay contains the components of a problem-solution text: description of a situation, statement of the problem, description of a solution, evaluation of the solution.

  - The description of the situation may have the characteristics of a short descriptive essay.

  - The statement of the problem may have the characteristics of a challenges section of a report.

  - The description of a solution may have the characteristics of a process essay (if the solutions require multiple steps). If you write about two (or more) solutions, the section may have characteristics of a compare and contrast essay.

  - The evaluation of the solution(s) may include expressions of critical thoughts, especially if the solution does not solve all elements of the problem or if one solution is inferior to another.

- The conclusion may have the characteristics of a persuasive essay as you try to convince the reader that one solution is better than another. The conclusion often finishes with a sentence that restates (but does not repeat) the thesis.

Example Problem-Solution Essay

Given that the overreliance on summative assessment is becoming
a problem for English language learners, propose and evaluate a solution.

WRITER'S PLAN	
INTRODUCTION	• definitions of summative and formative assessment (Brown & Abeywickrama, 2010)
SITUATION	• educational system driven by summative assessment • students constantly taking tests and exams to provide data on qualifications
PROBLEM	• overuse of summative assessment • students study for exams and forget • students don't receive feedback • students who don't do well on exams disadvantaged
SOLUTION	• move to more formative assessment • evidence of the assessment bridge (Colby-Kelly & Turner, 2007)
EVALUATION	• teachers worry feedback embarrasses students • students believe teachers not critical enough in evaluations
SOLUTION	• dynamic assessment description (Lantolf & Poehner, 2008)
EVALUATION	• hard to separate student ability from teacher assistance
CONCLUSION	• trend in assessment moving away from summative assessment • better for teaching, learning, and students

Formative Assessment as a Response to Summative Assessment

In the field of testing, assessments can be divided into two categories: summative and formative. According to Brown and Abeywickrama (2010), summative assessment is designed to summarize a student's achievement. It is typically an end-of-term test, has a high point value, and is high-stakes. The score of a summative assessment is recorded on a student's transcript, without any effort to provide feedback on his or her strengths or weaknesses. The purpose of a summative assessment is to produce a score for administrative purposes. In contrast, formative assessments are intended to facilitate student learning. They are typically end-of-unit tests or assignments, have lower point values, and are comparatively low-stakes. The score of a formative assessment becomes part of a student's final grade, but the test's main purpose is to inform a student of his or her strengths or weaknesses.

In many countries, educational systems are driven by summative assessment. Students of all ages require scores in order to determine their educational progress. Those with high scores attend better schools and the best post-secondary institutions while those with lower scores are streamed into regular or remedial classes with fewer opportunities for enrichment. Students are constantly being tested to generate scores. Educational administrators often make admission decisions based on a single score; that score must reflect the sum total of a student's skills and abilities. That score determines a student's future.

Is it really fair to judge a student's admissibility based on a single score? Could any single score, no matter how it is calculated, possibly reflect the complexity of abilities that any human possesses? This is the defining problem that results from an overuse of summative assessment. However, other significant issues also stem from excessive summative assessment. For example, students often prepare for summative exams by "cramming"—studying long hours and memorizing facts. This is not the best way to encourage a deep understanding of content. Students who cram for exams often quickly forget key concepts. Summative assessments are not intended to provide detailed feedback to students, so students lose the opportunity to learn from their work and from their instructors' expertise. Finally, some students simply don't score well on exams but do much better on assignments. These students are severely disadvantaged by an educational system's focus on summative test scores.

In the field of second-language learning and teaching, researchers and teachers are looking for ways to reduce the reliance on summative testing and develop alternative assessments that provide more feedback to students and allow them multiple opportunities to demonstrate mastery of core concepts. Both formative and dynamic assessment offer new solutions to the problem of overreliance on summative assessment.

Formative assessment, or assessment to enhance student learning, is also referred to as *assessment for learning* (AFL). Colby-Kelly and Turner (2007) state that AFL is characterized by increasing involvement of students in their own assessment. This includes self- and peer assessments as well as teacher feedback that enhances student performance and motivates students. Teachers who practise AFL modify their lessons based on the results of assessment; if results indicate students need more work on a particular concept, teachers revisit that concept to facilitate student learning. Colby-Kelly and Turner's study of a pre-university English for Academic Preparation program that employed formative assessment suggests that AFL can create conditions for enhanced motivation and learning.

One of the challenges of implementing AFL in the second-language classroom resulted from the conflict between theory and practice. In theory, teachers supported the use of self- and peer assessments and acknowledged their potential for involving students in their own assessment. In practice, teachers most often provided feedback directly to students, without emphasizing self- and peer assessment. Also, teachers worried that providing feedback might embarrass students; some teachers waited until class was over before speaking with students one-on-one in the hallways. Two students in the study responded that they found teacher feedback overly supportive; they felt that teachers were constantly encouraging and that teachers would be unlikely to provide negative feedback. While the benefits of AFL are substantial, Colby-Kelly and Turner's investigations point to challenges with its implementation.

Another movement in the second-language assessment field is a trend toward dynamic assessment, also a reaction to summative and standardized testing. Dynamic assessment (DA) involves diagnostic tests that are administered early in the term and designed to provide feedback and inform teacher planning. In their overview of DA, Lantolf and Poehner (2008) state that DA involves teacher mediation of student response. This explanation becomes clearer if DA is compared with summative assessment. Consider a speaking test in which a student speaks one-on-one with a teacher who assesses the student's speaking ability. In a summative test, the teacher has no flexibility to modify questions or responses to students, even if a student appears confused or answers incorrectly. With DA, the teacher could modify a response, asking the student to explain why he or she is answering in this way or encouraging a more detailed response. Teachers who use DA maintain they have a better understanding of student ability because they interact with the student during assessment.

While DA offers hope for improved diagnostic tests that can support student learning and inform teacher planning, critics suggest that it is hard to determine the student's ability to perform independently (Lantolf & Poehner, 2008). Teachers who use this approach to diagnostic testing acknowledge that some students require more help than others to complete the assessment. As a result, the assessment may not produce consistent scores.

Both AFL and DA are current trends in the assessment field, which respond to the overuse of summative testing in educational systems around the world. Although these approaches have implementation challenges, they offer new hope for more student-centred assessment that encourages feedback and enhances student learning and motivation.

References

Brown, D., & Abeywickrama, P. (2010). *Language assessment: Principles and classroom practices* (2nd ed.). White Plains, NY: Pearson Longman.

Colby-Kelly, C., & Turner, C. E. (2007). AFL research in the L2 classroom and evidence of usefulness: Taking formative assessment to the next level. *Canadian Modern Language Review, 64*(1), 9–37.

Lantolf, J. P., & Poehner, M. E. (2008). Dynamic assessment. In E. Shohamy, & N. H. Hornberger (Eds.), *Encyclopedia of Language and Education* (2nd ed., Vol. 7: *Language testing and assessment*, pp. 273–284). New York, NY: Springer.

PHOTO CREDITS

CENTRE FOR INTERACTIVE RESEARCH ON SUSTAINABILITY

p. 106: Martin Tessler / Courtesy: Perkins+Will

EPA (UNITES STATES ENVIRONMENTAL PROTECTION AGENCY)

p. 96

GETTY IMAGES

pp. viii, 136–137: © darekm101; pp. ix, 174–175: © Hero Images; pp. ix, 240–241: © JacobH

IROKOTV.COM

p. 44: Photo: @IROKO

SHUTTERSTOCK

p. 3: © ZuzanL; p. 4: © Rawpixel.com; p. 7: © Vic Labadie; p. 9: © Cameron Whitman; p. 10: © BEST-BACKGROUNDS; p. 13: © fizkes; p. 14: © Ollyy; p. 17: © Rawpixel.com; p. 19: © TTphoto; p. 21: © junpinzon; p. 22: © DisobeyArt; p. 25: © FashionStock; p. 26: © areebarbar; p. 29: © dboystudio; p. 30: © Rawpixel.com; p. 31: © Eugenio Marongiu; p. 33: © hxdbzxy; p. 35: © Yahdi Bin Rus; p. 36: © View Apart; p. 38: © Gorodenkoff; p. 41: © Dimitriy Domino; p. 43: © Kobby Dagan; p. 46: © David Crockett; p. 50: © Milles Studio; p. 53: © Maksim Shmeljov; p. 55: © Gaudilab; p. 56: © Dmytro Zinkevych; p. 57: © connel; p. 59: © Gaudilab; p. 61: © file404; p. 62: © Jacob Lund; p. 63: © Syda Productions; p. 65: © George Rudy; p. 67: © Sunshine Seeds; p. 71: © mavo; p. 72: © Odua Images; pp. viii, 74–75: © Aris Suwanmalee; p. 75: © nnnnae; p. 76 left: © TatyanaTVK; p. 76 right: © Vectorpocket; p. 79: © Monica Kulinska; p. 80: © alphaspirit; p. 82: © Ph.wittaya; p. 83: © GaudiLab; p. 85: © rudolfgeiger; p. 87: © ssuaphotos; p. 88: © ssuaphotos; p. 89: © Cbenjasuwan; p. 91: © Anatoli Styf; p. 92: © fizkes; p. 93: © xujun; p. 94: © Roman Motizov; p. 95: © Pavel Svoboda Photography; p. 97: © Ralf Lehmann; p. 98: © V J Matthew; p. 101: © Mike Focus; pp. viii, 102–103: © Moomusician; p. 103: © Tatiana Stulbo; p. 104: © ponsulak; p. 109: © Pixelci; p. 111: © Rawpixel.com; p. 112: © Ivan Cheung; p. 115: © Adon Buckley; p. 116: © asharkyu; p. 119: © gabczi; p. 120: © Physics_joe; p. 123: © Rawpixel.com; p. 124: © LStockStudio; p. 127: © happycreator; p. 128: © FLUKY FLUKY; p. 131: © Ron Zmiri; p. 132: © Monkey Business Images; p. 134: © GaudiLab; p. 137: © Scharfsinn; p. 138: © metamorworks; p. 141: © posteriori; p. 142: © ESB Professional; p. 145: © Yatra; p. 146: © FernandoZi; p. 149: © AppleZoomZoom; p. 152: © tkemot; p. 154: © GaudiLab; p. 155: © metamorworks; p. 157: © posteriori; p. 158: © Sirada Wichitaphornkun; p. 159: © njene; p. 160: © Kennedy Photography; p. 162: © pathdoc; p. 165: © Wisdom; p. 167: © Quality Stock Arts; p. 169: © Zapp2Photo; p. 170: © ARENA Creative; p. 175: © Irina Strelnikova; p. 176: © JP WALLET; p. 179: © TZIDO SUN; p. 180: © Rawpixel.com; p. 183: © Naresuan261; p. 185: © Sedgraphic; p. 186: © Rawpixel.com; p. 189: © Rommel Canlas; p. 190: © Aizuddin Saad; p. 193: © Ralwel; p. 194: © Rawpixel.com; p. 198: © Paranamir; p. 199: © Annette Schaff; p. 200: © Roman Samborskyi; p. 202: © GaudiLab; p. 203: © Dim Dimich; p. 205: © Phonlamai Photo; p. 207: © Jacob Lund; p. 209: © Big and Serious; p. 210: © Frederic Legrand—COMEO; p. 213: © Alexander Raths; p. 215: © DenisProduction.com; p. 217: © Stanislau Palaukou; p. 218: © Jacob Lund; p. 219: © Sergei Bachlakov; p. 221: © Montri Nipitvittaya; p. 222: © Lightspring; p. 225: © GaudiLab; p. 227: © thelefty; p. 228: © jörg röse-oberreich; p. 230: © Dave Smith 1965; p. 231: © Bobby Stevens Photo; p. 233: © Rocksweeper; p. 234: © Gustavo Frazao; p. 236: © GaudiLab; p. 239: © Neramit Buakaew; p. 241: © Sentavio; p. 242: © Steidi; p. 244: © josefkubes; p. 245: © StanislauV; p. 247: © AjayTvm; p. 248: © Ph.wittaya; p. 250: © gopixa; p. 253: © goodluz; p. 254: © Modella; p. 255: © hapelinium; p. 256 top: © NavinTar; p. 256 bottom: © Peter Hermes Furian; p. 258: © fizkes; p. 259: © Oleksiy Mark; p. 261: © docstockmedia; p. 262: © Avramenko Olga; p. 265: © Warot Pengpian; p. 266 top: © Davdeka; p. 266 bottom: © simamusume; p. 267: © Kateryna Kon; p. 269: © Lightspring; p. 272: © Rawpixel.com

UNSPLASH

pp. viii, 2–3: © Nathan Dumlao; pp. viii, 40–41: © Danielle MacInnes; pp. ix, 208–209: © Simon Conellan

TEXT CREDITS

CHAPTER 1

pp. 9–14 "Unemployment and Its Natural Rate" by N. Mankiw, R. Kneebone, & K. J. McKenzie. From MANKIW/KNEEBONE/MCKENZIE. *Principles of Macroeconomics, 7E* © 2017 Nelson Education Ltd. Reproduced by permission. www.cengage.com/permissions. pp. 25–29 "World Employment Social Outlook: Trends for Youth." Geneva: © ILO 2016. pp. 35–36 "The 'Jobless Recovery'" by D. Tapscott, & A. D. Williams. Excerpted from *Macrowikinomics: Rebooting Business and the World* by Don Tapscott and Anthony D. Williams © 2010 Don Tapscott and Anthony D. Williams. Reprinted by permission of Viking Canada, a division of Penguin Random House Canada Limited.

CHAPTER 2

pp. 44–47 "Jason Njoku and iROKO: A Success Story" by M. Matuluko. Muyiwa Matuluko, Techpoint.ng. pp. 50–53 "Entrepreneurship" by R. W. Griffin, R. J. Ebert, F. A. Starke, & M. D. Lang. (2014). *Business* (8th Canadian ed., pp. 110–119), Pearson Canada, reprinted with permission by Pearson Canada Inc. pp. 65–70 "Towards an Explanation of the Growth in Young Entrepreneur Activities" by S. Mboko. (2011) *Journal of Marketing Development and Competitiveness, 5*(4), 108–118.

CHAPTER 3

pp. 78–81 "So Fresh and So Clean" by J. Ball. (2012, May/June). "Tough love for renewable energy." *Foreign Affairs, 91*(3), 122–133. © Jeffrey Ball, Scholar-In-Residence, Steyer-Taylor Center for Energy Policy, and Finance, Stanford University. pp. 87–90 "Rooftop Power" by W. Priesnitz. (2010, September/October) *Natural Life*, 135, 28–32. pp. 96–99 "Geothermal Energy: An Introduction" by T. Rand. © 2010 Tom Rand, Eco Ten Publishing Inc.

CHAPTER 4

pp. 106–109 "Dr. Sustainability: Environmental Scientist of the Year" by T. Taylor. © Timothy Taylor. pp. 114–118 "China's Green Building Future" by C. Nelson. 2012, April–June). *China Business Review*, 32–35. pp. 127–132 "How Do Green Businesses Pay?" by B. W. Edwards, & E. Naboni. From: *Green Buildings Pay: Design, Productivity and Ecology*, Edwards, B. W., & Naboni, E. © 2013, Routledge, reproduced by permission of Taylor & Francis Books, UK.

CHAPTER 5

pp. 141–147 "Moving Forward" by D. West. (2016, September). Excerpts from *Moving Forward: Self-Driving Vehicles in China, Europe, Japan, Korea, and the United States*. Centre for Technology and Innovation at Brookings (pp. 1–32). pp. 150–151 Excerpt from: Greenberg, A. (2015, July 21). "Hacker's remotely kill a Jeep on the highway—with me in it." *Wired*. pp. 157–161 "Morality, Ethics of a Self-Driving Car" by T. Spangler. From Detroit free Press, Nov. 21 © 2017 Gannett-Community Publishing. All rights reserved. Used by permission and protected by the Copyright Laws of the United States. The printing, copying, redistribution, or retransmission of this content without express written permission is prohibited. pp. 169–171 "The Social Life of Autonomous Cars" by B. Brown. (2017, February). *Computer, 50*(2), pp. 92–96.

CHAPTER 6

pp. 178–182 "Using Technology as a Learning Tool" by B. McNeely. From *Using Technology as a Learning Tool, Not Just the Cool New Thing*. © 2018 Ben McNeely, *Educause*. pp. 190–195 "In-Game Culture" by J. Byetheway. "In-game culture affects learners' use of strategies in massively multiplayer online role-playing games." © 2014 *International Journal of Computer-Assisted Language Learning and Teaching 4*(4). pp. 204–205 "Can Artificial Intelligence Make Teaching More Personal?" by G. Blumenstyk. © 2018 *The Chronicle of Higher Education*.

CHAPTER 7

pp. 212–213 "Chris Froome Tests Positive, and Cycling History Repeats Itself" by J. Macur. From *The New York Times*, December 2017, © 2017 *The New York Times*. All rights reserved. Used by permission and protected by the Copyright Laws of the United States. The printing, copying, redistribution, or retransmission of this content without express written permission is prohibited. pp. 218–222 "Athlete Reference Guide." Excerpts from *Athlete Reference Guide to the 2015 WADA Code*, World Anti-Doping Agency. pp. 229–233 "Man and Superman" by M. Gladwell. "Man and superman: In athletic competitions, what qualifies as a sporting chance?" *The New Yorker*, Sept. 9, 2013. Reprinted with permission from the author. p. 237 Excerpt from: *The Sports Gene: Inside the Science of Extraordinary Athletic Performance* by David Epstein © 2013 by David Epstein. Used by permission of Current, an imprint of Penguin Publishing Group, a division of Penguin Random House LLC. All rights reserved.

CHAPTER 8

pp. 245–249 "Pharmaceuticals May Be Poisoning America's Drinking Water" by P. Frank. Credit for introduction: From Louise Gerdes. Pollution1E © 2011 Gale, a part of Cengage Learning, Inc. Reproduced by permission. Main text: Copyrighted 2007. Informa. 258052:0918SH. pp. 254–256 "Naming the Substances We Detect" by E. Callaway, L. Macpherson, & J. Simpson. "Talking substance about detection ... or naming the substances we detect?" *Influents*, Water Environment Association of Ontario. pp. 265–270 "Pollution of Aqueous Matrices with Pharmaceuticals" by K. Jindal, M. Narayanam, & S. Singh. Reprinted by permission from *Water and Health*, Sprinter Nature, Springer, India, Jindal, K., Narayanam, M., & Singh, S. (2014). Pollution of Acqueous Matrices with Pharmaceuticals. In P. P. Singh & V. Sharma (Eds.). pp. 355–359, 365–366, 368–369.

NOTES

NOTES